MILLION DOLLAR CROLLA

MILLION DOLLAR CROLLA

GOOD GUYS CAN WIN

ANTHONY CROLLA AND DOMINIC McGUINNESS

First published by Pitch Publishing, 2017

Pitch Publishing
A2 Yeoman Gate
Yeoman Way
Worthing
Sussex
BN13 3QZ
www.pitchpublishing.co.uk
info@pitchpublishing.co.uk

A CIP catalogue record is available for this book
from the British Library.

ISBN 978-1-78531-298-4

Typesetting and origination by Pitch Publishing

Printed in the UK by TJ International, Cornwall

Contents

Acknowledgement 7

Foreword 9

Introduction 11

1. Dark Nights, New Days 16

2. Derbies and Away Day Specials 37

3. Daylight Robbery 60

4. United Nights and Crolla Fights 66

5. Repeat or Revenge? 102

6. Down Time 176

7. I Love Manchester 188

8. Date in the Diary 202

9. Burns Night 224

Acknowledgement

TED Peate was Ricky Hatton's first amateur trainer. Sat in the café at the entrance of the Betta Bodies gym in Denton, Manchester, he's sipping his tea and talking about the kid he first spotted back in the day. He's just been watching the 'Hitman' pound Billy Graham's body belt as Ricky prepares for his bid to wrest the WBA welterweight title from Luis Collazo in Boston.

Questions are asked about Hatton and more follow about his own amateur career. Ted rattles off the gyms he boxed out of back in the fifties and sixties. A thought occurs, 'Did you know a Manchester fighter called Pat McGuinness?' Ted looks up over his glasses with a startled expression. 'How do you know Pat?' he says in high-pitched Mancunian. 'He's my father,' I say. Ted is silent for a second, looks me up and down and spits, 'Fuck off! Pat's your dad?'

I realise I'm a disappointment, but as Ted (or Eddie as he's known to the old man) regales tales from days gone by, I understand fully just what a fabulous lunatic my father was. All the fighting tales from boxing shows and demolition sites that I'd heard in dispatches are verified. And then some. Ted also confirms what I always knew – my dad is a star.

From the hills of Donegal to the streets of Moss Side, this book, Patrick Joseph, is just for you.

Foreword
Michael Carrick

I REMEMBER first speaking to Anthony at one of our 'Player of the Year' dinners at Old Trafford a few years ago. He'd come over for a chat about football and I bored the life out of him about boxing! What struck me about him straight away was just what a nice guy he is, so down to earth. We've kept in touch ever since.

I like getting the chance to meet other sportsmen and women from boxing, golf, rugby, or whatever sport. It's interesting. You're seeing that sport as a fan. As a footballer, you're a fan to an extent, but actually I enjoy watching other sports more. I like to get away from football. My habits have changed over the years and now I watch other sports more than I watch football.

I've always been a boxing fan. I used to watch the fights as a kid but it was only the really big fights that were on TV. The Benn vs Eubank fights and Benn vs McClellan stand out particularly. I remember watching that McClellan fight, going mad in my front room at home in Newcastle. In more recent times, along with the British fighters, I've always enjoyed watching Floyd Mayweather. I just appreciate what he's done and when someone's so good like that, there will always be people being negative all the time. But everyone he's fought he's dispatched, and most of the time he's done it with ease.

When I watch Ant, it's strange because I know him as a person and then I see him in the ring. The way he fights, he's relentless. You wouldn't think it from his character out of the ring. At what point does he switch? Does it come naturally to him or does he force himself to go into the zone? I like all that sort of stuff, the mindset of leaving the changing room and going into the ring, one on one. I wonder if you ever get used to it or if it's still a bit lonely at that first bell. You're standing there on your own.

With me, I start to change as the days are approaching a match. I'm probably better now than I was, but the day before a game, my missus will realise there's a game coming up. I'll be different. Sometimes I'm thinking about a game a few days before. The day of the game, sometimes you feel really chilled out and others you're a bit more tense. In the changing room, you have the warm-up and you're then really tuned into the game. But boxing is a totally different thing.

We've had people come into training to do some boxing. The younger lads here have boxing coaches come in to vary the training a bit. I've done boxing training in the past, using the pads as an exercise to get fit when you can't do other stuff with your legs. I've never been into a boxing gym, though – it looks too hard! I suppose it's like any sport, but boxers make it look so easy. I've got so much respect for them because it is brutal what they put themselves through.

It's great that Anthony's enjoyed such success and I know he's very well thought of at United. The more I got to know him, the more it actually surprised me just how big a United fan he is. I remember he went to Midtjylland a couple of years ago and I thought, 'Right, OK, you're a serious fan!' It must be brilliant for him to get the support and adulation from United fans even though he does a completely different sport.

When I first arrived here at United, Wayne Rooney was here and he was a big boxing fan. We were both ringside for the first Jorge Linares fight, but obviously it's not always easy getting to fights. It was fantastic to be ringside again for the Ricky Burns fight.

It was a brilliant atmosphere and great to see him get back to winning ways. I went into the dressing room afterwards to congratulate him. For Ant to bounce back from the burglary and the injuries and catapult himself to that level of world title fights and winning a world title, you have to have great motivation and unbelievable character to do that. It comes down to character and I suppose you've either got it or you haven't. Anthony has it.

Introduction

ANTHONY Crolla is the Manchester fighter widely regarded as 'the nicest man in boxing'. So how does this boy next door go about his business in the most unforgiving of sports? How has he trodden a path from prospect to has-been, from victim to world champion?

Written off by many, an office job beckoned for 'Million Dollar' before a devastating but defining fight put him back on track. His boxing dream was then shattered once again after a neighbourly deed threatened to ruin not just his career but also his life. But against all the odds, Anthony fought back to win a world title in front of his home town fans.

Covering key moments in a bumpy ride, this book attempts to give unique insight into the ups and downs and the preparations for the biggest nights of his boxing career to date – including the rematch with the exceptional Jorge Linares and the 'Battle of Britain' encounter with Ricky Burns.

It's access all areas, with insight into family life, media commitments, his love affair with Manchester United and, most significantly, his work at Gallagher's Gym. The book includes contributions from friends, team-mates and some of the biggest names in sport.

Spoiler alert: Anthony is a very nice lad.

* * * * *

Anthony Lee Crolla was born in Crumpsall on 16 November 1986. Raised in Newton Heath – the place where his beloved Manchester

United originated – until he was ten, the family lived on Regent Street next to Brookdale Park.

A happy child from a loving family, Anthony lived with his parents, Wayne and Maria, older brother Dominic and younger sibling William. He went to school at Christ the King RC Primary and stayed there for his final year when the Crollas moved to New Moston, less than two miles north.

We moved to a better house but I think the main reason was because my nanna Pauline died. She was me mam's mam and our house backed on to hers. She was an absolute lunatic and, without doubt, she would've been my number one fan.

She used to take me to church and she'd be lighting candles for the United players to make sure they did the business at the weekend! I used to go to Mass with her nearly every Sunday.

It was probably too hard for my mam to see that house every day. Me mam had found her as well after she realised something was up. They knocked the door down and found her there, passed away.

We're a close family. My mam and dad did brilliantly for us. I've only one grandparent left now, me nanna Margaret. She doesn't like the boxing but just wants me to be safe.

My grandad Roy [Crolla] was a great supporter of mine, too. In the early pro days, he'd wait up all night with the telly on and they'd maybe show a five-second clip of me at the end of the show! He passed away after my first few fights. He used to work at Sharp [Electronics] and a good few people who worked with him have come up to me over the years and told me about Roy.

Apparently, he'd always be telling them that his grandson would be a world champion one day! He really wasn't the type to brag or owt like that and I never knew he'd said any of this.

They reckon I get my strength from him. He wasn't big but he was ridiculously strong. He had big shovel hands and a big chest. My great-great grandparents on Roy's side came over from Naples and I do wonder if my will to win was passed down from them. They had it tough. Non-English-speaking and where they lived was a proper slum in Ancoats. There was battling all over the place. They must have been handy!

After Christ the King, Anthony moved on to St Matthew's RC High in Moston.

I loved it there. I genuinely missed school after I left. I did OK study-wise, but could've done better. I knew then I just wanted to box.

By the time Anthony started secondary school, he was already a familiar face at Fox ABC after being introduced by his dad, former professional boxer Wayne, who'd fought for an area title at 154lbs and finished up with a winning 16-12 record. Anthony caught the boxing bug early and quickly made a name for himself.

I don't want to sound like I'm whingeing, but I think I was very unlucky as an amateur. I won a schoolboy title and a senior ABA title, but I never really got my chance with England. I boxed for a north-west squad over in Germany and I boxed in a four nations tournament a few times. I boxed for England a handful of times, but I was around at the same time as Frankie Gavin. He was one of our best ever; he was around my weight and a great amateur.

I was always going down to squads but I felt I was just being used as a sparring partner. I'd get promised loads but nothing was forthcoming. I wasn't getting a chance and that's maybe because I was from a small club. I didn't want to play second fiddle.

I remember as a junior, about 17, I was fighting Dean Fieldhouse, who was on the squad, and we were fighting on the Thursday, so we were kept apart. Me and him were friendly, we trained together and he was from a gym near me [Northside ABC].

Anyway, there was a junior Commonwealth tournament coming up over in Australia, we boxed and I beat him. I beat him well. He got a call a couple of days later asking him to go to the Commonwealths. Do you know what I mean? I was like ... I'm not sure how this really works? I kept getting told things but I just wasn't enjoying the squads. I'd work hard, but I didn't feel I was benefiting from it in any way. I felt better doing my own stuff back home.

I always remember winning the ABA title. It was my proudest moment as an amateur – that or winning the schoolboy title. I was buzzing. My dad doesn't get excited by much but I remember winning the ABAs and the bell going and looking out at the Wembley Conference Centre and I could see me dad stood up roaring. I was like, 'Bloody hell!' Little things like that, making your dad proud, that means loads. Me mates all joke about how chilled out my dad is, but it was a big deal for me. I beat a kid called Chris Pacey, who was the favourite. I won and I won well – 29-16. He'd won the ABAs before, so it was a big scalp. When you go through the names from the year I won the ABAs, you go through the weights and there are so many good lads there like Stephen Smith, Stuey Hall, Jamie Cox, Tony Jeffries, Tony Bellew, Dereck Chisora, James DeGale ... people who've done all right! It was a mad year.

I'd just turned 19 a week or two before but straight after that fight, I turned professional. Ideally, I'd have had a few more amateur fights before turning pro, but I don't regret it.

The transition from amateur boxer to the professional ranks was a straightforward one. Fox ABC in Ancoats had been his home each evening; now his place of work in the daytime would be a short hop down Oldham Road to the Newton Heath/Failsworth border. The man who would mould the latest incarnation of Anthony Crolla was Anthony Farnell, a Manchester fighter of renown.

'Arnie' had come through at an exciting time for boxing in the city. Collyhurst-trained Robin Reid had won a world super-middleweight title while other rising stars included Mike Brodie, Michael Gomez – the Irish-Mexican – and a young lad from Hattersley called Ricky Hatton. Once Farnell's own boxing career had come to an end due to health issues, he turned his attentions to training.

Arnie was a young, hungry coach who gave me a lot of his time. His gym was very local to me and he had a good relationship with promoter Frank Warren as well. I was excited by the journey. I had 15 fights with Arnie, but he only worked with Frank Warren fighters and at the time I felt I needed a change of promoter. Arnie had a good stable and loyalties to Frank, so we just parted on mutual terms.

Change was considered necessary then in Crolla's quest for glory, but he was never going to stray too far from home.

Ricky came along with Hatton Promotions and I thought I needed to build myself in Manchester. It just made sense and I liked the idea that they were promoting locally.

I knew Joe [Gallagher] from the amateurs and was considering asking him to train me when I first turned over. It sounds unprofessional but if I'd have gone with Joe then, it meant getting a few buses there and back to Moss Side [Champs Camp], where he was training at the time.

When the time did come for a change, Joe was someone I'd always respected as a coach and he wasn't tied to any promoter. He'd just moved to

Denton [Kerry Kayes' Betta Bodies gym], so I went there. What I did learn pretty quickly is that if Joe had a restaurant, he'd be the greeter, the cook, the barman, the waiter … there'd be no other way he could do it!

I'll be forever in debt to him for what he's done for my career. He turned it around because at that time a lot of people were saying I was damaged goods and not going anywhere. He built up my confidence. I remember Hosea [Burton] saying how John Murray used to handle me in sparring, how he used to beat me up. But I turned it around and I think – and this is certainly no dig at Arnie – that certain trainers suit certain fighters and me and Joe work very well together. Everything happens for a reason.

Like all successful partnerships, it has to be mutually beneficial. Anthony Crolla embodies all the qualities that complement a coach who has similar ambition – endeavour, attitude, will and talent. Added to that is the 'Million Dollar' smile and the embodiment of a good role model.

'I've known Anthony since he was 12,' said Joe. 'He beat my kid [Dean Fieldhouse] in the Manchester schoolboys final. I went into the changing rooms afterwards and wished him good luck. I told him he had a great jab and shook his hand. He always stuck with me, stuck in my mind, so we do go way back.

'Speak to some of the lads in the gym and they'll say Crolla's my favourite. It's not the case. As a gym, we've all grown together and built together. We've built up friendships and bonds and I don't think you could pull anyone out as my favourite. Yes, I am associated with the Anthony Crolla story, but I feel the same about all of them.

'Maybe because Anthony's been in a lot of big fights, there has been a lot of one-on-one time with him. He's always had crossroads fights that he had to win. Some of the fighters in the gym haven't had those nights yet.'

CHAPTER 1

Dark Nights, New Days

Kieran Farrell

It's hard to find a turning point, but I think in many ways, the Farrell fight drove me on to realise my goal of becoming a world champion.

07.12.12

I was stood in the ring. I was gutted. I remember winning the fight, having the hand raised. Then I remember a noise – his mam.

He was getting carried away on oxygen and she's breaking her heart, holding on to the stretcher. The most horrible memory that will never leave me.

THE nicest man in boxing is trying to compute what has just happened. He's sat on a wooden bench against a grubby off-white wall, clothes neatly hung up on a rack with five pegs. There's a musty, sweaty smell mixed with some sweet-scented deodorant.

Exhausted, Anthony Crolla is slowly unwrapping his swollen, aching hands. The small, makeshift away-fighter dressing room is dimly lit. Other fighters from lower down the bill who've been sharing the room have boxed, changed and gone. The only people left now are a marked-up Anthony Crolla, his trainer Joe Gallagher, stablemate Paul Smith and Richard Thomas, an inspector with the

16

British Boxing Board of Control. It's anything but a winning scene, an unglamorous setting in a back room of the cavernous Bowlers Exhibition Centre, tucked away in the industrial bowels of Trafford Park, Manchester.

Anthony's just dished out the blows that have led to his local rival Kieran Farrell collapsing in the ring at the end of a brutal ten-round contest. The 22-year-old from Heywood slumped near his corner shortly before Anthony's arm had been raised as the unanimous victor.

Just minutes earlier, all around the ring, lairy, beered-up lads suddenly lost the vitriol in their voices. Whether Team Crolla or Team Farrell, they watched and chanted Farrell's name as a game young fighter, a man who'd recently become a father, was stretchered out to a waiting ambulance. A moody, fractured atmosphere turned to one of universal concern.

Crolla had made his way from the ring, thanking a stream of well-wishers as he desperately tried to get to the dressing room as quickly as possible, marching along the busy route – aluminium barriers keeping most of the punters at bay – Joe on one side, Paul on the other. Despite the win, Crolla struggles to find his 'million dollar' smile. It's an awkward walk at the best of times, with narrow stairs and long corridors.

In the dressing room, he knows Kieran's hurt. He knows how hard his opponent trained and could feel the hunger in his punches. He knows Kieran would've done anything possible to walk out of the ring with his head held high, pride dented, shouting that he'd won the fight and should've been awarded the decision. All of that maybe, but certainly ready to fight another day.

Anthony feels sick. He's won the vacant English lightweight belt, but hasn't bothered to pick up the red-brown strap off a floor covered with white, yellow and black tape, bloodstained cotton wool and empty water bottles. The shiny badge on the front of the belt has the St George's cross with the words 'Champion of England' emblazoned around it. It's eerily quiet.

After what feels like an age, but in reality is only an hour, now showered and changed into a black tracksuit, Anthony lifts himself off the bench with an audible intake of breath before walking gingerly from the room, through a gym weights area and down the stairs to the reception of the main hall. His partner Fran is waiting for him.

A poster advertising the fight with pictures of the two combatants has started to peel from the wall next to the toilets. On an adjacent wall, there are only drawing pins on view, still clinging to tiny bits of glossy paper. An eager souvenir hunter has clearly ripped off their night's memento.

A few remaining fans mingle with security and cleaning staff. Crolla's sore right hand is shaken a few more times. He winces with every congratulatory squeeze. He forces a smile for the last remaining selfies. But it's all a bit empty.

Outside the venue, the freezing December air strikes another blow. Anthony throws his kit bag into the boot of his little red Corsa in the now near-empty car park. Fran drives the couple to their temporary digs at her parents' home in Denton, a 15-mile spin anti-clockwise on the M60, Manchester's ring motorway.

* * * * *

Prior to the Farrell fight, Anthony Crolla, who'd turned 26 just a few weeks previously, was considered by many in the game to be damaged goods. He was supposedly on the way down and there was a young lion on the way up, desperate to make his name. So, it was agreed that Farrell would fight Crolla for the vacant English lightweight belt.

Billed 'The Battle of Manchester', the build-up to the fight had, for once where Anthony's concerned, been a touch acrimonious. Comments had been posted on social media and come fight night the mood was a little ugly.

But this was a fight Crolla desperately needed to win. He'd been written off following recent defeats to Derry Mathews and Gary Sykes, his second loss to the Dewsbury man, this time in the *Prizefighter* series.

I had to win this fight. If I didn't, I had a job waiting for me on Monday morning. My mate has a security company and he'd promised me a job in the office should things not go my way. My life as a full-time pro was completely dependent on me beating Kieran. Everything could have been very different.

Farrell vs Crolla was the main event on a night when promoter Dave Coldwell was launching his new Coldwell Boxing app. All the drama from an action-packed bill could be followed online.

Joe Gallagher remembers the night as vividly as his charge. There was so much at stake for both men, the trainer far from immune from criticism and fully aware that his tactics would again be questioned if the unthinkable should happen.

Once the undercard had finished, the main event fighters were called, but Joe wasn't happy. 'I was like, "Nah, we're not coming out of here until Crolla's warm," he recalled. 'I knew they could smell blood.'

It was freezing in there. Wasn't it freezing in there that night?

'Yeah, and you were giving it, "I'm all right now Joe," and I was saying, "No you're fucking not! We're not going out there until we're ready. I don't care about the TV app and the timings, this is all slanted against us and we go out when we're properly warmed up." So that's what we did.'

Kieran, meanwhile, was desperate to get going. He'd prepared, he was ready, he was angry. 'There was no argument between me and Ant. I was like, "Ant's a top fighter, he's a top lad" but it was fucking Joe Gallagher that was getting me going! I was like, "I'm gonna fucking kill him", you know what I mean?

'I've learned now that Joe can get into a fighter's head to take pressure off his fighters. They don't feel any pressure because everyone just wants to have a go at Joe. I remember being sat at our press conference and I said, "Ant's sound but his trainer's a fucking bellend."'

The temperature inside Bowlers was Baltic but the atmosphere was touching boiling point. The noise from the crowd could be heard from Team Crolla's dressing room. For a small hall show, the ring walk was a fairly long one, with corridors and stairs to navigate before entry into the arena. Farrell's fans, who'd congregated near the entrance curtain, were vocal in their assessment of Crolla's skills as he appeared. Unfazed, he sang along to Whitney's 'Million Dollar Bill' and headed for the middle of the room. Once up on the ring apron, on the outside of the ropes, Anthony had a little look around, a nod, a smile, then it was through the ropes and on with business.

I'd never had any animosity, never had a bad reaction off a fighter. Never. With Kieran, there was a bit of needle with me and his brother [Nathan]. We were having words on the way to the ring. His brother was hard work. I didn't know if I was fighting Kieran or his brother! He gave me the throat-slit gesture and all that.

Kieran followed Crolla, revelling in the attention from his supporters on his way to the ring. He bounced through the ropes and made a beeline for his opponent – standing in front of him, eyeballing him before heading back to his corner.

Joe had a plan. It had as much to do with mind games as game plans. 'I had to upset them [Team Farrell],' he explains. 'I thought … no! We're the experienced partner, I've got to get under their skin.'

Joe's preparations appeared to be on the button. Following referee Howard Foster's final instructions and the timekeeper's first bell, Farrell, wearing green shorts with his moniker 'Vicious' emblazoned across a yellow band, fired into Crolla at a fierce pace. The tone of the contest was set, with Crolla declining to go on the back foot and work behind his very fine jab, preferring instead to stand toe to toe – and so a domestic barnstormer took shape.

As the contest progressed, the pace remained frenetic. The plan had been to allow Farrell to burn himself out and while that didn't exactly happen, eventually Crolla's superior skills became evident.

'I got under Kieran Farrell's skin and he fought like a man demented,' Joe reminisced. 'In his corner I could hear, "Go on Kieran, that's it, go on lad! Go on Crolla, they [punches] don't hurt! Crolla's blown himself out!"

'Kieran then put his foot to the floor even more, giving it "Aaarrrggghhh!" Do you understand? I'd psychologically got inside his head. I spoke to Kieran afterwards and he said, "You fucking killed me that night. I was fucking hitting him and you were in the corner going 'cunt' and I was going 'Aaargh!'"

'But there you are, that's experience.'

Farrell withstood some heavy artillery in the latter stages of the bout but was never out of the fight and was there at the final bell. Both fighters were lifted into the air by their respective trainers but the three ringside judges scored it unanimously in favour of Crolla.

'I thought I won the fight, just through my workrate and aggression,' said Kieran. 'But I can see where the judges were coming from. Any round could've been scored either way. After the first five or six rounds, when I started feeling it on my head [bleed on the brain] – and that's not an excuse by any means but it's what happened – it started hurting me. Anything that skimmed past my head was hurting me.

'The pain slowed me down, my hands started coming down. I was coming forward relentlessly, but Ant was then picking his shots and when I watched it back I could see how those four rounds had gone to him.

'As much as I worked hard throughout, he was picking me off – "there's one for the judges", you know what I mean?'

Before the decision was announced, Kieran slumped in the ring and was manoeuvred back to his stool in the corner. Anthony had been stood on the ropes, arms raised, celebrating with his fans. As soon as he realised something wasn't right, he gestured to his supporters to calm things down.

There was panic in his corner. It was very worrying to see the way he went down. The result hadn't been read out but all I was thinking was, 'I hope he's gonna be OK.'

Kieran was placed on a stretcher with an oxygen mask covering his face. The mood in the arena changed dramatically.

'My last memory was when I was sat in the corner and the doctor was shining a torch in my eye and he was going "Kieran, Kieran, can you hear me?"

'I was looking at him with my jaw hanging down and I could actually see and hear what he was saying but I couldn't react. I was spaced out. I couldn't physically move. Then I started fitting.'

As the stretcher was carried from the ring towards the exit, the scorecard of 99-92, 96-94, 99-93 was read out by MC Simon Goodall. Anthony Crolla's arm was raised by referee Foster, but it was a surreal scene.

I was stood in the ring. I was gutted. I remember winning the fight, having the hand raised. Then I remember a noise. His mam. He was getting carried away on oxygen and she's breaking her heart, holding on to the stretcher. The most horrible memory that will never leave me.

21

It was weird but I just remember feeling empty. I had the belt which could save my career but I wasn't bothered. I wanted to just cry.

'When I was on the stretcher, someone said I was clapping. I wasn't. I was fitting. I was in the back of the ambulance fitting and my mum was in the ambulance screaming at me saying, "Stop it! Your dad's going to kill you!" You know, saying anything to try and make me come round.'

Serious injury in the ring, of course, affects both fighters. Whether the injured party or the one responsible, many are never the same again. Punishment had been given and received. The deep aches and pains aren't conducive to sleep at the best of times.

I went home and sat up all night. Chinese whispers start. I was constantly looking at my phone. I'd been in a hard fight so I was exhausted, but I kept looking at my phone and kept thinking. I went to bed but I couldn't sleep. I was shaking.

I was just flicking on social media all night. You'd notice this person say this and another says something else. Someone says he's taken a turn for the worse and I'm then looking at all sorts of medical stuff on the internet.

I was thinking, 'Do I go to the hospital?' Even though I knew there'd be no problem – his dad had come up and spoken to me at the press conference – I just didn't want to turn up when his son was in intensive care. Was it my place to turn up?

'I remember waking up, maybe six in the morning. My brother came in and he was like "Kiers, do you remember me?" I couldn't say anything. Then my dad came in and said, "You all right, son?" I said, "Dad, I just want to be world champion." He started crying his eyes out and I started crying my eyes out.

'When I came round the next day, I was like, "Nath, did you get my belt?" I thought I'd won the fight. He read me the scorecards, and I was, "Aahh fuck."

'My reaction might have been good for them but it was fucking horrific for me. I was like, "You what?"'

Early suggestions that Kieran was merely suffering from exhaustion were overly optimistic, but matters could have been considerably worse.

'In the hospital, they'd done scans to make sure the bleed had stopped on my head. There was a lot of blood. The doctor said it was a small bleed, but very significant in size. I looked at the scans and where the brain normally looks like worms and intestines, mine was black. Covered in blood. All of it.'

Recuperation was painful. The physical and mental wounds began to heal at nature's pace.

'Over the space of four months, it [bleed on the brain] had cleared up and gone. The last appointment I had, they were saying they'd have to operate if the blood hadn't gone. I was thankful they didn't have to cut my head open.'

I was always asking about him, and it sounds bad on my part, but I didn't see him for a while after he got out of hospital. I was always sending my well wishes and I wanted to go and see him, but I didn't. Then one day, I just went to his gym. I messaged him and said I was going to pop up and he was like, 'Yeah, come up.'

I was as nervous as anything driving to his gym. So nervous. It was sound within about 30 seconds, but on my way I wanted to spew it. It actually felt like I was going to a fight I was so nervous. I just didn't know what to say, what to do.

It had taken me a long time to meet Kieran after the fight and I wish I'd done it sooner, but now we're sound, we're mates. There wasn't any animosity, it was just awkward for a while. When I got there, all the kids were in and they were all asking questions. I wish I'd done it earlier but by the time Kieran was making a full recovery, I was going into another fight – Derry II. Selfishly, it wasn't the time to go and see him.

Kieran was mad dedicated and trained as hard as anyone. It's sad to see someone not pursue what he wanted to do. But, everything happens for a reason, and he's doing well.

And the brother?

You know what? Even years after the fight, he was always a bit stand-offish, but recently I've seen him and we had a chat. He's all right now. But listen, it was his brother and he's an emotional kid.

It was spelled out to Farrell, in no uncertain terms, that his recovery was miraculous but his fighting days were done. This message took a while to get through.

'I always thought I'd fight again. I tried keeping the belief that if I didn't get a British licence, I'd get an Irish licence. I kept that belief for a year and when I applied for a licence, I got a reply more or less saying, "Kieran, you've had a good career, just knock it on the head."

'I just couldn't believe I had the injury. Michael Watson rang me and said, "You're in the same boat as me." I was like, "I'm not in the same boat as you mate," because I just felt I wasn't even though I'd had the same injury.'

With his boxing career cut short, Kieran threw all his whirlwind energy into pursuing a new dream – having his own gym. With sponsors on board and cash raised from a benefit night – attended by his idol and former promoter Ricky Hatton and Jamie Moore, who'd been on co-commentary duty for Farrell's last fight – the dream quickly became reality. 'The People's Gym' is just a few doors up from the Farrell family home in Wham Street, Heywood.

New dawn, new day and a new outlet for his ambitions – the local community turned out for the opening and a thriving new gym for local kids was born. Regardless of the gym's success, the same old urges persisted. Despite all the experts and organisations that had told Kieran he could not box again, the temptation to prove people wrong, like he'd always done, was almost too great. Finally, the brutal reality of popular middleweight Nick Blackwell's head injuries, suffered in both his British title fight with Chris Eubank Jr and subsequent sparring sessions, helped drive the message home.

'I'll be honest. I'm not going to say I didn't have a spar, because I did. I sparred with pros, with everyone, and I was doing it regular right up until I got told he'd [Blackwell] been put back in hospital and that he had a bleed on the brain this time. He had a bleed on the skull the first time. He then got a bleed on the brain, the same as the one I got, and not everyone's so lucky with that. I was told that things were looking up for him because he'd spoken a word. I was like, "Fucking hell, he's spoken a word! It's bad, this." I saw a picture and I was fucking horrified. I thought, "You know what? I'll never do that [spar] again." I felt selfish.

'I've got a ninth-month-old baby and a four-year-old daughter, so for me to be getting in the ring like that, it's just my own selfishness. I needed to knock it on the head and I have done ever since November last year. It's no good.

'You just don't know what's going on inside your head and sometimes, even last night, when I was on a flight and with the pressure and all that, I didn't even know at one point if I could fly again. I know I can't drive because I can't keep in me head what I've got to learn for the theory. I am slowed down a little bit. If I go running, one side of me face will drop. Keeping fit's all right, but I can't keep up with the pros and that's what I've learned. I'm not a fighter now.

'My mum still suffers depression now and again from it [the fight]. It's like my brother. He put on three or four stone in weight. He got it all off eventually, but he tells me how he used to come and put pillows on my radiator next to my bed to make sure I didn't bang my head.

'It's the same now. He'll come to the gym and watch to make sure I don't go near the bag with my head when I'm hitting it. It's had a massive effect on my family. My dad's strong. He's never let it show that it's affected him but I know it affected everyone. They're all buzzing off how well I'm doing now.'

So, attention is now fully focused in other areas of the sport. Kieran is a coach, working with kids and professionals, along with dual roles as a promoter and matchmaker.

'I do everything. To be honest it's all in a day's work, but it's not normal hours. It's from six in the morning until 11 or 12 at night. I'm busy but I enjoy it. I'm craving a champion. That's all I want to do.

'When I trained for Crolla, I left no stone unturned. Everything I did was a million per cent and I had no regrets about having the fight, either. Shit happens and in life I think it's about your destiny. Overall, I feel all right. I get a headache now and again, like everyone. Mine probably get a bit worse. I might get a dizzy spell but nothing too major. If I do too much physically, it's bad for me.'

* * * * *

Fast forward three months and Kieran Farrell is at Gloves Gym, Bolton. Clad in baggy dark T-shirt and grey jogging bottoms, he has a towel over his left shoulder, right foot up on the ring apron, left hand holding a water bottle, the other clinging to the middle rope. He's shouting instructions at his fighter, George Brennan, a 20-year-old bantamweight from Altrincham. Farrell's brought the novice pro here to spar with former world champion Paul Butler. It's a lively tussle and Kieran's feinting and jabbing in tandem with every shot George attempts to land. Life as a trainer is suiting him more than ever now. He's in a happy place.

Spar over, he reflects on his renewed vigour as his former foe Anthony Crolla goes to work on a heavy bag at the far end of the square room.

'If I hadn't fought Ant, I wouldn't have met George and he wouldn't be doing this now,' he says, pointing towards Brennan as the fighter towels down. 'Other fighters wouldn't have had the opportunity over in Ireland. I'm doing a lot for other people and I got a British Empire medal off the Queen. Buzzing. That's me, happy days! Everything I'm doing now, getting kids off the street and all that, I'm happy.

'I think it's helped him [Crolla] because I've moved on from it. We've stayed in touch, we talk. If I ring him, he answers. If he can't get to the phone, he rings me back and says sorry for missing the call. He's bang-on. When people say he's one of the nicest lads and all that, well, I've never met a nicer lad than Ant.

'For Ant to keep doing what he's doing does me proud. Every time he wins, I'm like – "Yes!" I think first time it was a tight fight but Linares pipped it. Ant's now got the raging burn inside him to get that title and then unify the division. For me, him achieving that goal, you know what? That'll mean I only got beat once and that was by the unified lightweight world champion. I'll buzz off that.

'Not getting that win when we fought, it doesn't matter to me now. Just to be here and to watch Anthony do as good as he is, and be in a fit state to do that, I'm happy.

'At the end of the day, I'm glad Ant got the victory because if he'd have lost, it could've been him retired. I'd have still got a bleed on the brain. I might have won the belt, but I'd still have a bleed on the brain and would never box again.

'He's done it for both of us, for him and me. He's achieved world glory and that's all I ever wanted to do. I'm buzzing he's done it.'

Joe Gallagher walks past and smiles at Kieran, who nods and says, 'Cheers Joe.' Is this the same Joe Gallagher who had riled him so much? The same 'bellend'?

A boyish grin lights up Farrell's face. It makes him look younger than his years – a cheeky, freckly kid, his eyes wide open as he explains, 'Before the fight there were words said – it's one of those things. I was a wild man. I was 22 years old. I've calmed myself down a bit now, but back in the day I was a bit of a psycho, like.

'I've heard a lot of people say this and that about Joe, but it's because they're not in his circle, and it's a high circle to be in. There'll be gossip and stories made up but I know Joe's bang-on. I've been helping Joe with things he's doing and he's always helping me.'

Along with a busy diary – amateurs to nurture, professionals to find dates for and his own shows to sort – it's a year to look forward to for the one-time 'Vicious' Farrell.

'It couldn't really be better for me. I keep improving. Even though I feel 100 per cent now, I reckon in a year I'll look back at me now and think, "Fucking hell, look at me there!"

'I slur my words and I stutter but I keep seeing now that I'm getting better with all that. Walking down the street, I don't look any different to anyone else – bar the dodgy haircut, know what I mean!'

Derry Mathews II

Joe had been saying that I wasn't myself and that I hadn't been for a while. I didn't know it, but that's what he says. Kieran had had to retire and the lads in the gym were very supportive, but I couldn't stop thinking about it. It was bad.

It was the first outing after the Farrell fight. Emotionally, there were many questions to be asked and answered. The fact it was a rematch against Derry Mathews – the man who'd stunned him by inflicting his first stoppage defeat – only added to an already intense and draining period in Crolla's life.

For Derry, it was simple. He'd beat Anthony again and move closer to his dream of winning a world title.

The first fight, on 21 April 2012, was held at Oldham Sports Centre, just down the road from Crolla's home. The venue has since been replaced by a spanking new £15m facility, but on this night it was the old head who prevailed over the young gun.

Always a ticket seller, Derry had his usual vocal support, which added to a fevered atmosphere in the small but packed hall. He'd been saying all along in the build-up that he'd shock the boxing world and take Anthony's Lonsdale Belt. Along with trainer Danny Vaughan, Derry locked himself away in Scotland, away from his family and home comforts. He was hungry to prove everyone wrong. He believed he had a game plan to win.

While Derry was convinced, his previous fight, a crushing defeat to Ermiliano Marsili for the vacant IBO lightweight title, had left many questioning the Liverpudlian's future in the game.

Meanwhile, the career trajectory of Anthony Crolla was going only one way. He was on the up. He had a belt, and as Joe always says to his fighters, if you have a title you'll have work.

The British lightweight crown had been claimed in typical Crolla fashion. An opportunity had arisen while preparations were in full swing for a fight with Carl Johanneson. Gavin Rees was meant to be defending the title against Liverpool's John Watson, but injury forced the Welshman to vacate. Crolla was asked if he fancied stepping up from super-featherweight to embrace the challenge. He did. So, it was all about defending the belt. All looked well as a smiling Crolla confidently made his ring walk, with Whitney Houston's 'Million Dollar Bill', as ever, accompanying him in.

Anthony started well with a good tempo, landing the better shots as cries of 'Manchester, la la la' rang around. It was give and take until things began to unravel in the third round. A huge right uppercut put Crolla on the canvas for the first time in this career – amateur or professional – and a cut to the right eye didn't help matters.

Into the fourth round, a bad cut by his left eye added to Crolla's woes. It was toe to toe again, with Crolla finishing strongly. A decent fifth round in which Crolla landed some good body shots offered some hope. But a big left hand wobbled the champion and as Derry sensed blood, John Keane stepped in and waved the contest off.

'I remember the Hattons were promoting him [Crolla] at the time,' Derry explains. 'Ricky rang me personally and offered me the fight. I jumped at it. I knew I could beat him. I think that when I boxed him, and they might say I'm wrong, but Joe Gallagher's boxers all seemed to come forward in straight lines.

'He just kept coming at me, coming at me. I knew that if I caught him with an uppercut … we'd been working on it for five weeks in the gym and it paid off.

'The build-up to the fight was brilliant – Liverpool vs Manchester rivalry. All the social media stuff, Twitter had started and that was good. It was a great night.

'After the fight, I remember going up to him in the corner and just thanking him for the opportunity. I told him he'd come back a better man. He has. He's at a position at lightweight where I wanted to be.'

The Mathews defeat was the first high-profile TV loss of Crolla's career. A devastating blow. It was more surprising given the fact Anthony had gone into the fight following a dominant performance against Willie Limond in Motherwell a few months previously.

I went home and my dad had the fight on. I remember my brother [Will] saying, 'Dad, turn it off!' I was thinking I'd let everyone down and was watching it in tears. My dad's like, 'Look at this bit here, Ant, you're doing this wrong and that wrong.' He just kept talking at me, 'Look at this round.' I'm thinking, 'Oh dad. stop it!' Bloody hell. I was cringing.

I wouldn't change it now. It was a massive blessing in disguise. It shouldn't have been stopped, but it was the best lesson. If I'd have won, I would've boxed Gavin Rees next. If I'd have boxed like that, I'd have got flattened.

Next up was *Prizefighter* at the Olympia in Liverpool, a tournament that also included Derry Mathews, another old foe Gary Sykes and up-and-coming Mancunian Terry Flanagan. The draw threw up Anthony against local man Stephen Jennings.

He navigated that three-round hurdle to shake off the demons in front of a rowdy crowd and a live Sky Sports audience. The semi-final stage is where this journey would end. A points defeat to Gary Sykes, the Indian sign still hanging over Crolla. Meanwhile, Derry was outdone by Terry, who went on to beat Sykes in the final.

The *Prizefighter* gamble hadn't come off, but a defeat in the three-round lottery is never considered a crushing blow for any fighter. For Anthony, it was just another of life's experiences, then on to the next challenge. Kieran Farrell.

The Farrell victory set up another night with Derry and a chance for Anthony to avenge the loss and claim the vacant Commonwealth lightweight belt. Since their first fight, Derry had lost the Lonsdale strap after being stopped by Gavin Rees. Dirty Derry vs Million Dollar was chief support to Tony Bellew's WBC silver light-heavyweight title clash with Isaac Chilemba at the Liverpool Echo Arena. Lower down the bill were Anthony's stablemates Callum Smith and Scott Cardle, both enjoying routine victories.

Anthony started well enough, blocking most of Derry's shots or taking them on the arms and landing a couple himself when the opportunities presented themselves. Working off the back foot, the second round was positive, with cut-prone Derry leaking blood from a nick on his right eye. The third round was better again for Anthony as his shots were finding the target and silencing the Scousers temporarily.

A change in tactics saw Crolla press forward, seemingly in control of the fight as the middle rounds approached, but Mathews forced his way back in and started to land heavy blows, damaging Crolla's right eye in the process.

Mathews continued to enjoy a good spell, taking rounds until Anthony once again stepped up the tempo in the eighth, using the jab well.

Derry was still proving awkward and landed the most eye-catching punch of the contest in the ninth, but Crolla's fitness showed. He withstood it and came back stronger, dominating the final two rounds of an absorbing contest. Both camps celebrated at the final bell. A close fight was decided by Steve Gray's card of 115-115 after Marcus McDonnell judged in favour of Mathews, 115-113, while Ian John Lewis went for Crolla, 115-113.

Neither man could hide their disappointment at the draw.

'I thought I won the fight by two rounds,' Derry said. 'I watched it over and over again. But then, he'll say he won the fight by two rounds. It was one of them give-and-take-fights. I think it was round eight, I hit him with a right hand and he nearly went. I don't know how he stayed up. I think in the last round I had in my head that I'd won the fight, so I took my foot off the gas and tried to box. He won the last round and got the draw. It's one of them where I was frustrated, but at the same time it was a great night and a great fight.'

I felt I'd done enough. It was a great fight, a close fight, but I thought I won the championship rounds. But you know, Derry thought he'd done enough. I thought I won the early rounds because my shots were landing. He did catch me with some good shots but my fitness carried me through. The Liverpool crowd was great and it was the type of fight fans would want to see over and over again.

Liverpool people love their boxing and they've always been sound with me, even when I've been fighting their lads. The rivalry in boxing is obviously different to the football!

It's a sentiment Mathews agrees with. 'Ricky Hatton, Terry Flanagan, Anthony Crolla – I'd pay to go and watch them,' he said. 'They're the same as us, we're both fighting cities. The North West is the best boxing region in Britain. It's good to be a part of it.'

With his own inner-city gym, the 'Derry Mathews Boxing Academy', Derry is following in the footsteps of so many other fighters in making sure he does his bit for his community. Along with the familiar tale of kids coming in off the streets, the gym also delivers sessions for people with learning disabilities and conditions such as cerebral palsy, autism and spina bifida.

'I love the sport and the sport's been good to me,' he explains. 'I love getting up of a morning, half-five or six, to go training. I open the gym, I get the buzz. I do it because I love the sport.

'It's mad how boxing is. Me and Anthony went from a sports centre, fighting for peanuts, and I mean peanuts, to him becoming a world champion and me having world title fights. Anthony's a tremendous athlete and a great fighter. A lovely person, a family man like myself.

'If anyone can make money out of boxing, then they deserve a pat on the back. People who've beaten me, anyone in boxing, I just want them to win, not so much to get the win, but to get money to secure their children's future or their future.

'Anthony's a great fighter, one I've got a lot of respect for. He was and still is the Mr Nice Guy of boxing. The crowd love him. He turned his career around and he deserves a medal for that alone. I stopped him, but look at what him and Joe Gallagher have gone on to do.'

Gavin Rees

I always liked him, a tough, busy fighter with fast hands. If I could choose one person not to fight outside a boxing ring, out of all my opponents, it'd be Gavin Rees.

While not an ideal outcome, the second Mathews fight kept Anthony in the mix. Proving once again that he'd face any domestic opponent put in front of him, a fight with former WBA light-welterweight champion Gavin Rees was made at Bolton Arena. The venue was handy for Crolla despite 'The Rock' being the Matchroom fighter on a Matchroom promotion. With Eddie Hearn at the helm, it meant another night of live Sky Sports coverage and potentially another fan-friendly tussle. The Welshman was returning to action following a brutal TKO at the hands of then rising superstar Adrien Broner. No shame in that, of course, but at 33 what had it taken out of him?

Rees, as had usually been the case, would be giving up more than four inches in height to Crolla. Whether fighting at lightweight or super-lightweight, a lack of inches hadn't ever really hindered the tough-as-teak man from Newport.

I always liked him, a tough, busy fighter with fast hands. If I could choose one person not to fight outside a boxing ring, out of all my opponents, it'd be Gavin Rees. He's short, hard and takes a shot.

I was the opponent, even though we were in Bolton! Francesca was a few months away from giving birth to Jesse. My dad is old school and I used him for motivation. I remember telling him that Fran had fallen pregnant. I was 26 at the time and I remember him saying that I didn't have a house. It added motivation. I knew if I beat Gavin, there'd be a Matchroom contract waiting for me. Not officially, but I was sure there would be. But if I lost, then I'm an opponent again.

First child on the way, saving to get a deposit to put down on the first house. So much was riding on it.

If added motivation were needed, it was easily found in the fact the pair were competing for the WBO inter-continental title. It was, in effect, a world title eliminator that could set up a shot at Scotland's WBO champion Ricky Burns.

The build-up was, as expected, hugely respectful. Again, it was a Crolla fight where everyone could see the event for what it was – a well-balanced boxing bout. No frills, no nonsense, just two good lads who were ready to go at it.

A good undercard set things up nicely. There were stoppage wins for Crolla's pals Scott Quigg, who was too much for William Prado, and Paul Smith, the eldest of the fighting quartet of brothers, who settled an all-Scouse argument with Tony Dodson in the chief support.

Not surprisingly, Crolla was feeling the love from most of the supporters crammed into the venue, which sits in the shadow of the Macron Stadium – home of Bolton Wanderers FC. The fans who'd made the short trip from Manchester were creating a football atmosphere, constantly singing the familiar 'Ooooh Anthony Crolla …' to the tune of The White Stripes' 'Seven Nation Army'.

Once referee Phil Edwards got matters under way, Rees started busily, pawing away at Crolla's high guard without much success. Workrate had him edging Anthony in the early stages, although the cleaner shots were coming from the younger man, who picked off Rees as he applied constant pressure.

A clash of heads in the fourth saw Rees pick up a small cut by the left eye. This spurred on Crolla, who upped the pace in the fifth, forcing Rees backwards. The action picked up again in the sixth with good work from the Welshman.

As the fight went into the latter stages, both men were happy to trade. By now, they were covered in blood after another accidental head clash. Each man called on his resources for a final hurrah down the home straight as weariness took hold, Rees touching the canvas in the tenth, although this was ruled as a slip.

It was another close contest to back up the claims that Crolla's 'never in a bad fight'. Two judges made it 115-113 and 116-113 to

Crolla, with the third scoring it 115-115. It was a majority decision for the man from New Moston.

I thought I'd done enough, but you never know. Nothing surprised me about him. He's a tough, tough man. I trained so hard for that fight because I knew to beat a world-class fighter you have to put in a world-class performance. I felt I boxed well at times and boxed to a plan. I stuck to the plan and it paid off. When it got tough, the crowd really helped me home. Afterwards, it was one of the most emotional nights. It was the difference. It bought me some time to give us a start.

Along with a bit of financial stability, the victory paved the way for the tantalising prospect of Crolla fighting for a world title. To make that dream a reality, Ricky Burns needed to come through his fight with tough Mexican Raymundo Beltran, a man Anthony had sparred at the Wild Card Gym in Los Angeles.

New dawn

I'm delighted to join Eddie Hearn and Matchroom and I cannot wait for my first fight with them.

The setting is the Radisson Blu Edwardian Hotel, Manchester. This 'Palazzo' building – the Free Trade Hall – was originally a public assembly hall that turned into a concert venue. It was home to the Halle Orchestra and the Lesser Free Trade Hall (an upstairs room) is most famous for a Sex Pistols gig in 1976 that inspired a plethora of Manchester bands, including Joy Division and The Smiths.

History is all around then as Anthony Crolla is officially unveiled as Matchroom's latest signing. It's a sideshow to the main event, the press conference to promote Carl Froch against George Groves, an eagerly awaited super-middleweight showdown at the then-named Phones4u Arena.

Anthony was right. He knew that a career-best victory over Rees would result in a new, mutually beneficial partnership. Sitting at a table, posing for the cameras, Anthony looked relaxed. Casually dressed in a blue and black check shirt, pen in hand, Eddie Hearn leaning in on the left side with Joe on his right, Anthony flashed a big smile for the snappers.

I'm delighted to join Eddie Hearn and Matchroom and I cannot wait for my first fight with them. Froch vs Groves is a massive night and it's great to be a part of it. I am right up there in the reckoning now and I know Eddie believes I am close to major fights, so it's down to me to prove that, starting in Manchester on 23 November.

Eddie Hearn beamed about his new signing. 'His [Crolla's] victory over former world champion Gavin Rees has propelled him to another level, and beyond the huge domestic opportunities lies a world title challenge for him in 2014.

'He will be part of the huge Froch vs Groves show on 23 November, with the opponent and undercard announcement the week commencing 30 September.'

By this point, the projected Ricky Burns fight was off the table. The Scot had endured a 'life and death' with Beltran but somehow kept hold of his WBO belt following a highly controversial draw. Burns, who had his jaw broken in the second round and suffered a heavy knockdown, showed tremendous bravery but was left disfigured at the end of the contest and looked as surprised as Beltran was sickened when the scores were announced. Not the greatest advert for boxing officiating in front of a partisan Glaswegian crowd.

The seriousness of the injury – titanium plates were fitted the day after the fight – put a question mark over when, or even if, Ricky would return to action. So, for Crolla, it was on with another route.

Meanwhile, Joe was happy with Anthony's Matchroom deal and the relationship remains strong to this day, despite all the challenges professional boxing presents.

'Eddie Hearn, Frank Warren, Mick Hennessy – they're promoters who all want to put on the biggest shows, bring in the most money and pay the least,' Joe said. 'It's my job as a trainer and manager to get the most money for my fighters. We have games of tug-o-war – they'll pull one way and I'll pull another, but somewhere in the middle you meet. They have a responsibility to their broadcaster, whether it's BT, Box Nation or Sky, to deliver the best fights. It's up to me to make sure the fighters are well paid.

'Boxing is legalised killing. Dress it up any way you want, but it's legalised killing. At the end of the day, you're talking about someone's child. I have a responsibility to my fighters that they arrive home safely, with their health intact and with decent money for their work. The reward has to be worth the risk, that's why it's called prize fighting.

'Eddie Hearn's an ambitious young promoter. He's growing all the time. There's great competition now with ITV as well, so Eddie has to up his game. There's not a monopoly any more and there are probably a few Matchroom fighters looking at what everyone else is doing.

'You know, Eddie sometimes calls me the biggest pain in boxing but that's only because of the number of fighters I have. I might have a two-hour telephone call or discussion, disagreement, agreement over say, Anthony Crolla. But after that two hours we might move on to Scott Cardle, then there's another argument and then we move on to Stephen Smith.

'To Eddie, it seems that I'm always on to him, but most of the time we work things out, we get on, and the lads are all in big shows. He's delivering the titles and the fights for my lads and most of the time they're delivering the results for him.'

CHAPTER 2

Derbies and Away Day Specials

MANCHESTER is often described as a fight city, a place with boxing pedigree. So many bustling amateur gyms, emerging professionals and those that have affirmed their names in legend. Fighters who've crossed over to reach the casual fan and enthuse those who'd have a flimsy interest in sport at all. Ricky Hatton is one man who certainly captured the public's imagination way beyond his Hyde home.

No other fighter, surely, will command a 35,000-strong army to cross the Atlantic in the hope they'd get to see their idol light up the neon strip of Las Vegas. The Floyd Mayweather Jr vs Hatton fight in December 2007 was extraordinary. Most of the travelling fans had little or no chance of gaining entry to the MGM Grand, but were there anyway, draining Sin City of its plentiful liquor while the broken record soundtrack of 'there's only one Ricky Hatton' made the desert a peculiar winter wonderland.

Ricky's legend was long assured before he became a fighter-turned-promoter. Not surprisingly, he held a lot of sway when attracting local fighters to his promising stable – Crolla being one.

Other hungry and ambitious fighters joined more seasoned names, which helped Ricky and his team fix up a couple of handy local derbies.

An all-city scrap is always a winner for drumming up local press, shifting a few tickets and generally helping to create a buzz around town. Football often comes into it – red vs blue an obvious selling point.

Anthony has featured in five all-Manchester bouts in his career so far and come out on top in all of them. He started his run on his professional debut on 14 October 2006. Aged 19, Crolla outpointed Adbul Rashid, the fighting accountant from Withington, in a four-rounder on the Joe Calzaghe vs Sakio Bika bill at what was then the MEN (*Manchester Evening News*) Arena. This venue would always be special for 'Million Dollar'.

Michael Brodie

Crolla's first prominent all-Manchester match-up was against Michael Brodie in November 2009 – New Moston vs Collyhurst. A former world title contender and ex-British, Commonwealth and European champion, Brodie had helped lead the way for the likes of Ricky Hatton.

This was a fighter who'd done so much and got so far without any of life's advantages, a man who'd been so close at elite level, devastated at the perceived robbery against Willie Jorrin in his WBC super-bantamweight title challenge and twice more denied in his battles for WBC featherweight honours against In-Jin Chi. Their first meeting – a draw – was mired in controversy, while his second attempt ended in a stoppage defeat. One more crack at a world title ended badly again when Brodie was stopped by WBO champion Scott Harrison. Four years on from that defeat, Brodie was keen to find out what he had left.

Mark Alexander was Brodie's opponent at Manchester's Velodrome and for a time it looked like the ring return might end swiftly.

'The kid put me down five times, split me eye and all that, but I knocked him out in the fourth round,' recalled Brodie.

A few weeks later, at the same venue, Crolla outpointed John Baguley – his first fight working with Joe Gallagher – to set up a derby date.

We were with the same promoter [Hatton] at the time, so there were no excuses. I had to fight him, know what I mean? But he was someone I'd always looked up to. He was right up there with Ricky Hatton. Ricky was number one, then Brodie. I used to go and watch all his fights and we had a lot of the same friends, so it was one of those nights where the crowd was split and everyone was there just hoping for a good fight. Mike was also one of Joe's favourite fighters, so it wasn't nice we were kind of plotting to end his career. But it was just business.

'I would've liked to have a few more warm-ups before Crolla, then I think I would've been all right,' Brodie remembered. 'I'd been out the ring a long time. A few more warm-ups and it would've been a different fight.'

Robin Park Centre in Wigan was the scene for a night of action live on Sky Sports. Brodie vs Crolla was chief support, with the main event Anthony Small's defence of his British and Commonwealth super-welterweight titles against Manchester's Thomas McDonagh.

Brodie began the fight tentatively and Anthony went about his business. He took full advantage, landing shots at will and making Brodie look every day of his 35 years. It was a different story in round two, however. Brodie worked to the head and body, forcing Anthony to use his footwork rather than try to out-man the veteran.

While the second session was Brodie's, any hope his fans had of seeing the years rolled back were soon extinguished. Crolla's pressure forced Brodie backwards, the younger man now landing freely with big right hands before a right hook from the southpaw stance put Brodie on the canvas. He gamely beat Steve Gray's count, but the referee had seen enough and waved it off at the end of round three.

Michael Brodie's professional career ended that night.

'I was drained in that fight. I'd come down from 11st 7lbs to try and make 9st 6lbs. I didn't feel myself. Antony's a fit lad, so I knew I was going to have a hard fight. But I was drained. I remember spewing up after the weigh-in coz me stomach couldn't take food. I went to Nando's with Jamie Moore and only ate a bit of chicken, but spewed up everywhere. I felt hangin'.

'I still thought I'd beat him, but Anthony's a really good, fit kid. I take my hat off to him; he beat me fair and square. He proper battered me. I'm not surprised how well he's done because he's so fit and he listens. He's confident now. He's had world title fights and won a world title.

'I used to train with him when he was young. Listen, I love the kid and wish him all the best in the world. He deserves it, he puts the graft in. But, he didn't fight Michael Brodie that night. That fight would've ended a different way.

'It was hard to come back. After I got beat, I thought, "Fuck it, it's not me." I knew I was better than that.'

I boxed a shell of Mike. He'd been a big hero of mine and I've nothing but respect for him.

I saw him in a pub ages after. I was in there to drop off some tickets and as I walked past him, it was like 'Hiya!' We had a big hug. He was happy enough, well he certainly seemed happy enough, but you know, he just didn't get what he deserved.

It's been far from an easy ride for Brodie out of the ring. He went from the heady heights of world title challenges to the low of a prison spell, spending two months locked up on a charge of conspiracy to supply cocaine after drugs were found in his taxi. He always insisted he was innocent and, following a six-week trial, was found not guilty.

'I've been through a lot. I've had tough times, been divorced, been hung out to dry by people. But I've got three kids – I love my kids. I've got Bonnie, who's 20, Michael, who's 11 and lives in London, and my little daughter Grace.

'I'm helping my old trainer Sean Rafferty train the kids down at Terry Flanagan's gym now [Ancoats ABC]. I want to pass what I know on to the kids. I'm back involved coz I miss it. But I'm a proper lad and I need to work, so I've gone out and got a job on a building site. Listen, it's all right. It pays the bills.

'But I want to get more into the boxing again, it's all I know. Hopefully I can help a kid from Collyhurst come through, just like I did.'

Andy Morris

Routine victories over James Nesbitt, Sid Razak and Chris Riley followed the Brodie fight. The next Manchester derby put Anthony in with another familiar face and again a fighter he had great affection for. Once more, both fighters were in Ricky Hatton's stable and the match-up provided Anthony with an opportunity to win his first title – the vacant English super-featherweight strap. Standing in the way was Wythenshawe's Andy Morris.

Andy Morris was the most skilful fighter I've ever fought. I used to love watching him. When I was 12, I boxed his cousin, Anthony Binden, in my first ever fight.

Andy was like a little pro at 15. He always looked the part, dead-smart kit, and he was brilliant to watch. I remember sparring with him when I was about 18 or 19. He snotted me! Snotted me, he did! I was only an amateur giving him a few rounds, but I learned so much. It sounds cheesy, but I was buzzing just to share a few rounds with him. Covered in claret, like, but it was great. It was mad that we ended up boxing later on. But it was another big night. A big fight.

Morris was the more experienced of the two – a former British featherweight champion – but it was the kind of situation he wasn't too comfortable with. Ultimately, though, business prevailed and it had to happen.

'I'd say we were mates,' Morris remembered. 'To go into a fight against one of your mates, it's sort of a nasty situation. At that stage of my career, it was make or break. When you're fighting someone, you want to hurt them, do damage to them. It was hard to get that in my head with Crolla. Everyone else I'd fought I'd wanted to tear their head off. I wanted to hurt them, make a statement. With this fight, I just needed the win. I needed to do what I can do and get the win.'

That big night took place at Bolton Wanderers' in-house hotel (formerly De Vere), a venue fully integrated into the Macron Stadium, where apparently 'you're never far from the action', so the blurb goes. On this occasion, there were no eyes on the football pitch. All supporters were indoors, focusing on the squared circle rather than the centre circle. City fan Morris taking on Crolla the Red Devil, south Manchester vs north Manchester.

Morris was coming into the fight off a confidence-boosting knockout of Georgian journeyman Nugzar Margvelashvili. Before that, he'd suffered massive disappointment in failing to regain the

British title, dropping a unanimous decision to Crolla nemesis Gary Sykes.

The English belt was the only way back for Morris. Beating Crolla to win it would make a huge statement too. For Anthony, it was all about momentum. Five wins on the bounce since hooking up with Joe, no margin for error.

Vocal support for both men created a fierce din as referee Dave Parris called the lads together for final instructions. The 'Wythenshawe Warrior' started the contest well, boxing at distance, working the body.

It wasn't going my way. It must have been round four. I don't know whether Andy had had a decent round, or that the tide was turning, but I'd come back to the corner feeling sorry for myself. Anyway, Joe goes, 'Crolla, listen to me. These cunts won't give you another chance' – meaning Hatton Promotions! He said, 'This is your chance. These cunts won't give you another chance. Lose this and ...'

Joe was using siege mentality tactics to try and get Anthony fired up.

'The language makes it sound a bit harsh, but I did feel they all wanted Andy to win and Crolla needed a rocket up his arse,' Gallagher recalled. 'Crolla's had his back to the wall in a few fights and he needs that wake-up call. He needed to get out there and get a stoppage because the fight was slipping away from him.'

The plan had always been to weather the Morris storm and take over in the second half of the contest. Crolla, fresher and younger and with a phenomenal engine, eventually did just that, wearing Morris down before forcing a stoppage in the sixth round.

'I think in the first few rounds we were just getting a feel for each other,' Andy said. 'Then I felt I was winning the fight but diet, weight loss and everything else started to catch up. As soon as me eye shut, it was game over. You can't fight the likes of Anthony Crolla with one eye.'

Obviously, it was a shame for Andy, but again it's just business. I was delighted to get the English belt and it put me right on track.

After the fight, I found out that Sky Sports had picked up Joe bollocking me. Every bit of it! The Hattons asked me to meet up on the Monday. They said, 'Well done, Anthony, but Joe can't be saying that!' Joe wasn't at the meeting obviously!

We were both their lads and they might have been cheering for Andy on the night, but they knew him better than they knew me. Matthew Hatton was ringside cheering for Andy. I get on with Matthew, but I respect the fact he's a lot closer to Andy than me. He's his mate, but Joe didn't see it that way!

A dejected Morris, just like Michael Brodie before him, left a professional ring for the last time after defeat to Crolla.

'I think I was tired of boxing. It's why I retired afterwards. My heart wasn't in it. I wasn't capable any more. A lot of people said, "You're only young, there are plenty more fights," but it was time to call it a day.

'I always listened to me dad [Andy Sr]. He'd been at every single one of my fights, amateur and professional, every single one, and even he said to me before the fight that if I didn't win it was time to call it a day. He knew.'

Fortunately for Morris, hanging up the gloves didn't lead to other hang-ups. There was no craving for the crowd, no yearning for another run at a title, no desire to fight for money. He was content to walk away.

'It's no shame to get beat by Crolla. It's quite good to have someone like him on your CV. I'd like to think that during my career I could have beaten him. I was beating him but my eye shut. But if you're not into it, there's no point in coming back.'

With a fine amateur and professional career behind him, and no more exhausting battles in the ring, Andy's still digging deep as a drainage specialist for Cummins Civil Engineering, working on the smart motorway project in north Cheshire.

A family man, all Andy's spare time is spent with wife Steph and their three children. Four-year-old daughter Mila's a budding gymnast, while his two boys – Mason, 13, and Mikey, nine – have the boxing bug, learning their craft at Timperley ABC. Andy's happy to take a step back and leave the tuition to head coach Mark Davidson.

'He [Mark] does collar me from time to time and tells me to do pads or do a bit of coaching with so and so. I don't mind at all, but I couldn't go into coaching properly. I just don't have the time. When I can, of course I'm happy to help out.'

From Lonsdale Belt to Foster Jr

Opportunities present themselves from time to time. An English title helps eke out those chances in life. One such moment came a few months after the Morris fight. Gavin Rees was the British lightweight champion, but he had to vacate the title due to surgery on a nose injury. John Watson, who'd already lost in his previous bid for Rees's belt, was in line for another shot, while Anthony was invited to step up a division and take the fight with Watson on his home turf in Liverpool.

Crolla had been due to defend his English belt against Carl Johanneson – also an eliminator for the British title – but the temptation to move things a little quicker, regardless of the weight issue, was too great. Again, Crolla was doubted. How could he live with the much bigger man in the lion's den?

Sparring bigger lads in his own gym, like John Murray, had convinced fighter and coach that the underdog would prevail. He did. It was lively at the Olympia, Crolla's fans doing their bit in a hostile environment, their man involved in a bit of give and take before 'Million Dollar' cashed in with a brutal ninth-round stoppage.

Going into the fight as the underdog, Anthony's superior fitness and skillset proved too much for his bigger opponent. Crolla completely took over and from the sixth round it was simply a matter of when, not if, he'd have his hand raised. As it was, a wicked right hook did the damage in the ninth.

With the aesthetically pleasing Lonsdale Belt around his waist, options were plentiful. Gavin Rees had a European title, so that made sense, but it would have to wait. Next up for Crolla was Herve de Luca, a late replacement for Ghanaian Osumanu Akaba. It wasn't much of a fight as first-round body shots put the Belgian down three times before the referee waved it off.

The Strip

Boxing in Las Vegas is fairly high, if not top, on the list for every kid who ever laced on a pair of gloves. It was also a dream of the kid from

New Moston to get his name in lights on the strip. Part of that dream became reality in September 2011. He wasn't the star attraction at the MGM Grand, but did get to showcase his skills to the American public on the night Floyd Mayweather Jr controversially knocked out Victor Ortiz.

Anthony registered a split decision over durable Mexican Juan Montiel. The whole experience proved a little surreal as Anthony had travelled without his trainer. Joe Gallagher had opted to stay in the UK as Paul, Liam and Stephen Smith were all in action in Liverpool – the latter involved in a British and Commonwealth featherweight title defence against Lee Selby. While all ended well in the States for Crolla, it was traumatic for 'Swifty', who suffered his first loss as a professional via knockout.

Willie Limond

The Nevada adventure was followed by a trip north from Manchester two months later and a defence of the British lightweight title. Another visit to an opponent's backyard, this time an eager Willie Limond in Motherwell. The small village that is boxing meant the two men were well acquainted.

I'd been a sparring partner a few times for Ricky Burns. I remember when I was sparring Ricky, I stopped at Willie's house for a week or two. It was really nice; his kids were great. They'd come into the room every morning before school. But, bloody hell, didn't we end up boxing about a year later?

Niceties aside, the two men went to work. Crolla, 25, was seven years Limond's junior. There was a temporary blackout during proceedings, but it didn't last long and neither did Limond's serious ambitions of ripping the belt off the visitor from down south. It went the distance with Crolla a wide winner, much to the delight of his vocal travelling fans, but there was a little discomfort from the victor.

It was horrible. His kids were crying ringside. You meet people in all sorts of work, but Willie is possibly the nicest lad you could ever meet. He's a top lad. I still speak to him.

I went back up to spar with Willie a while later. I remember Callum Smith was up there sparring too and after training Willie was doing an interview with Scottish TV.

He was talking about having me up sparring and he was saying that with his Alex Arthur fight, he'd had a few problems going into it. The Amir Khan fight, his ear went and Amir had had a long count [Khan was floored in the sixth round], the Morales fight he was winning but the altitude affected him, and then he said, 'With Crolla, I didn't win a minute of a round.' He said it was his worst defeat.

While not a fight that will ever get mentioned in a Crolla highlights package, it was a night of particular satisfaction for Joe Gallagher. 'That was one of Anthony's best performances, but no one talks about it. To go up there and beat Willie and outbox him in every round? Not many do that to Willie. That was a massive win.'

I remember the journey home. It was a dead good win and I don't normally drink fizzy drinks, but Irn Bru's my fizzy drink. They love it up there. I remember getting two cans and we cracked them open as we set off on the way home. Good memories.

We'd gone up to Glasgow the night before the weigh-in and we drove straight home after the fight. It might sound boring, but we pulled over and got a couple of cans and that was it. British title in the back seat, Irn Bru in me hand, life was good!

From the sugar-high of Scottish soda to the brutal reality of a Scouse slap, the fine work at the Ravenscraig Sports Centre was undone by 'Dirty' Derry. Momentum was further jolted by the second Gary Sykes loss before results against Stephen Jennings, Kieran Farrell, Derry II and Gavin Rees addressed the mini-crisis and restored equilibrium.

Steve Foster Jr

By late 2013, the Matchroom deal was in place and Crolla's first fight with his new promoter was eventually arranged. Salford's Steve Foster Jr would challenge the holder for his WBO inter-continental belt at Manchester Arena as part of a stacked bill supporting the Froch vs Groves main event.

To the outsider, Manchester is one big urban sprawl stretching out in a ten-mile radius from the city centre. To those within that approximate boundary, there are all sorts of affiliations, rivalries and accents. Greater Manchester is made up of ten boroughs, including two cities – Manchester and Salford – divided by the river Irwell, which flows through the 'city' centre. Both have their own cathedrals, universities and idiosyncrasies. Crolla vs Foster Jr was therefore not a Manchester derby, as any proud Salfordian will argue. A Greater Manchester derby to be precise.

Local technicalities aside, the two fighters were familiar with each other having sparred together on several occasions. Foster was certainly a name. The son of Steve 'The Viking' Foster, he'd carved his own path in the game by claiming a WBU title in 2005 with a tenth-round stoppage of Colombian Livinson Ruiz. This was followed by arguably his best night in the ring when he demolished European champion Levan Kirakosyan five years later. Foster's recent form had been mixed, however, with crushing defeats to Ermano Fegatilli and Gary Buckland in European and British title fights sandwiched between victories over lesser lights.

The fight had come at short notice for Foster, preparations were hardly ideal, but it wasn't an opportunity he was willing to turn down.

'At the time I was drinking,' Foster recalled. 'I'd be going out and that was going on for weeks. I was even in the pubs up town with the older guys, me dad's mates, and I'd be drinking with them. On one Saturday night, I was out with them drinking Guinness and brandy, talking rubbish – drunk. On the Sunday night, I got a call from Jamie Moore [trainer] asking if I wanted to fight next week.

'I wasn't eating, only drinking, so my weight was OK and I said, "Yeah". Jamie said, "I haven't told you who it is or where it is yet!" He said it was Crolla at the MEN [Arena] and I said, "Yeah, I'll have it." He said he'd phone me back in the morning. Even though I remember being rough on the settee, watching telly, I said, "I'll definitely have it." I wanted to prove people wrong.

'I was in the gym for the five days before the fight. That was it. We just worked on the pads, that was about it.'

There was to be no last-minute fairy tale for Foster on what proved to be another good night for Crolla. With the jab working well and his defence dealing with Foster's hooks, Anthony stepped up the tempo through the early rounds with cute work to the body seemingly draining the ambition from his opponent.

Crolla could sense the end was nigh and continued with incessant assaults in the fifth round, a couple of hooks to the body leaving Foster on shaky legs. The Salford man came back and gave it his all in the sixth, but was exhausted at the end of the round and pulled out by Moore in his corner.

'I was obviously blowing and I felt I might humiliate myself carrying on, trying to do something I couldn't do because I wasn't fit. Jamie said, "Listen, call it a day, you've done your stuff, sort your boy out for Christmas, you're done." He was drilling it in my head that I'm done. He was saying there's no point, you've got your money for Christmas to sort your boy out.

'Once your gas is gone in boxing, nothing works. It's like you're throwing punches underwater. Timing's out, strength's out. It's frustrating, to be fair. In the corner, towards the end, Jamie's telling me to call it a day. He was telling me that I'd done what I could do, I'd helped out the show.'

I can only really remember little bits of the fight. It was an easy night to be honest, which I didn't expect. I like Steve and he'd come in at late notice but it was a comfortable fight. I'd had so many wars, there was the second Derry fight – fight of the year – Gavin Rees was a war and the Kieran Farrell fight had been a tough night. Then, wow, an easy fight – what's going on?

'I think I got my tactics wrong because I stayed off him and tried to box. I tried to be cute but obviously it didn't work. You can't do it if you're not fit. I should have just gone in brawling really and hope for the best. But that's how it is. All that was going through my head was, "I'm not getting knocked out, no way."

'I remember just thinking, "Let's get it on, ding ding." I even brought some of my mates into the changing room. We were having a laugh. The mad thing was, I've never felt so relaxed and that's what I was nervous about. I didn't feel right. I was just flat. At that time though, I did need the money.'

Steve's a good fighter and I've got a lot of respect for him. I felt I had more gears to go through on the night, though. It was a great night, great atmosphere at the arena and a good job done. Joe was happy too!

'Straight after the fight, I went out on the piss. I went to the Living Room [city centre bar] drinking. It still didn't sink in that I'd boxed

Crolla and what might have been. The doorman – he lets me in no matter what. I had me trackie and trainers on, but he just let me in.'

After that night at the arena, Foster boxed on for another year, his last fight a defeat to Jono Carroll in the *Prizefighter* series in December 2014. He intends to give the game one last hurrah after regaining his enthusiasm following a difficult period in his personal life.

'My son's 11 and he's always asking me about boxing. I want him to see me box. I want him to be proud of his dad, do you know what I mean? I want to do it for my kids and for the supporters that used to come to my fights. They've always been saying, "When are you fighting again, you've got it in you" and I've been like, "Nah, nah, I'm done. I've had enough." But then, for some mad reason, I went to watch my dad in a white-collar fight for charity and in the changing room I got butterflies in my stomach.

'I put the gloves on and said, "I'm having it again!" That just gave me the spark. I've been watching boxing videos and I've got the hunger for it. I mean, if I do it and nothing comes of it, then I've done it and I can sleep better at night.'

Foster is back in training at Champs Camp, Moss Side, under no illusions about fighting for world titles, but instead seeking peace of mind. In the meantime, he's happy for his former foe's success.

'When you mix with the best and you beat them, then you get all the credit you deserve. I give Anthony all the credit, all the praise in the world for what he's done. Get what you can out of boxing.'

John Murray

Before the Foster fight, there had been a lot of chatter about a Manchester derby that really would capture the imagination. John Murray was back after a two-year absence. His comeback fight, the night before Crolla vs Foster at Bowlers Exhibition Centre, had been an easy touch against Michael Escobar.

What really got the punters excited was John's dismantling of Scotland's tough John Simpson in his second fight back in Glasgow. Murray had scaled some heights previously as a British and European champion, a man who'd challenged Brandon Rios for a world title, but a failed brain scan had temporarily halted his career. Eventually, he received the all-clear and was desperate to regain his status as a top lightweight.

This derby pitted red against blue, New Moston against Levenshulme and the Murrays against Joe Gallagher. John and Joe Murray had been trained by Joe since they were kids, but a bitter fall-out added extra intrigue and spice to the event. There was no issue between the two fighters, friends and long-time training partners who'd sparred hundreds of rounds together.

The build-up during fight week was one of nothing but respect – at least between the fighters. Both Anthony and John couldn't even keep straight faces during the press conference head-to-head. Speaking after the formalities at the Radisson Blu Hotel in Manchester, both lads knew the script.

I've been in four Manchester derbies and won all four, but this is different because there are lots of factors involved.

John and I are good mates, we used to train together under Joe Gallagher and we support United and City. There is no problem between John and I, we will go out for a drink after the fight, but once that bell goes there won't be any friendship.

We are focused on doing a job on each other. I have been in John's corner before and he has been in mine. We have seen each other close-hand and have fought many rounds together.

There is only so much you can take from sparring, but we both believe we have seen strengths and weaknesses in each other. We both have the same friends so there might be a few neutrals in there on the night, but I hope to have the red side of Manchester in my corner.

If you can't get up for a fight like this, then I am in the wrong sport. It's a Manchester derby, I've been in them before and come out on top. This is the biggest one of the lot, though, but I am very confident of another derby night win.

This was always the fight I wanted and the demand there was for it showed how big a fight it is. I'm made up that it's happening; it's great for the city, too.

It's a great feeling knowing that I can walk to the ring on Saturday night with nothing more I can do about it. That's why I'm calm. It's rare that you'll ever get a fighter saying anything other than 'it's been a great camp', but that's what I truly believe, it's what I've had and I'm getting a little bit excited. I need to hold myself back.

I don't think it's personal. There might be malice towards me for the next few days but that's what John has to do to fire himself up. I've been in changing rooms with him and I know he'll be firing himself up. My way is to stay calm. I'm not going to waste energy, because I know on Saturday, once that bell goes [clicks fingers], I'm switched on.

I think his fall-out with Joe has given him an extra drive in training, but obviously he's got to fight with his head and not his heart. Without doubt, John wants to put one over Joe Gallagher; he wants to do a job on me so he can have one over Joe. But that's between them. I'm not interested. I've got aspirations of my own, dreams of my own and John Murray stands in the way of that.

To be involved in an event like this in Manchester is just a pleasure. It means the absolute world to me. It's a fight that's really captured the city's imagination and I know it's a fight I'll look back on in years to come.

I've been going to that arena ever since I was a kid, even before Ricky Hatton. I was watching Michael Brodie, Naseem Hamed, Joe Calzaghe and now I've got my chance.

When I was 11 years old, and I know it sounds cheesy as hell, but I used to think, 'I'd love to be that fighter one day.' I'd go home and shadow box. Now I've got my chance and it's going to be happening to me on Saturday night.

'Talking's cheap. I like to let my fists do the talking. I'm focused, training's gone perfect, everything's gone perfect. I'm so up for this fight. It's a massive fight. It's a massive arena in Manchester and it's going to launch my career into the stratosphere. Winning on points isn't enough for me. It has to be a knockout, it has to be brutal to show just how good I am and I'm looking forward to it.

'It's not about Joe Gallagher, it's for me. Anthony's a good kid but I see him as an obstacle in the way of my career. If I lose, Anthony's taken my career away from me. I need to win. Losing isn't an option. Anthony's in my way. My full attention is on him and doing a job on him. I can't wait for Saturday night. I'm so hungry, I'm so focused. I'm going to win and I'm going to do it in devastating style.

'I'm fresher and sharper in training than I ever was before the break. I genuinely believe I'm a better fighter now for two years out

51

of the ring. I had a very, very busy career with lots of hard fights and title fights one after the other. It took a bit out of me and I was flat towards the back end of my career. The sparring's perfect, really sharp, and I'm hitting very, very hard. I can't wait for Saturday night to show everybody just how good I am.

'It's a massive event. Everyone's interested in it. Anthony's a very well-liked person and I think I am too. It's a big, big fight, everyone's looking forward to it, and may the best man win.

'I think I'm capable of winning a world title. I'm hungry and focused now and I intend to use that to drive myself in training, work on technique and I'm confident I can win a world title before my career is over.'

Crolla's clash with Murray was part of a huge night of boxing in Manchester. Originally, the fight was supposed to be the chief support to Scott Quigg's second defence of his WBA super-bantamweight title against Tshifhiwa Munyai. But such was the interest in the derby bout that it was promoted to the main event.

A raucous crowd, under the lights at a packed arena, did their bit to create a memorable atmosphere. Ring walks complete, the action didn't disappoint.

To the surprise of nobody, Murray started fast and strong, targeting the body. For the most part, Crolla stayed out of range, settling in behind his jab and having some success with his right hand. Murray was trying to out-man his old mate, forcing Crolla back with some heavy artillery early on, catching him on the ropes.

Picking clever counter shots, Crolla was having some success, marking up John's right eye as he continued with his furious attack. A huge right hand in the fourth round looked to have put Murray in control, with Crolla's defence pierced.

By the fifth, John's tank was emptying a little. Crolla took advantage and established his jab to great effect as his opponent increasingly loaded up. In what was proving to be an excellent tear-up, Murray went for the showstopper again in the seventh, Crolla soaking up punishment. In a see-saw fight, the eighth round belonged to the man from New Moston. With each Murray offensive, Crolla was catching him more.

The ninth round saw the crowd screaming as Murray desperately looked to end the contest with a power shot, but was hampered by Crolla's uppercuts and hooks and a huge left. Now in control in the tenth, Crolla sensed his time had come as blood seeped from John's nose.

Crolla put a weary Murray to the canvas with a left hand and ended it shortly after with a barrage of unanswered blows as Murray was caught in the neutral corner. Referee Terry O'Connor intervened and an ecstatic Crolla leapt up on to the ropes, screaming 'Man-ches-teeeeeeeeeer!!!' to his delirious supporters.

Once the MC John McDonald had announced the official verdict, Anthony and John, two old pals, sat down together on the ring apron and spoke to Sky Sports.

It was even tougher than I expected. No matter how tough that looked, me and John were the luckiest men in this arena. I prepared for this fight like no other; John put the fear of God into me. I remember how tough those sparring sessions were and I knew I had to keep a cool head in a hot kitchen.

'I gave it my all, I was the best I've been in training and he's beaten me at my best. I want to take my hat off to Anthony because he was bang on. I don't want to make any excuses. As the rounds went on, maybe I began to feel the inactivity but full respect to Anthony. I had a full camp and felt great.'

It had been a special night at the arena. On a stacked card, gym pals Callum Smith and Hosea Burton enjoyed routine wins, Josh Warrington defended his Commonwealth featherweight title against Rendall Munroe, Tyrone Nurse got the better of Tyler Goodjohn for the vacant English light-welterweight crown and Olympic gold medallist Luke Campbell was victorious in his sixth professional contest. Meanwhile, Scott Quigg defended his WBA belt in devastating fashion, smashing Tshifhiwa Munyai inside two rounds.

The Murray fight was a sweet victory for Anthony and he knew it was the kind of performance, in front of a live audience and on TV, that could help catapult his career. It was also a night for Joe Gallagher to remember.

'In the build-up, I'd never heard Anthony say, "I can beat John Murray." Every interview I was hearing, "Yeah, the fans will love it, great fight, Manchester ... blah blah blah ..."

'I said to Crolla, "Can you beat him?" I had to force it out of him. "Can you beat John Murray? Can you knock John Murray out?" Eventually he says, "Yeah. I can knock John Murray out." I said, "Say it again! Say it again – I can knock John Murray out!" So, he says, "Yes. I can knock John Murray out."

'"Right," I said. "Now I've heard you say it, I believe you. Next time anyone interviews you, you say, 'Yeah, I'll beat John Murray, and talking about knockouts, I'll knock him out!' John will get riled and go, 'Cheeky cunt, you fucking can't,' and then John will be fighting harder than he should do." And lo and behold, come fight night, John came out and was like a fucking whirlwind for five rounds. But he shot his bolt.

'We'd worked on the finishing shots with Crolla and the exact shots that did for John, we'd practised and practised. After it, I thought, "Yeah. You did it. You believed it."

'After the Kieran Farrell fight, Anthony lost some of his nastiness in the ring. He lost his killer instinct. He lost it for the Gavin Rees fight and the Derry Mathews rematch. He was just happy to box, box, box, box. For Murray, I needed the old Crolla back. I knew that if he didn't have that edge, John would walk right over him, stop him and wipe his feet on him on the way out of the ring. I needed that hard, horrible, spiteful kid back. It came back for Murray.

'I'd deflected a lot of attention away from Crolla. I wanted the Murrays to concentrate on me and not Anthony. Every now and again, I'll take the bullets as long as it doesn't affect my kids. Let them all come at me.'

Regardless of the result and the realisation that it was the end of the road for his boxing career, John was content he'd given it a go. He'd enjoyed the occasion and played his part. The build-up and the barbs between himself and his former trainer didn't bother him, but as with every beaten fighter, there's always a case of what might have been.

'I'd tried not to make it all about Joe [Gallagher] because I knew that's what Joe would want. He'd want it to be about him. I said it a few times in the press conference. Crolla was the man getting in the ring; me and Crolla, not Joe. Nothing to do with him.

'I think if I'd boxed Crolla when I had the Simpson fight, it might have been a different fight. I was so up for the Simpson fight because I'd been out of the ring for so long and I was nervous. I trained harder. When it was Crolla, I didn't take my foot off the gas, but I wasn't nervous. Because I'd sparred him so much, I genuinely thought that as soon as I hit him, I'd get him out of there. I didn't think he'd be able to get me out of there either.

'We'd sparred a lot and I thought, "He can't hurt me." Obviously in the gap from when we trained together, he'd matured a bit and started hitting harder and he's game, man. He can take a good beating and still come back and give it his all.'

While Crolla enjoyed the adulation from his section of the crowd post-fight, it was a different story for the vanquished boxer. For Anthony, it was all back-slaps in the dressing room, while John cut a lonely figure in A&E.

'I remember going straight from the ring into the back of an ambulance and off to hospital. Didn't go backstage, didn't get anything, just straight out. I had a detached retina. My eye had been dodgy for a while.

'I waited in the hospital for about an hour and a half. It was like you'd just walked in off the street. I thought, "Shit, I've just been in the ring. My eyes are shut. I can't sit here for three hours." So, I phoned my manager, said I'd been seen and it was all right, so he picked me up and I went back home to an after-party. I couldn't go into town because I was still in me boxing kit.

'About three days later, I thought I'd better get to hospital and get my eye checked out. They kept me in the hospital that day and within a couple of hours I was on the operating table. I think I've had nine operations on my eye since that last fight. The retina keeps detaching and I'm practically blind in my right eye. I can see light and colours but I can't read anything. But you know, it is what it is. I had a good career and no regrets.'

In beating Murray, Crolla had once again retired a Manchester fighter. Unlike Brodie and Morris, who Anthony had followed and looked up to, the fight with John was more personal given their development together under Joe's tutelage and their friendship away from boxing.

Since that night, John has moved on with his life after fighting and is now a trainer with his own gym in Reddish. He is training kids as young as five right up to working with professionals such as Chris Conwell and his brother Joe.

'I'm still very good mates with Crolla, we get on very well. He's been down to my gym and helped out, like with the opening and that. I've not got a bad word to say about him, I like Anthony a lot. He's the most dedicated professional I've ever trained with. He lives and breathes boxing and he deserves everything he's got out of it, no doubt about it.

'He always seems to go into a fight as the underdog, doesn't he? He's done really well and, like I say, he deserves everything he gets. And don't forget, I taught him everything he knows! Every time he does well, I think I'm doing well!

'I'm thoroughly enjoying it. From the age of about 21, I was always worried about what I was going to do after boxing. Me mates were at uni. They [had] finished uni and were getting jobs. I was also thinking that by the time I'm 30, it's going to be over and I'm going to be a 30-year-old school-leaver and it panicked me. It's lucky what happened really. I failed my brain scan, had two years out of the ring and blew all me dough. I was lucky that I was given another opportunity to have a comeback. When I had the chance to make some money, I invested into my gym and I've got my own business. If it wasn't for that brain scan and two-year gap out of the ring, I might not have ended up with what I've got. I always try and take the positives out of things.

'I've got some real talents coming through and I'm really excited about them. I'll going to produce some top-quality champions coming through. I've got two beautiful kids and a missus and everything's going well. I'm in a good place. I'm happy and enjoying life after boxing.'

Maybe it's revenge for that night at the arena, but with a final parting shot John's keen to share a secret about Anthony – the very same all-round fine fellow and supreme professional.

'I know all about Crolla the big drinker! Everyone knows I like to booze, but I've been out with Crolla in town and that kid can drink me under the table! He'll give it, "Do you want a jägerbomb?" I'll be like, "Go on then, mate." It'd be a shot with each round with two or three more lined up on a table. He's like, "Bang, let's go again!" The man's an animal! He doesn't ever really get to go out, so I think he makes up for lost time. He even had me thinking, "Jesus Christ, this kid can drink!" Crolla the drinker! Not many people know that.'

Time to shine

Things were really kicking on now. Anthony was inching ever closer to his dream of a world title fight. An agreement looked to be heading ever closer for him to fight WBA lightweight champion Richar Abril. The plan was a September date – the reward for all the graft and hard work in climbing the rankings.

But these things often hit a buffer. Legal issues delayed proceedings, so the September date was premature. Instead, Anthony would face Gamaliel Diaz on 13 September in Manchester, while Abril looked set to defend his title against Edis Tatli shortly after. Should both Crolla and the Cuban champion come through unscathed, the fight could happen before the end of the year at the Liverpool Echo. But all didn't go quite as it should have.

It had been a typically thorough and arduous training camp and Anthony was ready to once more show off the progress he'd been making after all the hours of behind-closed-doors preparation. Instead, it proved to be a frustrating night as the contest ended prematurely due to an accidental clash of heads.

There was little between the pair in the opening two rounds. Crolla worked the jab well while there were eye-catching moments from the visitor. It all ended unsatisfactorily, though, when Diaz suffered a cut to his right eye in the third round and appeared to be reluctant to continue. He was in no rush to come out for the fourth round, almost inviting the ringside doctor to analyse the wound. The injury was deemed bad enough to leave the Mexican in no fit state to continue, so the fight was declared a technical draw.

He didn't want to know. The doctor ruled he was unable to continue, but I felt like he was happy with that.

* * * * *

Crolla soon had another date in his diary and a chance to take out any frustrations he had from the Diaz fight. The lightly regarded Hungarian Gyorgy Mizsei Jr was the nearest thing to a gimmee Crolla had faced for a good while – something of a gift on the eve of his 28th birthday. It was routine as expected, a points win over six rounds on a night when big-time boxing returned to Dublin.

Matthew Macklin, another of Joe's fighters, was topping the bill against Argentine Jorge Sebastian Heiland. What should have been a happy homecoming proved to be a disastrous night for 'Mack the Knife'. The industrious Heiland outworked, outgunned and ultimately spoiled the party with a tenth-round stoppage over a gassed Macklin, whose dream of facing Miguel Cotto in a fourth world title shot was left in tatters.

It was a different story for Anthony, who could now finally start planning for his defining world title fight. The long-awaited match-up with Richar Abril was confirmed by promoter Eddie Hearn – with home advantage to boot. Crolla vs Abril was set for 23 January 2015 at the Phones4u Arena. Matchroom had delivered and Anthony was more than happy.

To have the world title shot in Manchester is a huge factor. Without wanting to sound cheesy, it doesn't get any bigger than that. I am a Manchester lad so to be fighting in Manchester for a world title, I couldn't ask for anything more. The only way it could get better than that is to go out there and win it.

I have been watching a bit of Abril over the last year because we have been linked with a fight before, but I will watch a lot more of him after tonight. He is a very good champion; he is avoided for a reason. He came on to the scene when he fought Brandon Rios and everybody except the judges that night could see he won clearly. He is a very good fighter, a well-schooled amateur and nice and relaxed.

It is a very big ask but there will be a few factors in my favour, like being in my home town, which will bring an extra 25 per cent out of me.

In training, I will have an extra edge to me because I won't have a problem getting out of bed in the morning knowing there is a world title at stake.

I really believe deep down that I can win that fight and become a world champion. I am under no illusions. It is a tough fight and I go in a big underdog. But it is a fight I am capable of winning and the setting couldn't be any better. To do it in front of my home fans really is the stuff dreams are made of.

CHAPTER 3

Daylight Robbery

*M*ANN *Tracht, Un Gott Lacht* [Man plans and God laughs], so the old Yiddish adage goes. Problems, setbacks, accidents, illness and all manner of calamities can invade any life at any time. Fate can deal any man a cruel hand, and it did just that with Anthony Crolla. Maybe it's not so simple? Depending on whether the glass is half full or half empty, maybe fate played a blinder. That can only be argued in hindsight. On the face of it, on a mid-December day in Chadderton, 2014, Anthony's world came crashing down.

Training was going well. All focus was on Abril and all boxes were being ticked as Anthony steadily upped preparations for the night he'd always dreamed of.

Joe Gallagher said, 'He'd done a really good session in the gym and was due to do some track work down at City [regional athletics centre, Etihad Campus]. I didn't want him to overcook it, so I gave him the night off. I remember telling him to go home, put his feet up and chill. Spend some time with the family.'

Everything was normal. I remember going to get my phone screen fixed in Cheetham Hill. I was going to go straight to the track from there but then Joe phoned, so I went home.

I pulled up at home and as I was getting my bags out of the car I could hear an alarm going off. I was thinking that my neighbours Craig and Sophie weren't in, so I rang him and told him his alarm was going off. Jokingly, I said I'd check no one was breaking in!

Anyway, I opened my patio doors and looked over the garden fence into their garden. I could see a shadow, so I put the torch on my phone and noticed that there was a window smashed. A couple of seconds later, a head popped through the window. I was like 'What the fuck!' I started shouting 'Get out!'

I ran through my house, shouted to Fran, who was feeding Jesse at the time, and out through my front door. I ran around the cul-de-sac and I could see the two of them. I shouted 'Get back here!' They started running and I'm sprinting after them. I knew they weren't going to get away from me and I wanted to know what they'd taken. I remember thinking they [Craig and Sophie] were getting married, saving up for a wedding. So, I thought these lads could've taken anything.

I was closing in on them and all the time shouting at them. They turned down into a house and into a garden and I had them cornered. I was thinking that it might be hard work going back with two of them. I looked at one of them and thought 'I'll just walk him back.' If anything's gone missing ...

So, I've focused on one of them – the other one had run off another way – and the lad turns and starts climbing a fence, so I go after him. As he's climbing, there was obviously a loose paving stone, which he then dropped on me head. I remember going down on one knee and even though it was on my blindside, I knew he hadn't punched me. I knew he'd hit me with something. It was a different kind of feeling.

I went to stand up and I couldn't. I had a mad pain in my ankle and my leg kind of gave way. I still tried to jump up to grab him but his momentum took him over. My ankle wouldn't take any kind of weight. I was raging. Then, I felt blood trickle down my face. I went stumbling up the street fuming.

As I turned back up my street, Fran was walking towards me with a neighbour. She was asking what had happened and all I could tell her was that someone had hit me with something.

I got back in the house, blood pouring out of me head. Jesse was there looking at me but thankfully he was too young to know what was going on. I was just trying to joke about with him.

One of my best mates who'd come to pick up tickets, he turned up and was like 'What's gone on?' Next door had come back, there were a good few people in the house at this point. The adrenaline was still kicking in and I was just fuming thinking they've got away.

Me mam then ran round. She doesn't live far and someone had phoned her. She was going mad at me, all upset. Next door's mam was a nurse, she'd come round to try and stop the bleeding. She told me I had to get to hospital.

I was talking to my mate who'd come for the tickets. I was talking about training and sparring and how the head guard would cover the gash, and if the ankle was a bit sore I'd have to do a bit more swimming and cut running out for a week. I'm saying all this and my ankle had blown up!

As I was saying all this, I could see him and others in the room looking at each other. No one had the heart to tell me.

My uncle Darren then turned up and he wanted to know what had gone on. The ambulance had been phoned at this point but it was taking ages, so he said he'd take me and Fran to A&E in Oldham.

Got to the hospital and they put me in a room to check me out. At this point, I'm still talking to Darren about sparring and fighting but the adrenaline was slowly wearing off. They gave me a brain scan or x-ray, I can't remember, but they had a look at my head straight away. I just thought I had a cut and didn't know what the fuss was about.

My head and ankle were booming at this point, though. Anyway, I'm waiting in this room. Our Darren had gone by now so it was just me and Fran. A doctor came in and said, 'You're a boxer, aren't you? You've got a big fight coming up, haven't you?' I said, 'Yeah, fighting for a world title in five weeks. This is the last thing I need!' He said, 'Listen. That won't be happening.'

He said I had a fractured skull and broken ankle in two places. You know when you just can't get anything out? I don't remember saying anything. He asked if I was OK, and I said, 'Yeah, thanks.' He then said something about leaving us to it and left.

I was like, 'Ahh fucking hell' and I broke me heart; cried my eyes out. At that point, all I could think about was the world title fight. I hadn't thought about whether I could box again or not. I didn't think for a second about the injuries. I thought it was the end of the world.

Joe remembered, 'I was sat at home and I got a call from Rob Lewtas [Anthony's friend], who told me Crolla had been in an accident. My first thought was "Will?" and he said, "No it's Anthony." I said, "You what? He's had the night off at home!" Anyway, he told me he was in a bad way, so I found out where he was and headed off.

'When I got there, I went in to see him. I had a look at him and the first thing I said was, "You fucking dickhead!" His leg was in plaster, his head in a mess.

'I asked a nurse to move Anthony from the ward. He was in a room with loads of people in and around, visiting and all that. I asked if there was any chance he could have his own private room with just his mum and dad and Fran allowed in. I told them that there was no press allowed near him.'

I had my own room, own bathroom with Sky as well. I was lying there on me own on that first night and it kept coming up on Sky Sports News that I was in hospital after being attacked … it was weird. It repeats itself, so I was like 'Not this again', so I flicked it up a channel. I was all groggy and that on painkillers, but the first thing I see on BBC1 was me! It was on ITV too. It was mad. I was thinking, 'What's gone on here? How strong are these painkillers!'

Confused, still trying to come to terms with the magnitude of his injuries and all that that entailed, Anthony lay alone in his hospital bed feeling very low and very sorry for himself.

Unbeknown to him, long-time friend and sponsor Ged Mason – CEO of recruitment firm Morson, a huge supporter of amateur and professional boxing – had tipped off his mate Sir Alex Ferguson about the fighter's misfortune.

'I mentioned the incident to Alex, but he took it upon himself to phone him,' Ged explained. 'That's the type of person he is. Alex took it upon himself and he does that a lot. You don't ever hear about it, but he goes to more funerals and visits to hospital than anyone I know. He never tries to claim the glory or publicises it. He just does it in his own manner. I think Alex is a good judge of character, so he knew what Crolla stood for. That's why he made that call.'

I thought it was a wind-up. I got a phone call. He said he'd seen my story and said it was a great thing what I'd done. I was groggy and can't remember a lot of the conversation. We were talking about how frustrating it was watching the boys [United] at the moment. We had a lot of injuries at the time, so we were talking about that.

The press was all over the story by now. Owing to Joe and Anthony's relationship with the *Manchester Evening News*, Joe decided to act in an attempt to contain any unwanted attention.

Joe said, 'Pete Spencer [then sports editor] from the *Manchester Evening News* got wind of it all and asked me to take a couple of pictures. So, when he got a little bit better, I took a picture of Anthony with Fran by the bed and I gave it to the *Evening News*. I said, "That's yours, no one else is having it, so any money you can get for that picture, I want it for Anthony." I knew Ant was out of pocket, no fight and all that.

'Months later, Pete gave us a cheque for £600 or £700 that he'd raised from selling the photo to every publication. That picture had stopped photographers coming in the hospital looking for him.'

When I'd been in hospital, there'd been reporters knocking on doors on my street. Fran came home from work and there were TV trucks parked outside the house. When I got out of hospital, Joe had organised a kind of media day at my house. It was fucking shattering, but it was best to get it out of the way in one day.

Whilst Anthony continued to rest and recuperate at home, it was announced that his old rival Derry Mathews would take his place and face Abril at the Liverpool Echo Arena in March. It would be a first world title shot for Derry. Victory would surely set up a trilogy fight with Crolla.

That scenario would never come to pass. Derry's dreams were proving as elusive as Anthony's, with Abril pulling out of their scheduled contest due to suspected dengue fever.

A re-arranged date was set for the following month, only for the Cuban to once again pull out following a relapse – just two weeks before fight night.

In the meantime, Crolla's recovery was impressing the medics. Within four weeks he was out of plaster and doing everything possible to help his rehabilitation.

Joe was starting to believe the burglary incident and injuries sustained were a moment of fate that could work to his fighter's advantage.

'I'm a big believer that because Anthony had been through such a hard schedule – Gavin Rees, John Murray, Diaz and a warm-up in Ireland – it [the burglary incident] allowed his body to recover as he had to rest. We could've been bollocksed carrying on.'

As soon as he could, Anthony reintegrated himself back into the gym and the bosom of his team-mates. They welcomed him back with open arms – and a barrage of abuse.

'We know Crolla, he's not the confrontational type,' said Stephen Smith. 'If he walked into his own house and there were robbers in there, he'd make them a cup of tea. Honestly, he'd be like, "Come on mate, I don't think you wanna do this. Have a cup of tea!" I don't think he's the type to chase people down the street. He was definitely getting chased.'

All the lads were giving me grief – Paul [Smith] was asking what they [burglars] were doing out on a school night!

I'm over it now, although I do think about it. The one who stopped, he was cornered and I could see he was a bit scared. If I met him now, I wouldn't want to give him a good hiding. He could've been on drugs or whatever. What satisfaction would I get by giving him a good hiding? I'd probably want to handle it another way. It sounds daft, but I might get them to labour on my house, to do something positive.

But you know what, I've genuinely forgiven them. If one of them came up to me and said, 'I'm really sorry' – and I know it won't happen – but if they did I'd just speak to him. I'd take his number and speak to him because I'd respect the fact he'd come up to me.

In a weird way, it is a blessing in disguise.

CHAPTER 4

United Nights and Crolla Fights

Darleys Pérez

An enforced period of inactivity was working in Anthony's favour as his mind and body continued to heal. He passed a series of medical tests and was given the green light to box on by the British Boxing Board of Control. More good news followed and proved to be the best tonic for recovery after Eddie Hearn informed him that he would get his world title shot, if a little delayed.

His opponent, in place of the stripped Richar Abril, would be Darleys Pérez, the tough Colombian promoted from WBA interim lightweight champion.

Home advantage had also been secured and the news was made public at a press conference at Hotel Football.

The venue was significant for Crolla, with the building owned by United legends Ryan Giggs, Gary Neville, Phil Neville and Nicky Butt and set in the shadow of Old Trafford.

The fight was set for Saturday, 18 July 2015 at the Manchester Arena. To add a little drama to proceedings, the name of the opponent, while an open secret, wasn't revealed until the start of the first press conference. A large screen was shrouded in a black cover, which was whipped off to reveal the title 'High Stakes' and a moody bare-chested shot of Crolla alongside his rival.

I honestly feel I'm in the best shape of my career and I'm in a really good place at the moment. You would expect to hear those sorts of things ahead of a world title fight but without doubt this is the best I have felt.

My weight is fantastic and my training has been better than what it has ever been, so there will be no excuses on fight night.

After the injury, we cut down a bit on the long-distance running that I usually do but I feel more explosive for that as it has allowed me to do different bits of training instead.

I've got an unbelievable team around me that have been getting the best out of me during my training camp and I promise I will give 100 per cent against Pérez.

Top billing on the show was to be shared with his friend and gym partner Scott Quigg, who was to defend his WBA super-bantamweight title against Spain's Kiko Martinez.

To be doing this at the Manchester Arena alongside Scott makes this very special. He is without doubt the most determined and disciplined athlete I've ever trained with, and nobody deserves a big fight like that more than him.

We've been having two or three sessions a day together for months and he's been making me push myself to work even harder.

Crolla's story had captured the public's imagination and helped his profile soar. He now had the world title fight he craved and an unbelievable amount of goodwill from the Manchester public and beyond.

I got a little bit choked up in the press conference; I just can't thank the people around me enough and the support from everyone over the last six months. The best way to thank them is to go and win a world title on July 18 and that's what I'll do. I'll give absolutely everything I have to do that.

I think I know more than most that world title shots can come and go. This opportunity came up and I thought I'd be crazy to turn it down. In an ideal world, you have a few eight- or ten-rounders to get back, but listen, it wasn't that long ago I boxed and I believe the break's done me good. I honestly feel refreshed and feel I'll come back bigger and stronger than ever.

It's too big an opportunity to turn down. A world title in my home town; very few people get that opportunity. I've got it and that's why I'm going to make sure I make this dream of mine come true.

I can't explain now but I'm a big believer in everything happens for a reason. The support is going to be bigger than ever. More people will be there now.

He's [Pérez] a very good fighter. It's very rare you'd get a weak world champion. He's only lost to Gamboa. I've got my work cut out; it's by far the toughest fight of my life. Tougher possibly than what I've had to come through in the past six months. That's put me in good stead. On the night, I'll possibly have to go through hell and back to get it, but it's something I'm prepared to do.

* * * * *

Anthony went into full camp ahead of his date with destiny. All was routine with few niggles and disruptions. He'd had his fair share of drama for one year. Eight days before the fight, his growing popularity was evident at a public workout at the Trafford Centre. Huge cheers and a chorus of 'ohhhh … Anthony Crolla' greeted his emergence. Fans and shoppers gathered around the ring, punters straining for a peek from escalators and curious onlookers leaning over the food court rails.

Honestly, the nerves haven't set in yet. I think next week, fight week, a few might creep in. I'm pretty chilled out as a boxer, but it is a world title so nerves will creep in. I'm in a fantastic place, mentally, and I just can't wait for it.

There are better ways to raise your profile, but I know that after what happened with the burglary, there'll be a few more bums on seats on the night. I really appreciate those people coming and many will be coming to a boxing match for the first time.

It's got to be a career-best performance, make no mistake about that. He's a very, very good fighter and he does a lot of things very well. He's got a great pedigree back to his amateur days – he was a Beijing Olympian. I'm going in there the underdog, but I know with a career-best performance it's something I can do.

It's an unbelievable night of boxing, not just me and Scott in world title fights, but there's a lot of local talent. To be involved in a joint headline bill like this, I feel very lucky and blessed to be a part of it.

Fight Week

Most boxers find fight week tedious and tough in equal measure. Making weight, getting the last few pounds off, killing time as all the hard work is done. Nobody gets stronger or fitter in those final few days.

The final press conference is a fixture for any high-profile fight. The media obligations can be time consuming. Some enjoy them while others endure. For Crolla, it's a chance to have a first look at Pérez in the flesh as the Colombian wasn't at the first press conference at Hotel Football.

It's what I expected. I've got a slight height advantage, but he's got the look of a fighter who's trained hard and looks fit. He says he's had a fantastic camp, so on fight night you'll get the best Darleys Pérez and the best Anthony Crolla. I think we're in for a great fight.

It's an unbelievable bill and one of the best British cards in recent years. It's very special to me.

The venue for the second media event has switched to the Grosvenor Casino on Bury New Road, just a couple of hundred yards from HM Prison Manchester – or Strangeways, as it will always be known locally.

Among the writers and broadcasters gathered in the brightly lit function room at the back of the venue, away from the slot machines and roulette tables, is London lightweight Kevin Mitchell. On the wrong end of a tenth-round stoppage at the hands of Jorge Linares in his last fight, Kevin's in Manchester on other business, but has decided to drop in to the press conference – and to stir up interest in a potential future showdown with Crolla.

'I'm not being big-headed but I'm the biggest threat to the current world champions,' Mitchell said. 'I'd fight the winner of Pérez vs Crolla but hopefully Anthony beats him and we can get that fight on. Anthony's a top guy.'

Well, that would be great, north versus south. I was in the corner when him and John Murray had their great fight. Kev's a great lad, someone I respect massively, but my focus is solely on Darleys Pérez. I'd be a fool to overlook him but if I come through then it's a fight I'd happily take. Kev would be up for it and it'd certainly be a great British world title fight.

He's a good lad, Kev, I like him. He's one of those lads that I also remember when I was a schoolboy. He was someone who everyone stayed behind to watch. He was knocking kids over from an early age, so the talent and power's always been there. He's certainly one of the very best lightweights in the world.

The weigh-in was held outside in Cathedral Gardens, next to the National Football Museum, on a blustery summer's day in Manchester. After both men weighed in, there was a respectful handshake and a roar to the crowd, then it was off home to refuel and focus.

I think about my family at home and all the support I've had since the incident, particularly from across the city of Manchester. I'll be a very proud Mancunian to go out and win the title for them.

It's going to be some atmosphere and some occasion. For everyone that's bought a ticket – I'll be forever indebted to them for cheering me on.

An emotional night at the arena started well for Team Gallagher with routine victories for Marcus Morrison and Hosea Burton. It got better in an excellent prelude to Anthony's fight when Scott Quigg blew away Kiko Martinez inside two rounds. One world champion had retained his belt, now it was Anthony's turn to win one.

Before he could do that, he had a problem. He couldn't leave the dressing room before making the kind of decision that's crucial to a fighter like Crolla. Did he go for white socks or red socks to accompany red boots and white shorts with red trim? It took him an age, but eventually he chose white, to the relief of all around him. The kit matched, he looked good, he could now switch on, go out there and deal with Pérez.

A crackling atmosphere greeted Anthony's ring walk as he sang along to Whitney, as ever smiling and nodding to people in the crowd. Once Michael Buffer had introduced the fighters, as usual imploring everyone in the crowd and the millions watching around the world to get ready to rumble, it was time for the action.

Crolla moved, counter-punched and settled into the fight well, landing an eye-catching right hook in round two. He changed tactics, going on the front foot to exert constant pressure. There was a lull in the mid rounds before some clever work from the champion resulted in a cut appearing beneath Crolla's right eye.

Pérez stepped it up, sensing the fight was running away from him, but Crolla was always calm, landing clean shots and blocking blows with his arms. The visitor became increasingly desperate in the last two rounds, with two low blows penalised by referee Howard Foster with point deductions.

Surely then, it was to be a fairy-tale ending seven months on from the burglary?

Buffer composed himself before announcing the official verdict. To the dismay and disbelief of the crowd, the scorecards read 114-113 (Pérez), 116-111 (Crolla) and 113-113 – a split draw. The first score was incorrect and subsequently changed to 113-113. The amended result was a majority draw, but that was of little consolation to the challenger.

Crolla couldn't hide his disappointment. He knew he'd won the fight but his dream of winning a world title at his home-town venue had been shattered. Back in his dressing room, still in his kit, sweat beads trickling down his forehead, he stood, leaning against the wall next to a huge dressing room mirror. It was too early to take it all in. The smile still flashed, but the squint of the eyes as he did so gave the game away.

I've been asking people if it was a decent fight to watch. When you're in there, you don't realise. It was certainly a tough fight, but listen, I'll watch it back and see what I think.

At the end of the fight I thought I'd done enough, but certainly with the points deductions I thought I'd cemented it. But it's a draw and that's that. I give it everything I had in there tonight, so I can live with that.

I'm so thankful for the support I had in there tonight.

Me face is a bit sore, but other than that I'm all right. I'm just disappointed. I thought I was going to be world champion and I'm devastated really. But, like I say, I'm very fortunate to have walked out into that sort of atmosphere, to have the support of the city behind me, and hopefully I've done them proud.

It was surreal. I was waiting there and people were telling me, 'Don't let this crowd get to you,' but I knew that I couldn't let that play on me. They lifted me. There were times when it got tough they were that 12th man. It lifted me up and pulled me through those rocky patches.

*Everyone's reaction at the end was, 'You've got it, you've deffo got it!'
Then the draw … Aaagghh! Devastating, but you know, there's no point
crying over spilt milk, is there? You've still got to clean it up.*

*We'll fight again, but I'll just get on with it again. I'll come back bigger.
I've had setbacks before but I don't think I'd call tonight a setback. I've
proved I belong at world class. People doubted if I should take this fight so
soon, but I proved I belong. Honestly, I'll only get better. I'm 28, but I live
the right life and I'm always looking to improve.*

*People say we're warriors, but for me the warriors – and I'm not trying
to sound stupid – are the people who go out and try and save people's lives
every day.*

I'm just doing a job. I get paid for it and I give it my all.

Darleys Pérez II

It didn't take too long for the physical wounds to heal after the
controversial draw with Darleys Pérez. Mentally, it was a bit trickier,
but Anthony got on with things, ticking over in the gym until he
heard the news he'd been waiting for. The WBA had ordered an
immediate rematch following the public outcry over the result of
the first fight. Crolla felt vindicated and could now enjoy the rest
of the summer before plotting revenge on 21 November, again at
Manchester Arena.

A long training camp was planned and executed. All was on
track for another crack at the title. Another fight week, another well-
attended public workout, this time indoors at the National Football
Museum, followed by a press conference at the Radisson Blu Hotel
on Peter Street, Manchester.

Plenty of respect was shown by both camps, all looking forward
to another great night. The head to head, as always with Crolla, went
off with a handshake and a smile.

*I'm not the type of guy to read too much into having an eyeball with him.
I don't think I'm clever enough to understand body language. But listen, I
feel very good knowing myself that training's gone fantastic. I feel in a really
good place and I'm excited. I'm ready for it.*

*There's a great deal of respect between us. We shared 12 hard rounds
together and there's a good chance we'll do that on Saturday night.*

Last time I believe I proved I can more than hold my own with him and I think a lot of that was down to Joe's tactics and the way I carried them out. This time, we've made a few tweaks in the gym and I certainly feel I'll be a stronger fighter and a faster fighter. That can only be a good thing for me. I'll be even more confident that I'll be world champion.

I expect us both to start fast on Saturday night. Darleys will be looking to impose himself after the controversy of the last time out. He'll want to prove to everyone that he is a worthy champion. I reckon a faster start, yeah, but I'm not going to go in there reckless. With a good counter-puncher like Darleys, I'm only asking for trouble. If the opportunity presents itself, then I'd certainly like to jump on him.

Since the first fight Eddie Hearn had been looking ahead, planning the future for Crolla should he correct the injustice of four months ago. Kevin Mitchell had a date in December to take on Ismael Barroso in a WBA interim challenge, so an all-British affair could be made handily. Then there was Terry Flanagan, who'd picked up the WBO lightweight belt after his opponent, Jorge Zepeda, was forced to retire with a shoulder injury. A unification fight between two Mancunians – one red, one blue – who even went to the same school? It seemingly had it all.

Darleys is the only one to have my attention at the moment, but after the fight I can think about those other fights [Mitchell and Flanagan]. Those two fights would be very special. If it was Terry, it would be here in Manchester and we'd sell the place out. I've got great respect for Terry, but we'd happily put friendship aside for a deal to get sorted.

With Kevin, another fighter I've got great respect for, whether it was here or in London, it wouldn't bother me. It could be down West Ham way and I'm sure it'd sell well. Both fights I'd jump at but I've got to get past Pérez first.

Both men weighed in a pound under the lightweight limit the day before the fight, both reiterated their winning intentions, but Crolla knew this had to be *his* night. Unfair judging had stolen his dream once before. This time, nothing was left to chance.

Another raucous crowd were willing him every step of the way, but Anthony didn't let the occasion get to him. Boxing cautiously in a cagey opening, Crolla used his better footwork, moving well, making Pérez miss. Then came the explosion. In the fifth, with Pérez pinned to the ropes, Anthony fired shots to the head before switching his attack downstairs and sending the Colombian to his knees with a beautifully cruel left to the body. Pérez winced, shaking his head as if to dismiss his own chances of beating the count before referee Terry O'Connor signalled the end. It was a first stoppage defeat for the man from San Pedro de Uraba.

The crowd were frenzied, the Crolla song incessant as Anthony bounced around the ring, jumping up at each corner to scream 'Man-ches-teeeer!' to his delirious supporters.

Less than a year after suffering those terrible injuries when confronting burglars, the dream he'd visualised was finally real. It was a performance as shiny and regal as his white, gold and purple shorts.

It is an amazing feeling. It is a dream come true. Now I just want many more nights like this in Manchester. I've dreamed this dream since I was ten. I didn't know it was going to be this good. It is better than I ever dreamed it would be.

I was very confident I would get him out of there. I thought it would have been a head shot. I touched him with a right hand and sunk him with a left.

After the first fight, I went away and worked hard with the team. We have worked so hard in the gym. I just have to thank the team around me. Joe has turned my career around after so many people had given up on me.

I have come to this arena since I was ten watching Naseem Hamed, Joe Calzaghe and Ricky Hatton. To do it here is what I dreamed of.

Ismael Barroso

A battle of Britain fight with Kevin Mitchell was now a real possibility. To make that happen, Mitchell would have to come out on top in his WBA interim lightweight title challenge against Ismael Barroso at the O2 Arena, London.

He didn't. Crolla was ringside when Barroso proved that his dangerous reputation did not lack substance. The Venezuelan knocked out Mitchell in the fifth round of their December clash, and in so doing called time on the popular Londoner's career.

The mandatory challenger for Anthony's belt was therefore Barroso. While many suggested this was a nightmare fight against a heavy-hitting opponent, the champion was undaunted.

This is a tough task but there was no way I was not going to take the fight. I enjoyed a break since winning the title, but I have been in the gym for a while already and I am in a good place.

People said I was going to duck him but if I don't fight him I lose my belt, simple. Of course, I am going to fight him; I've worked too hard to become world champion to give it away.

With the date set for Saturday, 7 May 2016, it meant Crolla had a long build-up to ready himself for Barroso and could enjoy a family Christmas.

There was an air of déjà vu about the pre-fight publicity events. The Radisson Blu Hotel was again the venue for the press conference.

I'm enjoying fight week. There are press conferences and everything else but I think you've got to enjoy it. I'm enjoying my time as a world champion and I'm enjoying it too much to let it go.

It's like any other fight. You've got to stay calm and I'm not the type of fighter to get worked up at a press conference. I'm relaxed, Barroso's relaxed.

The press conference was moving along as normal when Barroso got his turn, speaking through an interpreter. He tried to ramp things up a bit after all the respectful platitudes from Crolla. Wearing a white baseball cap with large mirrored sunglasses, Barroso warned, 'I think you're talking too much for the amount of time you're going to spend in the ring!'

Anthony laughed and when Eddie Hearn pointed out that his man didn't do the whole trash talk thing, Barroso laughed and said, 'I don't like it either, it's just to make a fight!'

It was pretty funny. Listen, I know there's a language barrier, but Ismael seems like a cool guy. He does his talking in the ring, as his record suggests. I always say, when a boxer starts at a press conference, it's just a waste of energy.

It's very rare they're going to start rolling around and anyway they're not getting paid for it, so why do it? Pointless exercise, bad-mouthing each other. Nine times out of ten, you're going to shake hands after the fight. You should always be respectful, and anyway everyone knows this is a genuine fight – a 50/50 fight.

He's got power; he showed last time out that he cuts the ring off well, he moves his feet well, so he's not just bringing raw power. He's bringing boxing ability and skills and I know it's not just about avoiding a big left hand. He can hit with either hand.

I'm going to have to move my feet really well and I know there'll be times when I have to choose to box and times when I have to fight.

I'm forever in debt to the people that come out and support me. Having this city behind me, I just want to do them proud.

The man behind the fight plan, Joe Gallagher, was ignoring the prophets of doom. He'd been telling anyone who'd listen that Anthony was an improving fighter who had a sense of destiny. It was his time to shine once again.

'Barroso's a very dangerous challenger who presents a huge threat,' said Joe. 'That's Anthony's trick, isn't it? He always makes them feel comfortable then he gets in the ring and hits them in the head with a good right hand and a left hook! It's not in Anthony's nature, he's not a trash talker, he's just a nice kid. But he gets in that ring and he switches on. He worries me at times. I'm thinking, "He's too relaxed going into this, he's too relaxed," but he's got it mastered now.

'We've got to hit Barroso and hit him early. We have to see how he reacts to a shot. A few people I've spoken to in America say he's not too clever when you get to him. He doesn't fight as well up close, so it's very much up to Anthony not to be in middle ground. We've got to work our way in, counter things, but as we all know all game plans go out of the window when you get smacked on the nose.

'I think this has got the potential to be one of the fights of the year. I know that's an overused statement but Anthony Crolla's a very proud champion. He loves being world champion, he's going around the amateur clubs with his belts, and the kids are all having their pictures taken. If you looked in the dictionary for the words "world champion" I'd love to see a picture of Anthony Crolla because he replicates all that it is to be a world champion.'

There was no drama at the weigh-in, with both men coming in under the limit with ounces to spare. With all formalities completed, Crolla switched to fight mode and began visualising another great night at his number one venue. The Manchester Arena was Ricky

Hatton's fortress during a stellar career – his defining night against Kostya Tszyu in June 2005 is part of boxing folklore in the city.

The Hitman's fanbase was his greatest achievement. Thousands would flock to watch him fight anyone, anywhere, as was proved by the extraordinary numbers he took with him to Vegas, particularly for the Floyd Mayweather fight in 2007. But Anthony was doing his own thing and his vocal support had grown year on year. Unbeaten at Manchester Arena since making his professional debut there, it was his home now and Barroso would be his ninth fight under those familiar lights.

There is nowhere else in the world I'd choose to fight. It's a good hunting ground for me and is my favourite venue. It's been crazy how quickly the fans have got behind me and I honestly am blessed with the support I receive.

As has nearly always been the case, Anthony was once again going into a big fight as the underdog, and he'd have it no other way. Again, he'd prove the doubters wrong.

* * * * *

When a fight date is suggested, Anthony's first instinct is to4 check the football fixtures. Who are United playing? On this occasion, they were away at Norwich on fight day. Luckily, it was an early kick-off, so the many United fans who also follow Crolla could take in both events. It had been a long day for those who'd travelled down and up the country. Refreshments for many had been enjoyed since dawn's first light and the survivors in the crowd were in boisterous form. It all added to the occasion.

Barroso, as expected, came out strong and bullied Crolla in the opening three rounds. The tactics were to weather the storm, make Barroso realise that his heavy blows weren't having the impact he had anticipated, break his heart and watch him fade. That's exactly how it played out.

Crolla soaked up most of the punishment with his arms, the tight guard working well. By rounds four and five, Barroso's fire had been largely extinguished. He was gassing and Crolla went to work. It could've ended in the sixth and in the seventh it did. Again, a body shot was the weapon of choice – a fairly innocuous-looking right hit the spot and the Venezuelan couldn't drag himself up off the canvas to make the count.

Anthony's first defence had gone perfectly to plan. It was a sweet moment for the fighter whose star was again on the rise.

This is my house and nobody comes into my house and takes something away from me. I've shown I'm up there with any lightweight in the world.

He hit hard, but I've worked too hard for this. There was no way this title was leaving Manchester tonight. I knew within 30 seconds the way the fight was going to go. It was a case of not taking any silly shots.

I knew he was hurt. It was a matter of time before I got him out of there.

Anthony sat in the post-fight press conference, his face marked and swollen, a small nick visible under his left eye. Barely had the dust settled on the explosive fight when the inevitable questions were raised about the next opponent. Anthony said he wasn't bothered – that's for the team to decide. Eddie Hearn, seated to his right, ran through a list of options, including Barthelemy, Zlatacanin, Linares and Flanagan.

The win over Barroso, more than anything else, had put Crolla in control. Now, it would only be the biggest fights possible as Crolla set out to prove himself as the best lightweight in the world.

Jorge Linares I

After the Pérez fights and a first defence against mandatory challenger Ismael Barroso, Crolla could be forgiven for looking for an easier option next time out. That scenario didn't come to pass.

In mid-June, just over a month after the Barroso fight, a deal was made for Anthony to face the WBC 'Diamond' champion Jorge Linares, with the *Ring* magazine belt also at stake – the prestigious publication therefore backing the winner as *the* best lightweight in the world. The date was set for Saturday, 24 September, with home advantage once again secured.

Linares was no ordinary fighter. His journey to greatness is as unusual as it is interesting. He left his home in Barinas, Venezuela aged 17 for a new life in Japan under the guidance of promoter Akihiko Honda, a contact of Linares family friend Gilberto Mendoza, president of the World Boxing Association.

Linares began his professional career in a land as different to the dusty streets he called home as was possible to find. After learning Japanese, he settled into life there and has maintained his links with the country. Before every fight, he spends three months with Honda working on strength and conditioning before heading to Las Vegas to work on 'strategy' with trainer Ismael Salas. UK fans had witnessed Linares putting his plans into action with his dismantling of Kevin Mitchell. Crolla was confident his story would have a happier ending.

I'm so excited to have the chance to unify the lightweight division. Jorge is a fantastic fighter and it's another mountain to climb, but these are the tests that I thrive on and I've beaten two great fighters in Pérez and Barroso and I'm confident that I can beat Jorge too.

I've been a fan of Jorge Linares for years now and he's technically brilliant at times, but like any other fighter he has vulnerabilities. It's up to me to expose those vulnerabilities and I truly believe that I can and I will. Linares is a great champion but these are the fights you want to be in boxing for.

He looked well against Cano last time out but he hasn't been very active, whereas I'm coming off a career-best performance over Barroso. I really believe I'm coming into this fight in the form of my career and I'm capable of improving my game when I have to.

A broken hand picked up in training had hampered Linares' progress and forced a rethink. He had been due to defend his title against Dejan Zlatacanin but had to relinquish his WBC belt due to the injury. The Crolla fight would help piece things back together.

'This is my first unification fight and a great personal challenge for me and my career,' Jorge said. 'Last year was an unbelievable year. I had the opportunity to fight in England against Kevin Mitchell in front of a crowd of passionate fight fans in one of the greatest fights of my career. This fight is a great opportunity for me to fight in England once more, to be in front of a strong fight fanbase.

'Crolla is a very strong contender and I know with both our passions for the sport we will deliver an exciting fight for all the fans in Manchester. I know that Crolla is coming off a victory against my fellow Venezuelan countryman, so I am coming in with a lot of determination, pride and hunger for a victory.'

79

* * * * *

Session finished at the Gloves Gym, Bolton, home of Team Gallagher, Anthony's dressed in skinny blue jeans, white trainers and a grey hoodie. He's sat in the viewing gallery area of the gym overlooking his main place of work. Two of the Smith brothers, Liam and Callum, wander in. They sit opposite on a black, slightly worn, leather sofa facing Crolla, who's wolfing down couscous and roasted vegetables from his tupperware lunchbox.

In between mouthfuls, he's talking through his training regime to a backdrop of some gentle R n B and the less subtle grunts from the floor below as Hosea Burton rhythmically slams his fists into a heavy bag.

It's about routine now; diet and all that. I've had a good break. I'm looking forward to getting back to work. It's a bit like your first day at school; you're looking forward to seeing everyone but after the first week or so, the novelty wears off.

You're back working hard, so after a bit I'm thinking, 'I wouldn't mind being on a six-week holiday now!' The first few weeks are always hard.

When I'm out of training, diet-wise, I always try and be half-good. There'll be the odd day where I'll go out with the lads, but that's it.

After a fight, I'll have a few nights out. Once a year the lads will have a long weekend, but I'm not a big drinker. I'm not a lager drinker; I can't just sit there sipping away. It'll be a rum and coke for me. But days don't turn into weekends and weekends don't turn into weeks. If I've gone out, I'll do some kind of exercise the day after as punishment.

Food-wise, I make the weight easier than a lot of fighters. I'm growing into lightweight now and I'm getting bigger at the weight. I know it sounds sad, but for a treat I love going for a coffee and a cake. Sometimes I'll go on my own and I'll just sit there, quiet little coffee shop, often in the Northern Quarter [Manchester city centre].

It's a different crowd there, no one knows you – well some do. But it's quirky and I just like to people-watch with my coffee and cake. Must be the Italian in me!

Joe walks in talking about the hectic schedule ahead. Forthcoming fights dominate the conversation before gym tales of sparring sessions take over. Crolla giggles at a memory.

Ben Wager [Barnsley, super-lightweight] fucked me in sparring! I've had some bad 'uns, me! I always have a few bad spars. I remember funny things, like Joe going mad at me saying, 'This will be like a knife through butter with you and John [Murray]' and I was laughing. Joe was going, 'It's not fucking funny.' He'd lost it – gone mad at me.

Crolla turns to Joe, wide-eyed as if still surprised.

Do you remember when I had that bad spar with Maxi Hughes [southpaw, super-featherweight 16-2-2] before Barroso? After the first round, he just kept whacking me. I got snotted a good few times. About three spars before the fight it was and I could not get out of the bloody way of his right hand.

Joe switches to a positive, preferring to remember the more successful sessions. 'Liam [Smith] did a lot of sparring with Crolla earlier on in their careers,' he said. 'He did a lot for the Willie Limond fight. Beefy used to have a handful with Crolla. He couldn't deal with him.' Liam nods in agreement. 'Liam's been itching to get him back but he's too big now!'

The conversation moves on to gym tales from the Wild Card Gym in Los Angeles. Joe and his team of fighters have made annual pilgrimages to hook up with esteemed trainer Freddie Roach and his camp.

I'm a boxing fan as well and while Joe's my trainer and the only voice I listen to, it's great being around Freddie. He'd take us on the pads sometimes. He has a good relationship with Joe, so he'd help Joe out when it was a bit quiet. He's a brilliant pad man. He reckons doing the pads helps him and his condition [Parkinson's disease].

I remember my first day in the Wild Card. I thought I was living the dream. I'll never forget it. I was skipping next to Paulie Malignaggi, talking to him, and then the legend Shane Moseley's in the corner with his son just a few feet away. Kid Chocolate, world champion at the time, was shadow boxing, and then there was the local lunatic headbutting a punch bag. He was headbutting it, then talking to it. I just thought, 'Wow!' This boxing lark's mad.

Another former Los Angeles sparring foe of Anthony's is mentioned. 'What about that kid from Goosen's gym?' says Liam, pointing at Crolla, who rocks back into the sofa, laughing.

Oh yeah! For the first two rounds, he give me a good hiding. Probably the worst I'd ever had. I'd been British champion and he was just an amateur, a young kid. And he was a bit lighter than me.

I was looking at him thinking, 'Yeah, he's a bit flashy,' but then I thought, 'Hang on, he'll be a lot more concerned about me; he'll be thinking about sparring a professional.'

Well, he fucking snotted me! He just give it me. He didn't stop. Normally defence is one of my strong points, but me head was like a speedball. I got whiplash after it!

Juan Funez, that's him. He was getting ready to turn professional. We were doing six rounds and after four, he tried getting out just as I was getting on top. I was like, 'Don't you dare get out now!'

In fairness his uncle, who was his trainer, made him stay in for another round. Then, I give it him, know what I mean? I had to give it him. I battered him for the last round – man against boy – but for the first two … he was so fast and sharp. So sharp!

I remember coming back to the corner after the first round. Joe was like, 'Crol, what the …' and I was like, 'Joe, I know. You don't have to say anything.' Even Joe half giggled. Afterwards, we all laughed and still laugh about it now.

Another time, I'd had a few good weeks sparring at the Wild Card. I'd be sparring Ray Beltran [32-7-1, lightweight], Denis Shafikov [38-2-1, lightweight] and loads of other goods lads.

On the last sparring day, the Friday, Freddie Roach tells me I'm getting in with an African lad; can't remember his name. Freddie tells me he's a big puncher but I'd be able to outbox him. I'm not joking, he had these gloves on, they were like battered 12s [ounces], but we're really talking 10s, battered contest gloves. Aaaggh! He only hit me about five times, but oh my God…

I went back to the corner and Joe says, 'Stand your ground a little bit more with him.' I said, 'Have you seen his fucking gloves?' I was all right outboxing him but every time he hit me … I'd have rather he'd boxed with no gloves. It was that bad. The spar had started so I didn't want to spit my dummy out. It can be brutal out there, but I didn't want to start moaning.

I came out of that spar. I'd not had a mark on me after two weeks of hard sparring, and I was black and blue. I looked like a right second prize.

I had a go at Joe. I said, 'Cheers for pulling him on the gloves!' Joe just thought it was funny. I came home and everyone was saying, 'Bet it was tough out there by the looks of you?' I was like, 'Honestly, it was just the last day!'

* * * * *

It's overcast, miserable and dark, an August day in Bolton, and there's no sign of Crolla. It's 12.32pm and Gloves Gym is locked. Anthony was due to have finished his morning conditioning session around now. A phone call fails to reach him. Six minutes later, he calls back and realises he's missed a date in the diary. He's full of apologies, but no drama. He's not too far away, won't be long.

Crolla's changed his plans to ensure he fulfils the informal obligation that slipped his mind. He pulls up outside the back door of the gym at 12.52pm in his new, sleek black Merc. Once more, he apologises for his forgetfulness. It's genuine, the sad doe eyes mournful at the thought of letting somebody down. He hasn't.

The gym's still locked, so conversation takes place in the vanilla-scented, black leather-seated motor. He appears chuffed when complimented on the new acquisition.

Thanks. Just got it. Well, I've had it a few weeks. I don't even know what it's called, but it's clean inside and it's got a load of spec. Proper nice.

As is usually the case, football is the first topic on the agenda. Manchester United beat Leicester City in the Community Shield at Wembley the day before. For once, Crolla had to give it a miss due to training commitments and his little boy Jesse being ill over the weekend. He's not overly disappointed.

I would've liked to go, but I would've been rushing like mad to get down there and back. It's a glorified friendly at the end of the day. Just too much on really.

The Linares fight is seven weeks out. Along with the usual conditioning work, the regime is about to be stepped up.

We've done a bit of in-house sparring today for the first time, just to get our eye back in before the proper sparring starts at the end of this week. The conditioning weeks are the tough weeks, both in the gym and in the pool. You know that when you get those next few weeks out of the way, the sparring weeks fly by and it's fight-night.

With sparring, there's no one in-house I can specifically use for Linares. Like last time with Barroso, there were no southpaws, so I had to bring everything in. That's the way it goes. For instance, I would've been good sparring for Stephen Smith and his fight with Pedraza. He said it would've been perfect, but we couldn't do it because I had my fight around the same time.

When we do spar in-house, it doesn't get out of hand but it's not always the friendliest! You see Hosea Burton and Callum Johnson sparring and you think they hate each other. But it's not personal, it's business and they're helping each other. They're right wars, though. You'd pay to see them. Callum might batter Hosea for a few rounds, then Hosea will come right back and put it on him.

We'll be using Zelfa [Barrett, 11-0, super-featherweight] for this camp. We've used him before and he's a good lad. I always think it's good to use the young, hungry lads who'll put it on you. The prospects want to prove a point. I remember being that lad, being asked to spar. I wanted to make an impression because I wanted to come back. Sometimes you spar people at the same level and you coast. You have too much respect for each other. A few times I sparred Amir [Khan]. I know we're similar in age, but he was a lot more experienced than me. I was respectful but it was competitive. I saw it as testing myself. I was very grateful for the opportunity but I've never been star-struck.

The hard work's far from done, but I'm into it now. It's basically a 12-week camp. It's Monday, so that means bar, bag, punching, technique, tempo work. We normally have a hard punching session to start the week. We'll train for a couple of hours and it includes shadow boxing, floor work, skipping. Today we warmed up doing shadow and warmed down with skip. It could be the other way round.

This afternoon I'll go to the pool. With the swimming, we start with four rounds and build up to ten rounds. We might do sprints, short recovery, go again. Sometimes we swim continuous. It's all geared to three minutes – we keep it boxing specific.

Hosea's the best swimmer. The new kid, Paul Butler, he's the worst. He needs swimming lessons! Actually he needs armbands!

Training is varied for me. I'm not with Joe every day, mainly because of my injuries. I go up to Wigan three or four times a week to work with Martin Cullen. We do strength work and it's been a massive help since my lay-off.

Since the incident [burglary], there are certain things with the circuit in the gym that I can't do, so I make up for that with my strength work. I've had to adapt a bit. I do more bikram yoga and I'll go on the bike a bit.

For my first fight back for Pérez, I ran. But when I started my running for Pérez II, my ankle went. It was knocking on to my knee, so the physio said I was better off not running. I've felt better without it. I swim more and do other things. It was having too many knock-on injuries that were affecting the strength work on my legs.

It was a bit of a risk really because I'd never not ran before going into fights, but results weren't too bad and I haven't done any running for my last couple of fights. Early on in my career, I was crazy when I think about it. I was running six or seven miles a day, every day, and at a good pace. I was a good enough runner to be at club level, a decent level. I'd do cross-country races and stuff.

You can't reinvent the wheel, but I think boxing has been slow to adapt. Everything we do now is boxing specific. A lot of boxers are stuck in the past – run, run, bag, bag, don't do weights, they'll slow you down. Well, the right kind of weights will speed you up.

It's a science. For instance, I will lift some heavy weights, but I won't do loads of repetitions. Weights are a big part of it now. With Martin, I'll do different body parts on different days – legs, chest, shoulders, back, arms.

Anthony's phone starts to vibrate. He looks at the screen and says it's Saj [Team Khan] from the gym. He apologises and says he'd better take it.

'Hello mate … I'm sound mate. I'm locked out the gym, can't get in that's all … no I'm outside at the back. Been here a while … no, no worries, just give us a shout when you're back but don't rush … see you mate.'

Sorry, anyway, where was I? Oh yeah, tonight I'll rest up and tomorrow I'll go yoga then do my strength work.

The back door of the gym opens and out walks Saj looking around for Crolla. He spots him and shouts, 'I left me phone in the car! I'll leave the door open for you when you want to come in.'

Sound Saj! No worries.

'When you leave, just close the door like this …' Saj demonstrates and slams the door shut behind him. He turns and smiles, 'I've bloody locked myself out now!'

* * * * *

Hotel Football, Old Trafford was the venue for the first press conference – a month before fight night. The media gathering offered the chance for both men to have a good look at each other. There'll never be a Crolla press conference where playground insults are traded amid a sea of scowls, but this one was 'nice' even by 'Million Dollar's' standards.

Both boxers looked resplendent as they took their seats at the top table. Sporting blue jackets, white shirts and dark jeans, they were more suited to a night on the tiles than a dance in the ring.

He's a fighter I respect tremendously and seems a really cool guy. It's not the kind of fight that needs trash talk. Anyone that knows anything about the sport knows that it's a real fight. I just can't wait for September 24 to come around.

He has Robert Diaz, a great fella, over with him as well, so it's just massive respect. It's going to be a great fight. We're both going to bring our A-game.

Having a look at him in person, it gives you that little bit of a buzz. I'm going to go training now. I've trained hard this morning but I'm going to go and train again.

It gives you that little kick, that extra bit of motivation to see these beautiful belts on the table and think, 'I won those, they're on my mantelpiece and there's no way I'm letting them leave Manchester.'

The head-to-head for the photographers is all bright, white smiles and a warm handshake. Jorge gives the impression of being the South American equivalent to his rival.

'We're very similar characters and people. Outside the ring, look at us? We dress the same, we're very similarly dressed. It looks like we've been friends for many years. We could go out and have a meal together. He's very humble. He's been through a lot – ups and downs. He's very blessed to be where he is today, as am I. Outside the ring? We could be very good friends.

'Inside the ring, we're also very similar. Our styles will mesh very well and give the fans a beautiful fight, a clean fight. We both jab well, work the body well, we both attack, we both counter. Total respect for him.

'I'm very motivated. It's obviously a big compromise [fighting in Manchester] and there are a lot of titles at stake. That's the grand prize, fighting the best and walking away with those rewards.

'We're only 30 days out so I've got to go away and continue working hard, preparing myself to the fullest, so I can come out here physically and mentally prepared to steal the night, steal the show.'

Linares goes by the ring moniker of 'El Nino de Oro' – 'The Golden Boy'. As is only right, he's convinced he'll halt Crolla's recent run and maybe come back for another unification. 'My focus is on Anthony Crolla, but Terry Flanagan has crossed my mind,' said Jorge. 'It's a challenge, another world title. I'm not here for easy fights or easy opponents. I'm here to fight the best. Why not come back to Manchester? I'm starting to like the weather here. It's better than back home!

'I need to know that the day when I retire, I look back on my career and I know I've fought the best and beat the best.'

The fight had been easy to put together. Eddie Hearn praised Golden Boy Promotions and Robert Diaz, head matchmaker at the company. Likewise, Diaz revealed all negotiations were completed within a couple of days. All boxing matters were controllable, but Crolla had been concerned about the United game that day. Luck was on his side.

It's like I'm slipping someone a bit of money because it's perfect! Last time it was an early kick-off but away at Norwich. A bit of a road-trip, but massive respect to those that did both. It's going to be easier this time and I think we're going to get three points as well! It's Leicester, the champions, at home, so it's going to make it even more of an atmosphere. I want to deliver.

A lot of them [United players] are into the boxing and I'll be very thankful for any that make it.

Once all interview requests had been satisfied, Linares and Diaz headed off to the airport for their flights back to Vegas. Joe Gallagher was still in the function room, still talking enthusiastically about the challenge ahead.

'The two best lightweights in the world are going to meet head-on, nothing more to say really. The way they both apply themselves,

dress themselves, you'd think they were both off to the GQ awards!'
Joe laughed.

'It's a great fight, a great opportunity and another great night to
look forward to in Manchester. He [Linares] has boxing skills, and
plenty of them. A world champion at three different weights, he's
technically very good, he composes himself very well and throws
lots of good shots.

'Barroso was all power, power, power and trying to take Anthony
out. He didn't have the skill Jorge Linares has. Linares carries power
and skill. It's a different fight again. It's a difficult fight for Anthony,
but we'll put a game plan together and I'm sure we'll come through
on the night.

'Me and Robert Diaz follow each other on Instagram and we've
been putting on little bites. I put on a picture of Anthony swimming
and he gave it, "Tell Anthony not to swim too far away – we're
coming." Linares was on there running, so I was, "Tell Linares not
to run away." It's just between me and Robert, banter you might call
it, but for the fighters, they both know they don't need any trash talk.
They're preparing well and they don't have time and energy to waste
on trash talk.

'Up on the table there was the WBA belt, the WBC Diamond
belt, the *Ring* magazine belt and I said to Anthony, just as the press
conference finished, "Let's make sure, when we announce our next
fight, that the three belts are on our side of the table." That's what's
driving him, the chance to prove himself as *the* number one in his
division.

'It's great what he's achieved up to now, but he's fighting the best
and he wants to go in there and beat the best. Imagine how good
Anthony's story will be after what happened last year. To be a *Ring*
magazine champion? There haven't been many from this country. It's
a hard award and a hard belt to win.

'We've been in the gym, practising stuff, studying, we've had
sparring partners throwing Jorge Linares-style shots. We're being
the best we can be. We don't think being brave wins this for Anthony
Crolla; he's got to have his skills. Anthony was a good amateur, an
ABA champion, and he's going to need his amateur skills in this fight

– punch selection, sharpness, feet. Linares is going to look to give Anthony problems with his boxing skills.'

* * * * *

Preparations have gone well, the hard sparring has been done and everything is now being tapered down. The only issue is a minor problem Crolla has with one of his so called team-mates. Callum Smith's made no secret of his admiration for Linares.

He needs to pick sides. I've told him! He's a big fan. But in fairness, if I was telling a young kid in the gym to watch someone, I'd say watch the way Jorge Linares does this and watch the way he does that. He is technically brilliant at times. But in the fight, it's going to come down to a lot more than that. Not just about who wants it more, but tactics, and I think I've got a great man in my corner to sort them out. But he is a great fighter and that's why Callum's a fan.

Fight week

It's Monday, the start of fight week, and Anthony's still found time to go back to school. He's at the MCMA Academy in Blackley, a large secondary school just down the road from his New Moston manor. The event's been organised by the Manchester United Foundation in partnership with local charity The Sport Community.

It's unfamiliar territory for Anthony, addressing hundreds of schoolchildren in a question-and-answer session, but he handles it with ease, doing his bit to inspire and motivate the next generation to follow their dreams. After the talk, he headed to the gym to do pads with some of the keen young boxers. That part of the morning was right back in his comfort zone.

It's been an absolute privilege. I was really impressed with the facilities but with the kids as well. It was great meeting them and speaking to them, they were a great bunch. Hopefully, they see a local lad who's achieved his dream and it might inspire one or two others as well.

* * * * *

The Palace Hotel [since renamed The Principal] is a building steeped in Manchester history. The former home of the Refuge Assurance

Company is an iconic, Grade II listed Edwardian landmark on Oxford Road in the heart of the city. An elegant venue, then, for a classy pre-fight conference.

Every boxing bill has a title. This one is being sold as 'When Two Worlds Collide'. There's a huge poster picturing the combatants fixed to a screen at the back of a function room, set away down a maze of corridors from the reception area. Both men appear on time and have dressed down since their first press conference – Crolla in a black tracksuit with red trim, Linares going for the military look with a khaki army-style shirt and black jeans. They're not matching any more.

Rumours abound that Jorge might be a bit tight at the weight. There have already been suggestions from his camp that he may move up a division to super-lightweight following Saturday's fight, whatever the result.

Regardless, the Venezuelan and his team give the impression of supreme confidence, and Jorge is determined to honour a promise he made to a dying friend and countryman.

'Gilberto Mendoza [former WBA president], he was like my grandfather. I am where I am today because of him and his son Gilberto Mendoza Jr,' Linares explained.

'This is something I promised him. I promised him the WBA belt, to bring it back to him, so yes I have that on me and because I know that I'm preparing well in the gym to come and fulfil that promise.

'There is a lot of respect for Crolla, but once we get in the ring it's on,' Jorge said. 'This is the most important fight of my career, but I am ready and on Saturday I am taking all of the belts.'

Joe Gallagher was equally defiant and used the press conference as a rallying call for Manchester to again turn out in force and back their man. Describing Manchester as the capital of British boxing, Joe compared Anthony's night with Hatton vs Tszyu. Anthony didn't feel any added pressure with the comparison.

Saturday is going to be a special night and I feel blessed to be taking part in it.

There will only be one Ricky Hatton but for this fight to be compared with Hatton's fight against Kostya Tszyu is an honour.

Any concerns about Linares and his weight were quashed at the weigh-in a day later at the Radisson Blu Hotel. The 31-year-old came in lighter than Anthony, nearly a full pound under the 135lb limit. Anthony too had ounces to spare.

Fight night

It was another very busy night for Joe Gallagher at the arena. Along with making sure Crolla was relaxed and ready, he had other lads fighting on the bill. Hosea Burton and Marcus Morrison went on early, both putting in good shifts with early victories over Fernando Castaneda and Matiouze Roye respectively.

Anthony was his usual relaxed self in the dressing room, shaking out to Joe's dance music in the background. Sky Sports camera crews and BBB of C officials were coming and going and when Crolla sat down to have his hands wrapped, United captain Wayne Rooney popped in to wish him luck. The Reds had earlier beaten champions Leicester City 4-1, but Rooney had been dropped to the bench and ended up playing just seven minutes as a sub. Still, he was here to back Crolla, just like the fighter had supported the striker over the years.

Back out in the arena, Callum Johnson added to the Team Gallagher feelgood factor by claiming the vacant Commonwealth light-heavyweight title with a ninth-round stoppage of the fabulously named Willbeforce Shihepo of Namibia.

The chief support was an intriguing middleweight contest – John Ryder vs Jack Arnfield for the WBA international belt, the latter coming out on top with a unanimous points decision.

So on to the main event. MC Craig Stephen called the challenger to the ring, prompting a chorus of boos. Kitted out in a maroon baseball cap, fluorescent yellow T-shirt and black shorts, Linares looks a picture of concentration as he navigates the route to the centre of the arena.

Moments later, as Linares bounces around the ring, Crolla's face appears on the big screens, his entrance imminent. Sight of their man leads to roars all around before the familiar chorus of 'oooooh Anthony Crolla' takes over once again. It's a remarkable sight with

17,000 excited supporters in attendance – all supporting a fighter who had been challenging for an English title just a few short years before.

The action got under way, with Linares firing out early jabs and Crolla manoeuvring himself into the centre of the ring, trying to force Linares back. A couple of snappy shots from Linares to the body hint at a long night ahead for the champion.

Clever work from Linares follows in the second round, his classy combinations causing Crolla problems and the crowd already sensing that all isn't going to plan.

Moving into the fourth and fifth rounds, the Venezuelan is building up a lead, although low blows annoy many at ringside and referee Terry O'Connor warns Linares, but no points are deducted. An overhand right from Crolla gees up his supporters and leaves blood around the left eye of his opponent.

Into the sixth and Crolla's constant pressure appears to be affecting Linares, who looks to be tiring a little. Anthony's in control of the round before Linares lands a beautiful overhand right to send Crolla wobbling, befuddled and hanging on for the bell.

After a minute on his stool, Anthony somehow summons the mental and physical strength to take the fight to Linares again, winning the seventh and displaying incredible workrate in the eighth. The challenger's work is cute, though, and he gets on his bike in the ninth and tenth but dazzles with enough combinations to catch the eye of the ringside officials.

The final two rounds left Crolla looking for something special or the belts would no longer be his. He tried desperately to make a dent in Linares, who was managing to deal with everything Anthony threw at him.

The final bell was met with a warm embrace between the two fighters. Crolla had taken some lumps, landed his own and was always competitive, but his body language was telling the story everyone knew. His reign was over, a reality confirmed by the scorecards of 115-114, 117-111, 115-113 all in favour of the winner and new ...

Speaking to Sky Sports shortly after the verdict, Anthony was down but defiant.

It was close. You work hard. I've got no complaints. I'll watch it back. I made a few mistakes and walked on to a few sharp counters. I'm disappointed in that and I'm disappointed I couldn't win those belts for Manchester.

He rocked my world. I'm not going to lie. My head's still spinning now. I'm in great condition and that's what pulled me through it. It's a pleasure to share the ring with a great like Linares.

He's the best fighter I've shared the ring with. I came so close to beating him, so it shows I belong at that level. A few mistakes can cost you dearly and that's what happened tonight. I'm gutted.

The way this city turned out, I've got to make sure I win a rematch. It's something I'm so thankful for.

When Linares took to the mic, the boos had been banished from the crowd. Not quite a scene from a *Rocky* film, but the respect from the fans was evident in the applause for the new champion.

'First of all, I want to tell the people of Manchester thank you so much,' Jorge said. 'Anthony once told me that he was a fan of me, and I am a fan of his. We gave Manchester a beautiful fight, and we should do it again.

'I hurt my hand in the sixth round a little bit, but I backed off and played it well strategically. I then decided to close in the final three rounds, and I think that gave me the victory.

'I think I hurt him a couple of times and I saw him rock, but I didn't want to be too aggressive. I wanted to be intelligent. And that's what I did.

'Now I want to take a good break, and to make sure my hand heals. And then why not come back to England? And why not come back to Manchester? I love it here.

'I want to thank my team, my corner, my wife and my family. I promised Gilberto Mendoza I would bring the belt back, and I did.'

Linares had made it clear immediately after the fight that he'd happily do it all again. Promoter Eddie Hearn confirmed that a rematch would happen.

'There's no question, there will be one, there's an agreement. This young man is a credit to Manchester. He's never moaned once. He'll dust himself down. He will fight Jorge Linares again and he will beat him.'

* * * * *

In the days and weeks following the fight, Joe Gallagher had watched the action over and over again. Poring over every fine detail, he had to work out what had happened, what worked, what didn't and what they could do better next time.

'You've got to hold your hands up, Jorge Linares is no mug. He's a three-weight world champion and he's one of the best pound-for-pound fighters in the world. He's had a few speedbumps on his career, a couple of losses, but that doesn't take away from the fact he's a quality fighter.

'Last time, it showed down the stretch that he had that experience of being in the big world title fights. He danced and ran away with it the last couple of rounds. He'll come back with more confidence, knowing he can hurt Anthony, but we'll have a game plan. This is boxing at the top level, this is physical chess, this is second guessing. We're second guessing what they're going to do and obviously they're studying Anthony.

'That's what makes it such a beautiful sport. When the game plan does come off and you've out-thought them, it's great. Sometimes it doesn't come off and they've had your number. They had it last time, but I'm trying to put things right to make sure we'll have their number this time.'

Rest, recuperation and family time. That's what Anthony needed following the Linares fight. He had a break but rarely spent any time without the wily Venezuelan invading his thoughts. What could he have done differently? The consolation was the chance to give it another go against a man he had even greater respect for now.

He's a cool guy. I know I say it about everyone, but I watched Linares for years. I'm a bit of an anorak. I didn't think there was a chance of fighting him until I won a world title. You know what – he's a nice guy.

I know anyone can be a good winner, but after the fight, we were talking and his missus was there – and she was lovely too!

As time passed after the fight, Anthony ticked over in the gym and enjoyed one of the perks of being out of training camp. Manchester United is an enduring passion for him and a little room in the diary gave him the freedom to follow his team home and away.

94

I've always been a United fan, always gone. I've always had a season ticket but I started going to more and more away games with a mate of mine. Away tickets are bloody hard to get, aren't they? I go with me mate Shaun and I think a lot of Reds see me at these games all the time and realise I'm a genuine fan.

Whenever I go to away games, I tend to travel on the lively supporter buses – there's the O'Neill bus, the Betty bus and the Monkey bus. When we are on European trips, I'll always meet up with the lads who come and support me.

'We sit in the top left section of the K stand at Old Trafford,' Shaun explains. 'Anthony was kind of anonymous until after he fought Derry Mathews the second time. It was evident there were a lot of United fans in the Echo Arena that night supporting him and his support grew as he was getting recognised more and more at away games.

'Since the Mathews fights, there's always been lots of Reds wanting to follow Anthony. Where we sit, everyone buys tickets for his fights, from young kids to old women and lads who wouldn't normally go and watch boxing.

'Crolla's just one of their own. There's a United supporters' branch in Newport in south Wales and they bring two coachloads to his fights. There are Reds who fly in from Norway, a minibus that comes from Edinburgh and lads who travel from Merthyr Tydfil for his fights.

'The *United We Stand* magazine have their own coach and they fill it every time he fights, plus the Cockney Reds always come and cheer him on. There are about 80 United lads from Burnage who make every fight a big night out by bringing their wives and girlfriends.'

While boxers like Crolla are huge football fans, many footballers are fascinated by the fight game. Wayne Rooney's a familiar face at Gloves Gym – he counts Crolla and fellow Scousers the Smiths as friends – and both he and then-United colleague Michael Carrick were ringside for the Linares fight.

While not the same as scoring a goal at the Stretford End, Crolla's taken to the turf a few times, enjoying an ovation from the Old Trafford crowd when showing off his WBA belt pitchside. He's often featured in the matchday programme, is a regular on MUTV and has even been the subject of two documentaries produced by United's in-house TV station. To cap it all, he even has his own fan club within the United following, who bring a special flag to matches with 'United Nights and Crolla Fights' emblazoned across it.

I was made up when I saw that. I first knew about it when United were playing PSV a couple of seasons ago. Loads of people started sending me pictures of the flag. It was mad. I didn't even know the lads behind it – I do now. Mad.

The United connection has certainly helped to raise his profile, with many fellow Reds buying tickets for his fights, whether they're boxing fans or not.

I have amazing support from United fans and it is genuinely humbling to meet them at games, or to have a photo and drink with them. A lot of them tell me about which of my fights they've seen.

When the rematch [with Linares] was being negotiated, there were two dates being discussed. One was 11 March and that was the same day as Southampton away, which would have been a nightmare! The other was 25 March, during the international break, so that was always the preferred choice in my eyes.

Everyone will have the weekend off from football and can hopefully enjoy their Saturday night with me. You never know, I might have 75,000 fans interested in coming now there's something to do!

For the 2016/17 season, United had failed to qualify for the Champions League and were instead competing in the Europa League – a rung below. New United boss Jose Mourinho was doing his best to rally enthusiasm among supporters, who weren't particularly taken with Thursday night football when the elite tournament had been their staple for so long. Anthony saw things a little differently. With training not in full flow, he could travel to some lesser-known destinations that the Europa League throws up.

Zorya Luhansk were in United's group. United had beaten them at Old Trafford earlier in the season and by the time they were scheduled to meet in the return, the Ukrainian side were bottom of the group with qualification beyond them. United, on the other hand, were almost assured of progressing.

The match was taking place more than 400 miles from Luhansk due to the conflict in eastern Ukraine. The coastal city of Odessa, in the west of the country, was the venue. The 'pearl of the Black Sea' proved a memorable destination.

I had a drink on one of the nights. Everyone went to an Irish bar – I think it was called O'Neill's. Don't get me wrong, I wasn't steaming or owt like that, but I had a few drinks. I met so many people, it was so busy. It was brilliant.

Cheapest place I've ever been. It made Benidorm look expensive! I was shocked. But the town was nice, it was decent. We were staying about 15 minutes out of town, but one night we went in to a restaurant, and it was a very nice one. We had a starter, main and dessert and a few drinks and it was about £15. It was a mad place. Cold as well, but great.

United fans had been advised to take special measures when in Ukraine due to known hooligan elements that had previously targeted foreign fans. Those travelling were urged to avoid certain areas, avoid wearing any team colours and refrain from attracting attention.

As usual, Burnage Red Shaun O'Donnell travelled with Crolla.

'We did the overnight trip and stayed in a decent part of Odessa, but it was clear it could be dodgy because there were so many police and military. It was moody but spirits were high in the pub [Mick O'Neill's] and it was dirt cheap to drink and eat over there. Crolla's arrival in the pub was met with the usual "oooh Anthony Crolla" and the obligatory photo session with Reds from all over the place.

'There was a colossus of a man on the door and Crolla was still having selfies so this big bloke asked me who the little guy was. I showed him a picture on my phone of Crolla in the ring holding the belt and the doorman went over and literally picked Crolla up with a bear hug, he was so happy to be with him. He rang for a car to pick us up and take us back to the safety of the hotel. We got in the car but unfortunately Irish Tony missed the door handle when he was trying to get in. We were halfway up the road before we realised that he was spark out in the middle of the street!'

Anthony's United obsession is a sporting distraction away from the harsh realities of the boxing game. Watching his team allows him to switch off from training. His love for his team is something his gym mates are used to although Team Gallagher is divided. Liverpool fans now outnumber the United contingent, with Morrison and Cardle beholden to City and Celtic respectively.

Football is never usually an issue in the gym, just a verbal stick to beat your mates with when things go right or wrong, depending on results. Sometimes, though, it can get a little fractious.

When we played Liverpool the other season, Paul [Smith] rang us when we were on the way down and told us to park up at his grandad's house. He said he'd give us a lift to the ground and then give us a lift back after the game. Unfortunately for Paul, we beat them 1-0 and Rooney scored. Paul then conveniently turned his phone off and left us to do the victory walk miles back to our car!

Another time when we beat Liverpool away – Mata scored twice – we were kept in after the game and we had parked the car a good distance from the ground. Eventually, we got out of the ground and were walking to the car but we seemed to be the only United fans on the road. We were on the other side of Stanley Park and a car went past and [someone] shouted something out of the windows. They pulled over further up the road and got out. Shaun said, 'Here we go Crolla, this lot are looking for it!' But they all had their phones out for a selfie! They were Scousers and us Mancs, but they were giving it, 'We love you Crolla!'

* * * * *

Christmas holidays were not long forgotten and camp had begun in earnest. Interest in the rematch was slowly growing and Anthony and Joe had been invited by BBC Radio Manchester to take part in the station's *Red Wednesday* evening show. It's all things Manchester United, a subject as familiar to both men as boxing.

They're joined in the studio by former United striker Danny Webber, a much-travelled player now forging a career in the media. News has broken regarding the impending departure of United forward Memphis Depay. He's off to Olympique Lyonnais and nobody's particularly bothered.

'He's sixth or seventh down the pecking order and not fighting for a place,' Danny chips in first. 'He's not trying to fight for a place

– he's just there. Manchester's a working-class city and fans want to see effort from the players. If you're swanning around Manchester, earning a lot of money and not representing [the team] on the pitch, then you're going to upset people and that's what Memphis did.'

There was a lot of criticism for David Moyes when Marouane Fellaini came in, but he always does a shift. With Memphis, I don't know, you just didn't feel he was putting in a shift. It seems like good business.

It's Joe's turn now and he has another target in mind. '[Anthony] Martial avoids an awful lot of stick. I mean, £31 million we paid for him! I'm sure there'll be people looking at him saying, "You've got to perform or Rashford will be given a go." Memphis didn't perform. We've got some talented kids in the youth team that are dying to break through.'

The radio chat is taking place just a few days after United's disappointing performance at home to their most hated rivals, Liverpool. The same day, United's record signing Paul Pogba launched his new emoji. It's been a big talking point and has raised many questions about the modern footballer.

He's got enough pressure on him with the price tag. If you're going to have the emoji as well, the way social media is these days, he's putting more pressure on himself.

There are a lot of people giving him stick after the Liverpool game. He seems a big character, he's very flash and I think that works for him. Sitting back and being humble might not work for him. He's loud, he's brash and usually he walks the walk as well, so I don't mind it.

Listen, all these clubs giving him stick – if they could afford him, they'd have got him. Obviously with him being a United player in the past, them letting him go and bringing him back, it adds to the stick, but I'm a big Pogba fan.

Conversation turns to Anthony's match-going habits. There are a few United away days in the Crolla diary, but there could be another clash on the horizon. Presenter Bill Rice asks Joe if Anthony needs to be careful about going to games in the run-up to a fight.

'One hundred per cent. It could be anything. You don't want to be in and out of a football stadium, falling on steps, twisting an ankle. Anything could happen. Anthony goes to a lot of away games, anything could be thrown and hit him on the head. You know what Anthony's like for getting hit on the head with things!'

Do you know what? Funnily enough, last time I was at Hull, we got a late winner and I copped for a coin on me head there!

'There's Hull away gone next week! You can forget all about that! You've got to stay away and look after yourself. As much as he'd like to be there, everyone understands that Anthony's got to get in the ring and perform. He's a professional and you'd expect him to act like one.'

The hour-long football chat eventually turns to boxing and Anthony's night of destiny – and the odds stacked against him.

I've been in boxing a long time and I've had it where my career's been on the line, and listen, I'm a realist but I don't think, 'What if I lose?' If things didn't work out, I'd go away, improve and make myself get up there again for another opportunity. But I'm just thinking about this fight. It's all that's on my mind and it means absolutely everything to me.

Joe picks up the chat again. 'It's another big night in Manchester. Last time, Carrick and Rooney were ringside; it's international weekend and I know a few of the players have already been on to Matchroom and Anthony for tickets. Hopefully Jose, the Special One himself, will pop up this time as well. I know he's a boxing fan. It will be a great night in Manchester, with a great atmosphere, so that's what you want.'

The hour-long show flies by and the lads leave the swanky new Media City studios and head for home. Anthony still has United on the brain as he makes his way out of the building. He loves the connection with his club but like Ricky Hatton before him is keen to have the goodwill of everyone in the city, whether red or blue.

I'm a proud Mancunian. I don't want to turn half the city against me. I'm a Red obviously but I do really appreciate everyone supporting me, whether they're City or United. I know there've been United songs at my fights, which is great. I get amazing support from United fans, but I don't want to alienate anyone.

The Georgie Best song before the Barroso fight was amazing. But everyone loves Georgie Best! It's funny but while I was waiting to come out at the end of the tunnel for the fight, and there's all this noise going on, all I could hear was one bloke shouting, 'Crolla!!' I was trying to get in the zone and he's shouting, 'Crolla!' He was relentless and eventually I looked up and he looked at me and shouted, 'Crolla! Do it for Eric! Do it for Eric!' It was funny. He was deadly serious!

Eric [Cantona] was my hero. I love a story I heard about Sir Alex and the United players at a black-tie do they were at. I don't know if it's true, but I can imagine it is. He goes to Giggs, 'Ryan, sort your tie out,' then he spots Nicky Butt and he bollocks him. 'Nicky, your dickie bow's all over the place.' He was bollocking all the young ones. Eric walks in with a white suit on and red trainers. Sir Alex looks at him and says, 'That's class!' All the other players are looking at each other going, 'What the fuck?' Eric got away with murder!

Apparently, on the night Eric did the kick at Crystal Palace, all the players got the hairdryer treatment. Sir Alex went around the dressing room and give it everyone, 'You this, you that.' He got to Cantona and said, 'Eric, you can't be doing that, son.' That was it. Got away with murder.

CHAPTER 5

Repeat or Revenge?

Jorge Linares II

It's 9.54am. The flashier cars are parked near the back entrance of Gloves Community Gym, Amir Khan's name prominent above the door. The back of the building looks like all the other industrial units surrounding the car park. The brown wooden door's been left slightly ajar. It's good to get inside, away from the typically damp, cold morning air of a January day in Bolton.

Once through the first dimly lit, empty gym area with a vending machine on the right and a ring on the left, it's through the second door and into the place of work for Team Gallagher. The lights are bright and the heat immediately hits the senses, as if walking fully clothed into a sauna. It's stifling. A huge heater above the ring to the left is belting out hot air. All part of the plan, of course. The room isn't particularly musty, no strong odour of sweat, just a slight tinge of disinfectant. It's Monday morning and the place is clean for the working week ahead.

Heavy bags rest still. Mirrors surround them on two sides of the square room. The rest of the gym has brick walls painted black, with graffiti superimposed. There are Khan's branded initials, bolts of lightning, a tiger's head and an image of Bolton's most famous fighter in action.

All around the walls are framed fight posters depicting glory nights from home and abroad. Mayweather features prominently.

There's Tyson vs Holyfield, Canelo vs Khan, Morales vs Barrera and two huge banners strung to the side of the ring – one for Canelo vs Smith, another for Crolla vs Linares.

From somewhere, music fills the room. It's an old house track. Joe Gallagher walks out of the changing area first. He's dressed in a black T-shirt emblazoned with 'Gallagher's Gym' in gold on the front, plain black shorts and black Nike trainers with thick white soles. When asked about the music, he says that he's in charge of the playlists. The stuff he's put on for the morning session, apparently, is old-school Marbella tunes.

Anthony has changed into his black and red kit – including matching leggings – and has a black baseball cap on backwards. He's followed by Hosea Burton, his nickname 'The Hammer' writ large across his blue top. Marcus Morrison and the newest member of the stable, Paul Butler, complete the training quartet. Burton clambers into the ring and starts slinging out jabs and hooks in front of the mirror.

Joe calls Anthony to his position next to the ring. His laptop is showing the Crolla vs Linares fight. 'Look Anthony, he's always throwing the left hook to the body,' Joe says, pointing at the screen. 'He threw every shot in the book.'

Butler walks towards the pair, wrapping his hands as he peeks over at the footage. Joe catches him out of the corner of his eye, turns to him and laughs, 'Fucking Swansea! I told you, the wheels have come off!' (Saturday, 21 January, Liverpool 2 Swansea City 3).

Joe continues to throw bits of advice in Crolla's direction, even after he's moved away to start skipping. The stopwatch is out and the session begins in earnest. Instructions are given, 'Skip ... double up ... skip.'

After ten minutes, all fighters get gloved up. Joe moves around them, talking all the time. The subject matter veers from disbelief that none of his young charges have seen *Trainspotting*, to mock anger when James the caretaker walks past with a pizza box.

All get to work on the bags with all manner of grunts, groans and screams as gloves connect. Butler's the smallest, but the loudest.

Another ten minutes in and Joe's strapped on the body belt. A circuit's in full swing, with fighters moving stations from bag to bar to burpees on the mats; speedball, tyre flip and sledgehammer on tyre. Each takes turns with Joe on pads. There's a loud screech as Anthony catches the top of Joe's finger at the end of a rapid combination. A minute's recovery and all is well again.

Half an hour into the circuit and the fighters pair up. Crolla and Burton clamber through the ropes and take turns firing a medicine ball from across the ring into each other's chest. Joe's voice can be heard above the music, 'You're trying to throw him out of the ring! Throw it like a basketball, not a tart on the beach! Stop fucking about, move your feet! To his chest! You're trying to take his fucking head off!'

Next, there are four fighters in four corners of the ring and a brutal-looking abs session begins, followed by press-ups, a chin-up competition (Crolla wins with 35) and stretches. Work over for the day, Burton, Butler and Morrison make their way into the changing room. Crolla continues with extra dips, chin-ups and press-ups and more stretching.

Close to 1pm and the first part of training is over. Crolla heads for the shower. Ten minutes later, Anthony walks back out of the changing room, stripped to his underwear. He's smiling and patting imaginary love handles.

I'm fat! I'm a few pound heavy on my back. But I've got two weeks to get down to ten stone nine before sparring.

Joe moves back to his laptop to once again analyse round 12 of Crolla vs Linares. The action finishes and he sits on the ring apron, leans back against the ropes and talks through his schedule.

'They've just announced Flanagan vs Petrov, April 8. Petrov's a kid I was looking at as a voluntary for Crolla if we didn't have Linares. It's on the same night as Beefy [Liam Smith] against Liam Williams.

'Obviously Hosea and Marcus are on the Manchester bill with Anthony, while Paul Butler is fighting on the 8th with Liam. That's another big night to look forward to, but Crolla's the focus now. That was a good conditioning session today. It's about putting the pedal to the floor now. They were doing six rounds of very anaerobic, short, explosive work.

'I keep on top of them. I'll give it "Crolla, don't be lazy!" But he isn't like that. Crolla leads the way in many respects in the gym. Some days, though, when he isn't feeling it, the other lads will pull him through. They've done their conditioning session now, so they can have something to eat, get a couple of hours' rest and then we'll do a swimming session.

'Tomorrow, Anthony will do some work with his strength and conditioning coach Martin Cullen [in Wigan]. 'He'll work on legs and other strength work with free weights and he'll do yoga as well tomorrow. Wednesday, he'll be back in here and we'll do an hour on pads. We'll work on technique and go through loads of stuff from the first fight. I have that fight playing all the time because sometimes you can watch it and become numb to it. Sometimes I'll look up and catch it and I'll see something clearer. I used to watch rounds one to four, then four to eight, eight to twelve. Now, I'll just see little snapshots.

'Look [points to the screen], Anthony was throwing singles and doubles and Linares was always coming back with counters of threes and fours all the time. We've got to make sure we put more than one and two together. We put a three and a four so when Jorge lets his hands go we come back with a counter that's more than a single.

'With Anthony, it's very constant, relentless pressure. Chip, chip, chip away. To the naked eye it might not look good, but when you're in there, Anthony invades your space. Just before Linares caught him, Anthony was beginning to break him and make him wilt, just like he did with Pérez and Barroso. But, you saw Linares and the class that he has. He was able to keep the distance and put Anthony on the back foot at times.

'We've got to be a little bit cuter and smarter with our feet, make sure we don't come out with our head in the air and get caught. Anthony needs to be a little bit looser and more supple. I'm not saying we stand there with Linares and match him punch for punch. Linares has impressive shot selection that will catch a judge's eye. There seems to be no effort in his shots when he's throwing them.

'Anthony can make changes. If you look at his fights, he was on the front foot with Derry [Mathews] but in the rematch on the back foot, using his boxing brain. He boxed well on the back foot against John Murray. With Barroso, he went back to what he's known for, coming forward with his hands up, and now with Linares, with him being such a skilful fighter, we'll adapt again.

'Before the first fight, people were talking about his [Linares'] vulnerabilities in the Kevin Mitchell fight. I wasn't buying into that. I think Linares and his team had looked into Kevin Mitchell and seen that he'd lost to Ricky Burns and Michael Katsidis and thought, "Nah, we'll beat him." They weren't on it.

'They were aware of Anthony because Barroso used to be in Linares' camp and they knew what a big puncher he is. They knew it'd be a 12-round fight, so they were fit and conditioned to do 12 rounds. That showed down the straight.

'I know Linares has been away in Japan [training camp]. He's back in Vegas again and he's a proud champion. He's got the *Ring* magazine belt and he's got huge nights and fights ahead. He doesn't want to give the belts up on the first time of asking. I think he'll come fitter again. Can he be as good? I think he can, so it's up to Anthony to raise his game.

'It was fine lines and fine margins in that first fight. That's the difference. We've got to make sure those fine lines and fine margins fall our way this time. Imagine if he does it? That would be an unbelievable story. He didn't fight the best in his division and get blown out in two rounds or three rounds or four rounds. He went in there and gave a great account of himself. That's a success story in itself.

'Maybe we're being a bit silly and foolhardy and believing Anthony's better than he is. Some people would say that. They'd say he got found out. We got found out on that night, but we were up against one of the best pound-for-pound fighters in the world in my opinion.

'He's had a few speedbumps in his career, Linares, but I saw a quote from Emanuel Steward, God bless him, that Jorge Linares was one of the best combination punchers he'd ever seen since Sugar Ray

Robinson. To get that kind of accolade from a respected trainer like Emanuel Steward just shows you the quality he has. I think Linares showed everyone on the night what a good fighter he is. Can he do it again? It all remains to be seen. Can Anthony Crolla raise his standards again? I think he can. It just needs one of those famous body shots that beat Pérez, beat Barroso, to land.

'One thing away from the ring we need to address, and I feel it's been going on for the last few fights, is Anthony being the nice kid he is. He likes to give the personal touch with tickets, to meet everyone and all that, but I've got to try and stop that for this fight. I need Anthony to isolate himself and be nasty, be the nasty Anthony Crolla, to think about Anthony Crolla, and the people that are used to getting the tickets off Anthony personally, they've got to understand he's not doing it this time.

'It's very much like *Rocky III*. He's got to be a bit like Mr T, to isolate himself and be nasty. If he does that and wins, the fans that buy tickets off him are going to have another huge Anthony Crolla night defending the belts. If he doesn't win, then where does he go? I'm sure everyone understands Anthony has to be selfish and if they don't, then they're not real Anthony Crolla fans.

'Also, there's the media. Now, this gym, the fighters, myself, we're all quite media friendly. I don't mind Matchroom coming up, Sky to do videos, Manchester United doing the documentaries on Crolla coming back from his injury to his world title win. I'm quite accessible, but it's always a pain when it gets to three weeks out and they say they want to come and do some filming.

'Nah ... the last thing I need is people phoning Anthony, getting him walking around Moston, visiting a school teacher, doing anything other than training, home, rest. If they want to do that type of stuff, I want them to come early on in camp, get what they need and then let us concentrate on the fighting.

'Some might say it's a nice distraction for Anthony to have a bit of time out, talking and that. But I'm a bit more ... "Nah!" Especially for this fight. No access. You'll see him at the press conference and the weigh-in and that's it. Do you know what I mean? If Anthony was away in a camp somewhere, they wouldn't have access.

'It's the first press conference tomorrow. Jorge Linares against Anthony Crolla, I think the fight sells on what it is. Two great fighters and two gentlemen inside and outside the ring. Mutual respect. They'll shake hands before it then they'll go in there and give it their all. Then they'll shake hands after it.

'You don't need trash talk to sell a fight like that. It'd be totally out of character for both to trash talk. For me, I don't want to be upsetting Jorge Linares. He's good enough as it is without being upset! [laughs]. And it's poor Anthony taking the punches. We'll be respectful, no mind games, he's got a very good trainer [Ismael Salas]. I don't want Linares to go away and think, "That cheeky cunt! Did you hear what he said?" He might then pull that extra ten per cent motivation. I'd be giving him the motivation. Very much like when Macklin fought Sturm – very polite, very nice.

'Listen, away from the media, I'm bollocking Crolla hard. If you think we're taking this lightly, we're not.

'In past fights, like Kieran Farrell, Derry II and Murray, I felt they were baying for Crolla's blood. They were psychologically having the edge on Anthony before fight night. That's when I thought to myself, "Nah! Anthony's not giving anything back. They're bullying Anthony." John Murray was doing interviews and going, "I'll knock Anthony Crolla out. He knows I'll knock him out." Ask Anthony, and he goes, "Yeah, me and John, we're good mates," and all stuff like that.

'Remember Scott Quigg and Carl Frampton? I sat back in the first presser and it was all, "Carl's a nice kid, Barry McGuigan's a legend, Shane McGuigan's a young kid coming through," and I thought, "Fucking hell, we need a bad guy to sell this. It's pay-per-view, they're small kids," so I volunteered. I'll be the dickhead. So I started and Scott started, but Carl's very sharp with the tongue. I thought he was going to have Scott over, and although Scott did all right, half the time they were talking about me! Me and Barry were having it and me and Shane were having it.

'It all kept Quigg out of it a little bit. It was about Gallagher, the prick. McGuigan against Gallagher. But listen, you're selling the fight, doing pay-per-views, getting bigger numbers, so the kids get bigger purses and everyone gets paid more. That was totally out of character for me. I put myself out there but it wasn't really me. It was an act. I haven't had a run-in with anyone since. I've vowed to be nice to everyone for a while!

'I learned a lot in America about psychological warfare. I watched Freddie Roach and Floyd Mayweather before Pacquiao vs Mayweather. People were saying the Mayweathers' ruined him, calling him cockroach and all stuff like that. It took him a while to come back.

'Now, I know people were calling me a prick for having a go at Barry, but it did work. Barry bit, Shane bit and I did have them riled. Barry was fuming but it was all tongue in cheek. Listen, Frampton won *Ring* magazine fighter of the year [2016] and I thought, "Fucking hell, that's brilliant." Tyson Fury won it the year before, then Carl won it and I thought, "That is fucking brilliant for UK boxing; fucking fair play."

'He beat one of my lads and then beat Leo Santa Cruz. He did a really good job, so I sent him a congrats message and a good luck in Vegas for the Santa Cruz rematch. There's no animosity. The fight was a fight and that's it. I've got no problem with Carl. Barry's still a legend and Shane's an up-and-coming trainer who's doing well.'

First press conference

Eddie Hearn does his usual scene-setter, including revealing the news that the fight will be on Showtime in the USA, as well as Sky Sports in the UK. He then introduces the top table gathered at the back of the Halle Suite in the Radisson Blu Hotel. They're sitting beneath a banner proclaiming 'Linares vs Crolla II', with an image of Linares in action to the left of the title and a similar image of Crolla on the right (it's now Linares vs Crolla rather than Crolla vs Linares for the first fight).

To Eddie's right is Jorge Linares with Robert Diaz, head of matchmaking at Golden Boy Promotions. To his left are Anthony and Joe. The table is bookended by Brian Rose and Jack Arnfield, the promotion's chief supports. It's an interesting middleweight clash for the WBC international belt. These men of Blackpool are friends and former gym mates. Both speak well and respectfully of a bout that will split a town in two. In front of the top table sit, Jason Welborn, who's set to challenge Team Gallagher's young middleweight prospect Marcus Morrison.

It's then on to the main event. Joe's introduced first. As planned, he gets a few things off his chest.

'I'd like to welcome Robert and Jorge Linares. We've bumped into each other a few times, at the WBC convention over there [Hollywood, Florida], and look, we all know it's a great fight.

'It didn't go Anthony's way last time, but when Jorge sits back and looks at his fight collection, that will be one of the standout moments. Can he do that again? He's training hard, he has a good coach and Robert Diaz did a fantastic job babysitting him last time. Cheerleading from ringside – I want you [looks at Eddie Hearn] to put him in the top tier next time!

'This is a fight for the *Ring* magazine belt, the WBC Diamond belt and the WBA [title]. Not many fighters in Britain get a chance to fight for the *Ring* magazine belt. Anthony's had one chance, and we didn't win it. Now we've got a second chance. I will say Anthony's better in a rematch. His career shows that.

'But, I want to say to a few people going into this fight … if anyone wants a ticket off Anthony Crolla for this fight, go to the website or go somewhere else. Leave Anthony Crolla alone for this fight. He can't say no.

'If you really care about this kid and you want other big nights in Manchester, leave Anthony Crolla alone. I want Anthony to be a horrible, nasty person. I need him on the job.

'Please, anyone out there – and this includes Sky and ITV – anyone who wants any promo work, come and get it done now, straight away. Because then he's not available for anything. I want a selfish, angry Anthony Crolla. We need the best Anthony Crolla, and then some, to beat Jorge Linares.

'Leave him alone, no dishing out trophies, nothing else. No United games. He's got to be fully focused.

'I'd like to thank Eddie Hearn for delivering this opportunity and Jorge Linares for giving Anthony the rematch. It's going to be a great night and I'm sure the Manchester fans will come out and roar Anthony home this time. Thank you.'

Eddie thanks Joe and smiles. Joe flashes a wry smile back and polite laughter ripples around the room as members of the press react to Joe's passionate speech. Anthony chips in with a chuckle. *'There's a day trip to St Etienne for the United game if anyone wants it?'* More laughter.

Robert Diaz gets a brief build-up before addressing the room …

'I didn't know how Jorge was going to react to the fans, as I know that Anthony has great fans. I think that Jorge won a lot of fans that night and he'll have his share. Anthony didn't have to take the fight, he could've gone elsewhere and got some wins, but that shows what a man this guy is. He wants the belts and we expect a better Anthony. I said you would see the best Jorge ever and you did – he's going to be even better this time.'

As is the case with these things, the men who'll make the sacrifices, train like demons, take the risks by trading leather, they speak last. It's Manchester, it's Anthony's patch, he's a Matchroom boxer, so naturally he's first on the mic. Dressed in a three-piece navy suit with white shirt, he leans towards the table, eyes darting around the room.

I want the belts back, simple. Fighting for these prizes is huge. I'm so lucky to have a second chance and it's one I have to take. It was a special night last time, great crowd, and it'll be even bigger this time. The setting was perfect but I lost my belt. I lost to a great fighter but I don't celebrate losing. I don't want to feel it again and I want to go down in history by beating a great fighter. I am better in rematches and I'm locking myself away to work harder and smarter to make sure these belts stay here.

Jorge is the best and I want to be the best – beating him stakes my claim. I didn't win the first one but I had success and I can work on that. We've both got great teams behind us. I believe if I make the right changes for the fight, I will take the titles.

Finally, it's Jorge's turn. He cuts a very different figure from his last visit. Maybe it's the air of confidence gleaned from knowing exactly what to expect from Manchester and Anthony Crolla. Maybe it's the white polo neck, dark zip-up jumper, heavy black hoodie and thick, black-rimmed specs. He looks more like an urbane geography teacher on a field trip than one of the world's finest boxers.

'I wasn't supposed to win but I'm glad I did, so I can come back. Manchester treated me so well and I am so happy to return. The belts mean so much to me and my country, and I am going to work very hard to make sure that I take them home again.

'It's a new year and a new day. Anthony is going to be better and hungrier, and that means I will work harder, come with more skill and an even better game plan to win. I hope to see another huge crowd in Manchester and we're going to provide the fans with another beautiful fight.'

When all the talking is finished, the two tables disperse for photos. Head to heads for Morrison and Welborn, on to Rose and Arnfield, then Linares and Crolla step forward to face off.

No security needed. No insults, indeed no words spoken. No danger of flying fists or tables, for that matter – this being the very room that had hosted the infamous Dillian Whyte vs Dereck Chisora press conference a few months earlier. There wasn't even a scowl or a staredown. Two lads with faint smiles looking into each other's eyes with nothing more than respect, yet a complete understanding that no quarter will be given or received. Pure boxing.

Boxing press conferences are always split into two parts. The introductions and speeches from the personnel seated at the top table, followed by questions from the floor. Formalities over, promoters, trainers and fighters break off for one-on-one interviews with TV, radio, the written press and the growing band of online video, blog and podcast sites. Joe's 'leave him be' speech has inspired further questioning.

I've very lucky that I have a few friends that help me with tickets, but sometimes I'm stupid and I think I'm still doing four-round fights in leisure centres. I've done it all my career. It's stupid. I want to give myself the best possible chance on the night.

Joe wants to see me like I was in the John Murray fight, with the nastiness in the ring that I showed on the night. That's what we're working towards. It's not in my nature to go around all moody and snarling at people. I've just got to be smart.

I was gutted I lost my world title but I gave it everything on the night. I made a few mistakes that were costly. I got over the disappointment, though, because I lost to a future hall-of-famer on a good night as well. He had a good night.

I'm not happy to be a good runner-up. I'm fighting for the three best belts in boxing. Winning those puts you on a very elite list.

If the worst was to happen, there are plenty of big fights out there for me. I've just got to keep on improving and being involved in those big fights. Obviously my career won't last forever. How much longer? I don't know. But at the moment, while I feel good and while I'm improving, I've not put any time on it.

Most of the remaining journalists are focusing on Crolla, understandable given the local interest and language barrier with Linares, who can get by in English but prefers to conduct interviews in Spanish, with Robert Diaz translating. The visiting pair stand alone to the left of the stage. Linares is still happy to chat a little more, happy to play the media game.

'To come and travel so far, for all the hard work that I've done, to lose my belts? I can't afford it. I don't want to start over. I know what I want. I want bigger and better things, so I think it's going to be an even tougher fight than first time but it's going to be my fight. I'm going to win the fight.

'We stole the fight that night [first fight]. Even though the fans didn't have their fighter win, I think they walked away happy knowing that they had seen a fight for the ages.

'I feel like I have a bigger responsibility to come again to his backyard. That adds that extra motivation, knowing that I have to do even more to walk away with my hand raised and my titles.'

But what about the rumours that you're struggling to make lightweight?

'No. I feel very comfortable. I feel at the best moment of my career at 135lbs. Yeah, there are possibilities of moving up to 140lbs in the future, but why move up there now when there's still so much to accomplish at 135lbs? I'm going through one of the best moments of my career, so I'll stay here until it's time.'

And the promise to Gilberto Mendoza?

'I'm always in contact with the family. I'm very happy and fortunate that I was able to accomplish the promise that I made to him. Now it's not just about winning it, because that was done. Now it's maintaining it. That's something that I continually promised him, to maintain it, and to maintain it in Venezuela.'

Why do you and Crolla appear to like each other so much?

'We're very similar. Anthony and I are very similar. He's very respectful and humble, very polite. But inside, we're very tough warriors and that's why we're able to do what we can do. I don't think it's necessary to bad-mouth. I don't think it's necessary to do all the talking back and forth. Maybe some fighters need it, for insecurity reasons. We don't. We know what we provide.

'He's always sending me messages, saying hello to my family. I send him messages saying hello to his family. But, at the end of the day, it's what we do and we've got to do our job on 25 March.'

Robert Diaz has been an integral part of Oscar De La Hoya's Golden Boy Promotions for more than a decade. Before that, he was a well-known and respected boxing manager. A Californian of Mexican descent, Diaz is no stranger to Manchester due to his involvement in some of Ricky Hatton's big nights.

'I don't think anything compares to Manchester. When Ricky [Hatton] came back in his return against [Vyacheslav] Senchenko, those two or three years that we'd missed of Ricky, just to be back in that moment, and unfortunately it was just one night, but I was so honoured to be part of that. I've never seen fans like the Manchester fans. It was incredible to live it, I'll never forget it, and I think we saw something very similar in September with Anthony Crolla.

'Anybody would be different to Ricky. There's only one and always there will only be one! What he did was ... well, you couldn't even write it in a book or a movie. You couldn't even visualise the thousands and thousands of fans. They weren't boxing fans, they were Ricky fans. That's the difference.

'Anthony Crolla, besides what he represents to Manchester for what he's done, what he's done in the community, for what he's gone through in the past and we all know the story. But what he brings inside the ring is a will to win, conditioning, strength, heart. He was hurt in the last fight, looked like he was going to go. Next round, he came back like it was the first round. That talks about his conditioning, his will, his heart. It's very hard to give up when you have that army of support.

'People say, "Why are you and Jorge going back to Manchester? You're getting set up, you're going to get robbed." And I asked Jorge, we talked about it and he said he'd rather fight in arenas, even though he's the villain, the bad guy. He'd rather be in arenas and events like this than where he's the favourite but not have that big of an event.

'We feel very well treated and fairly treated here. I don't see that changing. We thought about it and he does have to do that bit extra just for security, but I think at the end of the day you have some of the greatest fans in boxing worldwide because the fans are with you, win, lose or draw. That's a real fan; they're not just on the bandwagon. And they respect a fighter even if they beat their fighter. Jorge's been receiving nothing but love and respect, through social media and even through the airport coming into the UK. People recognise him, which has a lot to do with Kevin Mitchell and Anthony Crolla.

'A lot of fighters, when they've beaten an opponent already, they go into the fight thinking that it's going to be easy. Jorge's not looking like he's coming to defend titles. Jorge's coming like he's going to win titles. He's coming like the challenger, because he's in his [Crolla's] backyard and he's expecting a tough challenge.'

A third fight?

'I think that's a very good story ending for the Manchester fans, but I'd like to end it on this one. Hopefully by knockout, so that there won't be talk of a third [fight] and so it's not such a tough fight for Jorge. I'm not predicting that, though, because we know we have our hands full come 25 March.'

Joe Gallagher has conducted several interviews and is now waiting for Crolla to finish his obligations. He's pleased with the press conference and the immediate response of the press. He knows his plea will get the attention he wants, so all can concentrate on the fight.

'People don't see Anthony as this big, huge sports star. They've got to separate the difference and leave him well alone and let him prepare.

'Anthony's very good but I just feel that he should be left alone to train, then we can all enjoy Anthony Crolla being a success.

'I think Jorge Linares will either come to finish Anthony early or he might come southpaw, switch it up a little bit, which he's done in the past. It's all mind games. I don't think it's going to change too much.

'We're going to be second-guessing him at the highest level. But lives and careers are at stake and Anthony cannot afford to make any slip. Jorge is very fast and counters very well.

'We've got to be precise with our punches – fast – bring our punches back and don't give Jorge Linares any opportunities. If he comes to try and knock Anthony out, then great; it means Anthony's got a better chance of hitting him.'

So what happens next? Should Anthony win, is it over to Vegas for the decider?

'There won't be a trilogy. Anthony will win. Me, I'd love Anthony to retire. I think it's a great time to retire – all the belts and out at the top. It doesn't get much better than that, does it?

'Listen, if there was a trilogy, a Vegas night, I'm sure they'd love it in his back garden. We could bring Manchester over there and we could have a "Hatton" night in Vegas.'

The event is being marketed as 'Repeat or Revenge'. From a Matchroom promotional point of view, the first fight worked on every level bar the result. Not surprisingly, ticket sales have gone well, with Crolla's popularity ensuring a similar-sized crowd at the arena. Eddie Hearn appears content and confident in equal measure.

'I think there's a different dynamic in this fight. It's challenger versus champion and a few times during that press conference, Crolla sort of looked down at the belts as if to say, "I remember them, they used to be on my mantelpiece!"

'I think he'll be more determined in this fight. Last time, it was like a celebration of champion versus champion. He's going to be more determined in this fight. He was determined last time as well, but Jorge Linares, let's be honest, was just too good.

'Robert Diaz said that last time was a career-best performance from Linares, but this time he's going to be even better. That's quite unusual at his age and with his experience to put in a career-best performance and another one in the fight after.

'Part of me is hoping for the same Jorge Linares or a slightly worse one because then it'd be a lot easier for Anthony. But I guarantee, you will get a better Anthony Crolla in this fight.

'Sometimes he has to pinch himself at what he's achieved and where he is and sometimes you may go into a fight with someone like Linares and think, "Can I mix it with this guy at this level?" He's shown he can. Yeah, he lost the fight.

'I had him two or three rounds behind Linares, but he still mixed it with him. After seven or eight rounds, I was really confident but he got tagged, I think at the end of the eighth, and it swung momentum. Linares went on like a train after that. But I don't think Linares will put in a performance as good as that again.

'I'm more confident in this fight, and I know it sounds bizarre, but I'm more confident now than ahead of the first fight. People were saying that Crolla was the 4/7 favourite and I was thinking, "Really?" I was thinking it was a pure 50/50 fight.

'Now, they've got Linares the favourite and rightly so, but I'm more confident because he's been in there with him, he's shared a ring with him and he's smart. Gallagher's smart. They know exactly how to beat him this time. It doesn't mean they can do it, but they know *how* to beat him. Before, they had an idea and they had to go in and try and do it, but they couldn't do it.'

If he should fail?

'You get to the stage with a fighter where you start looking at the exit. A lot of these fighters that have been around a while. You're talking about four or maybe five more fights.

'I'm already thinking, "Beat Linares and if it's an epic fight we'll do it again." Maybe that would be his pay-per-view fight. If not, we'd maybe fight Terry Flanagan. If not, we'll go again in Monaco, take some Mancs out there!

'I know the next steps for Anthony Crolla – win, lose or draw. That's my job. I don't want him to be fighting when he's 35 or 36. I want him to make his money, achieve his dreams and then get out of the game. He's on his way to doing that.'

Barcelona

No distractions. That's been the key message all along from Joe Gallagher. He wants Anthony focused on the fight and the fight alone. Because of his 'can't say no' nature, the trainer doesn't trust the fighter to turn down the usual requests outlined in his press conference speech. When not training, Joe wants Anthony resting and nothing else.

A decision has been made to uproot, break the monotony of home and base the camp in Barcelona for a few days. Joe's done his research and Team Crolla (Joe, Anthony and Marcus Morrison) is staying at a four-star AC Hotel in the Diagonal Mar district, a few miles north of the city centre – beach on one side, shopping mall on the other. It's an area transformed in recent years from wasteland to modern hub of residential, commercial and leisure complexes.

It's Wednesday evening and Joe and Anthony are eating sushi in a Japanese restaurant on the edge of the mall. Marcus Morrison has dined alone elsewhere. The democratic choice is a little too exotic for him. You can take the boy out of Hattersley and all that.

The pair polish off salmon sashimi and chicken teriyaki with rice before coffee and a short walk back to the hotel. It's just after 9pm. Anthony heads to his room to Facetime Fran and Jesse while Joe heads to the top-floor bar.

It's a vibrant hub, a mix of hotel guests and locals in the dark, swanky bar, with views on one side over the beach. Water and latte, that's it, no cheating from boxers or trainer.

'It's spot-on here,' Joe says. 'I wanted to get Anthony away grafting. I wanted people back home to say, "Oh shit, he's away." I want that disconnection, so when he comes back they know to leave him alone. We've sort of broken the routine. I was telling the lads earlier, I'd be tempted to do a couple more weeks out here.

'I'm in my element, we're getting good training and we're studying. I'm really happy. We're fortunate in Manchester that we never have to go away for big camps. We've never had to move a full camp abroad, but I'm really enjoying being away. The location, gym, sparring are all great.

'As a gym, we like to do a yearly trip to the Wild Card in LA and sometimes a January trip to Marbella. Los Angeles is great but with jet lag and everything, it's a killer. I thought we'd have a look at Barcelona. It's not known for its boxing but it's working well.

'It's good having Marcus working alongside Anthony. It's a bit like when Anthony was coming through. John Murray was having the big fights and Anthony was part of the team, watching. Anthony's now in that position. I let people know now that Anthony's number one in the gym. He's the priority for this fight.

'It seems like we're chasing time out here. Before you know it, it's 6pm. Breakfast, gym, come back to the hotel. Then it's 2pm, we train again then another day done. I know Anthony's not flying here, there and everywhere. He's resting when he's not training.

'I really would stay out here another two or three weeks, as long as it helps him win this fight. Redemption – it means the world for me as well as him.'

Anthony walks in and takes his seat. He's quickly followed by Marcus. The pair are room-mates for the duration of the trip.

I've just had a dinner date with Joe and, before that, me and Marcus had Ed Sheeran and Alicia Keys on in the room.

'You would've liked the sushi,' Joe tells Marcus. 'You could've had the teriyaki.'

* * * * *

Barcelona is bathed in sunshine. A perfect Catalan winter's day that feels like the best of a Manchester spring. It all adds credence to Joe's plan to get away from all distractions. The addition of vitamin D is a bonus.

It's 10.30am. Anthony is dragging his kit bag out of the boot of a small, battered silver Seat. Joe and Marcus are already inside.

The car's conveniently parked fully on the pavement of the Entrena en Barcelona (Train in Barcelona) on Carrer del Perú, maybe five feet from the entrance of the gym they've been calling home for the past three days. The exterior of the black-painted building, once a motor repair shop on a street of industrial units, has two large steel shutters, one raised to reveal double glass-mirrored doors.

The doors open up into a large square room, reception desk to the left, shelves above it stocking all manner of protein products, hand wraps, training gloves and gym T-shirts. No discernible aroma hits you on entry: it's almost sterile and well-ventilated.

The unit could snugly house four Olympic-sized rings, but there's just one ring in the north-east corner of the gym. Directly in front of the ring are rows of bags of all shapes and sizes hanging from the rafters. The left-hand side of the room is set out for circuit work. Climbing ropes and gymnastic rings hang close to the wall, there's a large JCB tyre with sledgehammer resting on it, a selection of kettle bells and all manner of pull-up bars and other torturous-looking pieces of kit.

In keeping with the exterior, the walls, floor and ceiling are painted black. The darkness is lifted by a series of hanging fluorescent strips and a huge window at the front of the building lets in a large shaft of light.

The gym is owned by local trainer and promotor Oriol Peña, who's been a fine host for Team Gallagher, helping the camp run smoothly. The gym is handily placed, a 15-minute walk inland from the hotel or, as is the case here, a couple of minutes in Oriol's car. He was at the hotel to pick them up this morning as agreed, but all hasn't gone quite according to plan.

Joe had wanted to be at the gym before 10am and isn't happy. 'I swear to God Crolla's like a woman! Me and Marcus were ready on time. We had to hang around in the lobby waiting for him. Fuck's sake!' he shouts with a grin.

Today is a conditioning day. Circuits, pads and bags. The two fighters change and start wrapping their hands by the side of the ring. A group of local keep-fitters are working the bags.

The circuit is tough. Oriol's putting Marcus through his paces with battle ropes, kettle bells, press-ups and abs work. Crolla shadow boxes in front of the mirrors to the right of the ring, dancing in and out of the floor-to-ceiling bags.

Marcus is doing a circuit before pads with Joe. Crolla's warming up ahead of his pad session, singing along to Adele's 'Hello'. He knows that what lies ahead with Oriol will be the most painful element of the day. Motivation has been chalked out on the floor – Oriol's written 'Linares revenge' in big capital letters.

He's a good guy, good to do bits with. Obviously there's a language barrier, but he know his stuff and everything we've been doing, circuit-wise, is boxing-specific.

He's a good trainer, so hopefully he'll have some good fighters. Boxing's not so big out here, but he seems very good. MMA seems to have really taken off out here, so I think boxing has a long way to go.

There are three professional fighters based at the gym – Abner Lloveras, Rafael Pujol and Guzman Castillo – and a dozen amateurs, four girls, eight boys. It's a one-size-fits-all kind of place, with boxing, MMA and crossfit all accommodated.

As Crolla begins his circuit with Oriol, there's a random reminder of home as out of the dressing room walks a young man wearing a 'Smiths' T-shirt – the Manchester band, not the fighting brothers. On the front is the iconic Salford Lads Club image. The T-shirt's owner is 20-year-old Vinny Damasceno, originally from Salvador, Brazil, who's just arrived in Barcelona on an internship. Speaking excellent English, it transpires his father's a Baptist missionary who moved the family to Albania, before settling in Norwich a few years ago.

* * * * *

Work done, and the three amigos are back at the hotel. All have eaten and are feeling refreshed ahead of an afternoon taking in some Barcelona landmarks.

A cab is called for Plaça de Catalunya, the main city square – the Catalan equivalent of Trafalgar Square. Once there, Joe's retracing his steps. He was here back in the 90s but can only really remember the Hard Rock Café. He sat down with his wife to eat at 7pm with almost nobody in the restaurant. He thought Barcelona must be the most boring city in the world until he noticed the place filling up the later it got.

The square is bustling; the lads mooch around not quite sure where to go next. The temporary Catalan surroundings are suiting everybody.

Camps can be long sometimes, it's part of the job. It's nice to freshen things up with a change of surroundings and no one knows me out here, so there are no distractions.

Even the food's great. We're near the sea, I love seafood and it's fresher. It's the Mediterranean way of life. No rushing around, no being stuck on the motorway. I'm the most laid-back man you can meet but I'm not missing being in a rush, getting stuck in traffic jams. The M60?

It's a lovely city. It's certainly somewhere I'll come back to for a city break.

After Crolla's posed with the pigeons in the square, Joe gets his bearings and remembers how to get to Las Ramblas, the popular tree-lined boulevard that leads from the square to the sea. A 15-minute stroll later and the marina stretches out in front of them. Hunger's kicked in again but local eateries aren't on the same wavelength, so after failing to find a place to eat it's all in a cab and back to the shopping mall next to the hotel.

Around ten minutes later, all hop out and head inside the building. It has a mirrored glass exterior while inside it's a three-story mini-Trafford Centre. To keep Marcus happy, it's agreed they'll have their tea at a fairly nondescript pasta place. They've been here before. It's a small restaurant with a cartoon chicken stencilled on the window. It's positioned on a narrow corridor on the first floor, with an upmarket burger joint opposite. It's 5pm and there's nobody else dining. It'll be another four hours before any locals are remotely interested in their evening meal.

Anthony orders salmon with roasted vegetables, Joe goes for the mustard chicken while Marcus opts for chicken and pasta, all washed down with agua sin gas (still mineral water) and a full-fat coke for Joe. As they munch away, chat turns to longevity of careers. Joe has a plan and he doesn't envisage being in the training game long term.

'I look around the gym these days and I think "Right, he'll be retired in a couple of fights, he's got a year in him and that'll be that." When the younger ones like Marcus are done, I'm done.

'I don't want anyone being in it for the sake of being in it. I don't want anyone fighting for money. Get the belts and the money will come. If you don't have a belt, you're not in work. You have a belt and you have to defend it against someone.

'You've got to be careful with kids' careers. Look at Callum Smith. I don't think he's had ten hard spars. He's not done more than ten and it's the same with Marcus. One spar that stands out with Callum was with Hosea. They did ten hard rounds and they were both on it. Hosea won five, Callum won five, there was no give and take. It was brilliant.

'Anthony's had hard spars but now it's more set-piece spars. I'm always wary about bringing kids in that are too big and strong. Got to be careful with sparring. I think Anthony's got two fights left.'

We'll see. We'll see how I feel. I'm still improving but I am wary that you can get problems later in life when you've been in a gym all your life ...

'People get into a routine. Boxers get into a routine. Paul Smith's lucky because he's got a Sky gig [as an analyst]. He knows he's got work and he knows what time he has to be there. In boxing, the lads know they have to be here or there for training at set times and when they leave boxing, it's, "What am I doing today?" They've got fuck-all to do. They think they'll blow some money, that'll make them happy, but it doesn't make them happy. They'll pay for their friends to come and play, but that won't make them happy. They'll be in their forties with no money, skint.

'It's like school. When you're at school, you didn't realise you had so many mates. You play football with everyone in the playground and it's the same in boxing. When you're away from the gym, at home with just the missus, your other mates are working when you're not. They're not there any more.'

When I'm done, I'll stay in boxing somehow. I think about the Fox [ABC] and getting involved, but it's a big commitment taking on an amateur club. I love working with the kids but Monday, Wednesday, Friday and the rest?

'I've experienced this. I missed Curtis's [son] school plays. I missed his parents' evenings. I missed everything. I was always taking John Murray sparring or Joe Murray sparring. I'd be going to Leicester for Rendall [Monroe] or Chris Aston's in Huddersfield. Now I'm adamant I won't miss anything of Sophie's [daughter].

'It's dawned on me. I used to miss all my kids' stuff just to make sure the fighters got everything they needed. You can't buy that back. With an amateur club, it's hard.'

I'd love to get involved in a club and have chief coaches or it takes over your life.

'Once you get on that wheel, it's very had to get off because you feel like you're letting everyone down. I can't walk away from ten fighters. You've got to be in it. I'm in it with this lot until it finishes. Seven years from now and that'll be it. I'll be done. I don't care what superstars come along. That's it. I want my life back then. I want to travel. Hopefully, I'll have earned enough money to go to places like Australia and spend time with my family.

'At the moment, though, on Sunday afternoon, I start packing my bag for the gym. I'll sort my stuff and text the lads about times, sparring and all that. I can't wait to get in the gym. I'm driven round the bend in the house. Bored shitless, climbing walls.'

I've been boxing a long time, had tough fights. I don't want to be in the game too long. I've had the injuries, so I have to think about that.

That said, I've never once worried about my head. I know I can't do, but I haven't worried about it anyway. I have a brain scan and as long as that tells me I'm OK, that's good enough for me.

For my first spar back after the incident, I remember thinking, 'Will I be able to take a shot?' It sounds stupid, but I was looking forward to getting hit to see what would happen. Within a minute I'd been belted and it was all forgotten about. But I know I have to be careful and not hang around in the game too long.

* * * * *

It's Friday. Anthony's lying on the floor of his temporary gym, stretching.

This morning I watched Linares again, so I'm just thinking about certain shots I need to throw in the fight. I want to bring those shots into the sparring today. Now's the time to practise, get it right in sparring then get it right in the fight.

There are times in sparring when Joe starts getting annoyed with me. You just have to keep thinking and reminding yourself about the things you've watched and put it into practice.

I'm sparring Marc Vidal [featherweight, 8-1-4] again today. What's good about him is that he's hungry and ambitious. He wants to leave an impression. Sometimes when you spar kids, there's a bit too much respect. Not with this kid! He's going for it and he throws some similar shots to Linares.

When you spar someone for the first time, you probably get a little bit nervous because you might have heard something about power, you might have heard he can whack or something. You want to feel it out.

But it's a very different kind of nerves to a fight. When you're an amateur and you go to another gym sparring, you have nerves then because it's a little bit like having a fight, whereas now, I feel I've been doing it long enough.

If things aren't happening in a spar, as frustrating as it is, I always try and get the best out of it. Mistakes are going to happen in the gym, so I don't beat myself up about it. I used to, but now I don't.

For some fights I've had nothing but bad sparring, but then I've put in some of the best performances of my career on fight night. As long as the sparring's right style-wise, specific, it makes sense.

I raise my game. Early on in my career, I might have left a bit in the gym. Now, I fight a lot better than I spar. I leave mistakes in the gym and put it right on the night.

Before I fought Andy Morris, I remember a water bottle flying at the wall from Joe [he lets out a loud chuckle]! It was an amateur kid who was snotting me. It happens when you're working on things.

Maybe it's me overthinking things. That's what you can do sometimes. When I fought John Murray, he went on about the sparring quite a lot. But I knew I'd raise my game. I'd improved an awful lot since we'd sparred, so it was a bit irrelevant. If you want to take comfort from sparring sessions, then fine. But it's very different when you've got gloves on half the size, when you can't take as many shots.

Warm now, with hands carefully wrapped, Anthony climbs through the ropes and bounds to the blue corner. Joe eases the red gloves on to his hands, ties the laces and binds them with silver gaffer tape. Final instructions are given. Anthony rolls his head from side to side, yawns to stretch his jaw muscles then bites down on the gumshield.

Vidal has been ready for a while in the opposing corner. At first glance, the black leggings and sleeveless grey vest look more akin to a dancer's attire. On closer inspection, the camouflage pattern on the top and the words 'La Guerra' (war) emblazoned in bold red letters hint more at the day job.

He's bouncing, stretching, leaning on the ropes and then tapping on his gumshield with his right glove. He listens to Oriol whisper in his ear whilst accepting another squirt of water. He nods, touches his toes before fixing his head guard one last time. The clock beeps, round one.

Eight good rounds in the bag with the loose, snappy Vidal and it's the turn of local boxer Alejandro Moya Mendoza to offer a different challenge. Whilst Vidal delivered flashy combinations and constant pressure, Mendoza is more upright and orthodox, his amateur style still evident as he prepares to make his pro debut in a couple of months' time.

He does well in some give-and-take sessions and is delighted Crolla's turned up at his gym, as he explained in good English.

'I've been training and fighting over in London with Repton. I won the Harringay Box Cup, but I'm back here to turn professional at 64kg [super-lightweight].

'I enjoyed the spar, it's a great experience. He's a top man. The best punch off Crolla is the body punch. He has a great body punch. But I think I have a good left uppercut, which I caught him with a few times.'

Marc was lively and aggressive. I know he felt some of my shots, but he bites down on the gumshield and he flies back at you. He really puts it in. Some sparring partners will come in and are happy to just pick up their wages. He's a good, fit kid. He's given us what we needed today and the other days we've sparred this week.

Good 12 rounds in the bank today. Good to bring Alejandro in for four rounds, too. He's technically good, as you'd expect being from Repton, but he's only just starting off. It's good to have someone fresh and hungry at the end of the session.

He felt a few of my body shots on Wednesday and he was like, 'Aagghh', but he had some success with the left uppercut and that's a shot that Linares likes. These are positives. I can't be getting hit with those uppercuts, but it's better to be caught now than on fight night.

I did think, 'Fucking hell, he's caught me again!' It's one of Linares' key shots. I'm not going to beat myself up about it, but I was getting caught too much. I've just got to be aware. Sometimes I stayed on the ropes a little bit too much. I should've moved off a little bit more. That said, my uppercut was coming off also and it's a hard shot to get off. I was boxing well behind my jab too.

I wasn't trying to win the spar, just work on things. Some things were coming, some need a lot of work, but I've got six weeks to do that. I think we're in a good place.

Conditioning-wise, we're in a good place. I've done a lot of rounds this week, which is tough, but it's been good to have that in the bank for when we get back.

Joe's overseen the action and packed his things away in his black bag. He has a quick chat with Oriol then returns to the ring apron, sits back and gives his verdict on today's work.

'Sparring was good, we did some good things. Five or six weeks out, you don't expect the complete job to be there. If it was there, I'd be a little bit worried. There are things that I can see he's trying to do in sparring which he got off sometimes and other times he didn't.

'I just need to keep reminding him to stick to what we're doing instead of trying to win a spar. I think he got too square on the ropes; he needs to keep moving, not sit on the ropes. He's got to stay smart and keep a clear head. But he's had 12 good rounds with two good kids, plenty of punch output in the spar, a good day and a good way to end a hard week.

'He's lively [Vidal] and throws very good shots. He hooks to the body well, is loose-limbed and puts combinations together well. He's a kid we're considering bringing over to the UK for sparring.

'I don't want heavy sparring. I don't want bigger, heavier kids punching holes out of fighters. He's a similar height to Crolla, a little bit lighter, but he's putting the shots together. He's keeping Anthony sharp and tight. Linares was quick and fast, very sharp, but I think he's going to be aggressive in this fight as well. That's why we might bring him [Vidal] over.

'Alejandro was a different style. We had one kid who can spar like Linares in bursts and one who's like Linares stood up, who can use the jab, simple shots. Best of both worlds.'

Marcus takes his turn to spar. His training has been co-ordinated with Crolla's as he's defending his WBC international middleweight belt against Jason Welborn on the undercard. He won the vacant belt by smashing Jefferson Luiz de Sousa in two rounds on the night Anthony stopped Barroso.

Facing him in the opposing corner today is Abner Lloveras, a hard, seasoned combatant from an MMA background. Now 34 and starting out in the pro-boxing game, he has one fight and one win under his belt at super-welterweight. In the ring, 'Skullman' looks mean and grizzled. He'd be well cast as muscle for the mob in a Prohibition gangster flick. But with the feisty, competitive spar over, he's all smiles and friendly fist-pumps, the kind of lad who helps old ladies cross the street.

Marcus has enjoyed the experience, but is glad it's nearly over. 'It's the end of the week and I feel a bit tired, but it's good to get the rounds in. I did ten rounds on Monday and Wednesday and eight today. In between that, on Tuesday and Thursday, we've been punching bags, doing pads. Oriol's been doing circuits as well, so I am tired. These are the days you've got to grind it out.

'The sparring today was good. He's [Lloveras] a tough operator from a UFC background. He's been around the likes of Conor McGregor, been around the block. He's tough and doesn't stop coming forward. It's good.

'Going into the fight with Welborn, we know he's going to keep coming forward and the lad I've been sparring over here, from the MMA background, is tough – knees, elbows, the lot! It's just what I need for Welborn. He's going to be there [for] the ten rounds.

'Welborn's not a great boxer, he's not technically great, but one thing he will keep doing is come forward. He's rugged and he'll swing and swing for ten rounds.

'Barcelona's been good, though. It was a good week and has broken camp up. I'd been in training for four or five weeks prior to coming out here and now I'm refreshed but tired. It's a good week's training in the bank.'

* * * * *

Marcus Morrison is all packed and ready to depart the hotel. He's sat in his grey tracksuit on a grey sofa in the airy lobby. It's grey outside,

Anthony at BBC Radio Manchester with Joe Gallagher, Danny Webber and presenter Bill Rice.

Anthony's fashion crisis before his first world title fight vs Darleys Pérez – is it red or white socks? [Richard Thomas]

Warming up at Entrena en Barcelona.

A United away day. L-R: Anthony, Terry Hall (friend and frontman of The Specials), Will Crolla, Shaun O'Donnell.

Catalans backing Crolla for Linares revenge.

Crolla in Barcelona with the Brazilian Smiths fan from Norwich.

Downtime in downtown Barcelona with Marcus Morrison.

Playing with pigeons in Plaça de Catalunya.

Las Ramblas with Joe Gallagher and Marcus Morrison.

A café con leche by the Barcelona waterfront.

A left uppercut lands during Crolla's Manchester derby win over friend and foe John Murray. [Getty Images]

The body shot that did for Darleys Pérez. Finally a world champion! [Getty Images]

Barriso down as Crolla tames the tiger from El Tigre. [Getty Images]

Anthony back at St Matthew's RC High.

Leaving the dressing room for Jorge Linares II.

Linares – a class act in and out of the ring, proves to be too much again. [Getty Images]

It's a huge win for
'El Niño de oro'...
[Getty Images]

....but dejection
for Anthony.
[Getty Images]

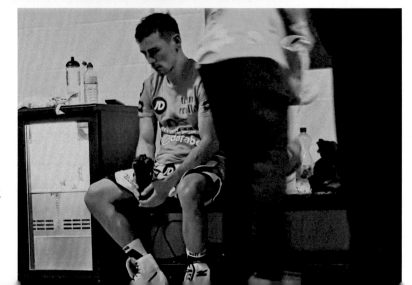

Pain of
defeat
in the
dressing
room
after
Linares II.

Anthony in Albert Square being interviewed on Five Live Drive.

Crolla post pre-fight Ricky Burns press conference with Sky Sports' Adam Smith and Fraser Dainton.

Anthony waiting for a brew at Altrincham Market.

Kieran Farrell lending Anthony his support ahead of the Burns fight.

That winning feeling! Anthony overcomes terrible nerves to put his career back on track on an emotional night in Manchester. [Getty Images]

too. He's fiddling with his phone while Joe and Anthony are stood at reception checking out.

After a week away, Marcus is now looking forward to getting back to home comforts at the house he shares with his mum, his girlfriend and their dog in Hattersley.

'I've got three older sisters who've moved out, an older brother who lives with his girlfriend and kids and I've got a younger brother, but we've got different mums.

'For the time being, I'm happy at my mum's. She won't like me saying this, but she does everything for me. I don't have to lift a finger. She does my cooking, cleaning and everything else for me, which makes training life a little bit easier.'

Anthony's completed his formalities at the desk and wanders over. He too has opted for the grey tracksuit look – with compulsory baseball cap.

It'll be nice to see the family. I know I could easily stay a bit longer because it's good work and no distractions, but I've got my little boy and whether it's one week, two weeks or one day, I miss being around him. Like most fathers, you want to be around your children. He's at that age where he's coming on so much. But it's one of those things where you think you have to be with your family, but you're doing all this for your family.

I'll get to United tomorrow [home to Watford], if I'm allowed! Yeah, I'm going! I'll get home then, chill out and go to yoga on Sunday. Back in sunny Bolton on Monday. Joe! Have you seen the fucking weather forecast for next week? Fucking shite!

Back in Blighty

It's 2pm, Thursday afternoon. The Market House is bustling – it always is. The building was once just a dilapidated part of Altrincham market. The communal wooden tables, with their long wooden benches, are full with mothers and pre-school children eating coal-fired pizza. Businessmen are holding meetings with a fancy red and micro-brewed ale.

There's a late-lunch office crowd scoffing a homemade pie or simple sandwich. A huge success story, what is essentially an upmarket food court has transformed the fortunes of a town. Anthony visits this spot once a week, tying it in as a treat before a session of muscle therapy at nearby Complemed.

I like it here. Nice little eateries. I remember after one of me fights, the fella over there [points to the corner of the square room] came over with steak, eggs and chips for me. It was lovely. It was that one, the Tender Cow. He came over the other week and said, 'Listen, I know you're in training or I'd bring you some food over!' I was, 'Ah, no problem mate, thanks anyway.'

Anthony arrived home from Barcelona late on the Friday night. It was a day of rest on Saturday and such was the importance of recuperation and family time, he even missed the United vs Watford game.

I was shattered. I had a rest day and Jesse wanted to see me, so I missed the match. I got back after 11.30pm and Jesse was still awake. He'd had a bit of a sleep after nursery, so he got all giddy when I came in.

Did the yoga on Sunday, was in the gym on Monday doing a tough conditioning session and on Tuesday I did strength and conditioning work with Martin [Cullen] in Wigan. I did a bit on the bike as well.

I was back in the gym in Bolton on Wednesday for a big pad session with Joe and a big swimming session with Hosea. He's a good swimmer, so I was trying to catch him. He's built for it, to be fair.

Today, I've done more yoga and more S&C with Martin and I'm heading over to see Abbas [musculoskeletal consultant] after here. I also go to physio on a regular basis to make sure the ankle's still OK.

Every Thursday, I do the session with Martin and I come here. I always get an hour before I go to Abbas, so I get a flat white.

Crolla's wearing a navy baseball cap and is all decked out in Under Armour gear – red hoodie with grey trim, grey tracksuit pants and grey trainers with red trim. His obsession with colour co-ordination has made him a marked man in the gym.

Callum Smith always says, 'Crolla, did you get dressed in the dark again? Did you grab whatever was on the side?' I try and match whatever I wear. I'm a bit scruffy today because I've come straight from the gym, but I still match.

Whether I get up early or do it the night before, I always get my clothes ready and matching. I just feel a bit better. I'm not trying to impress the boys in the gym or being too vain, although my missus and mam would argue differently. I just feel better in nice, matching clothes and I think it helps me train better.

Even if my kit is smelly, it can be smelly as long as it's matching.

Before my first world title fight [Darleys Pérez], it was the day before and Joe was trying to get me to change the gloves. I'll be honest, this sounds really unprofessional, but I'd got all my kit matching perfect then Joe says, 'I think these gloves are a better glove.' But the colours? I was wearing red, white and gold shorts and these gloves were black and illuminous green! They were Everlast gloves and I'd ordered red and gold Grants. Different type of glove, different make.

I said that I'd try them and have a look but the moment I saw those gloves, they could've been the best gloves ever but I wasn't wearing them! It's so bad and I laughed with Joe afterwards. There wasn't a chance I was wearing them.

I made out to Joe that I liked the other gloves better, better fit and all that, but it had nothing to do with that. Really unprofessional, but that's just me.

It sounds vain, and when I'm getting punched in the head I'm not thinking about looking pretty, but wearing those other gloves would've played on my mind. It would've done. For that fight, I changed my socks two or three times. I didn't know whether to wear the red sock or the white sock with the kit.

[Scott] Quigg was fighting in the arena at the time, I was in the dressing room getting ready to go on next and I just couldn't decide. I'm not one bit superstitious. I could walk under a ladder on the way to the ring, it doesn't matter, doesn't bother me and I wouldn't say I'm OCD, it's just the way I am. I've got to look right.

I normally get Melissa from Suzie Wong [fightwear designers] to do two sets of shorts for fight night in case colours clash. Melissa's a mate and I usually get her to design kit based on old United kits. This next kit I'm wearing for Linares II is white with green and yellow trim for Newton Heath, or black with green and yellow. Not decided yet.

I always walk out with a matching T-shirt, of course. I go for the T-shirt rather than anything else as it's good for the sponsors. It's easy.

My mates slaughter me. I'm not as bad now but I've got a missus and kid, so I'm not going to be as bad. But the lads used to always tell me to be ready an hour earlier than when we were meeting. It's not being vain, don't know what it is. Well, I am a bit vain, I'm not going to lie, but I try not to be.

Fashion's possibly an area I could go into after boxing. I spend a bit of money on clothes and I spend far too much on designer trainers, stuff like that. I get a lot of things for free, some of the big brands, which is great. But buying trainers is a guilty pleasure.

* * * * *

It's been agonising, but Anthony's finally made a decision that will impact on his immediate future. After weighing everything up, he's turned down the opportunity to go to Wembley on Sunday for the United vs Southampton EFL Cup Final. Not only that, he's resigned to watching St Etienne vs United on the telly tonight instead of being with his pals in France.

Can't do it. I went to Blackburn last Sunday but that's just up the road. St Etienne was realistically always a non-starter and going to Wembley, it's a long day. Even me mate I go to the match with told me not to do it. He said it was too much. My mates are looking out for my best interests. I'm just going to watch it at home. I might have one or two of me mates round and cheer the boys on from home. Setting off early, late back, in the gym early Monday morning? Not great preparation.

I've got a great set of mates and they always look after me. Not that I would, but if I was ever tempted to go out for a night out close to a fight, they wouldn't go out with me. I'm very lucky like that. They've always got my best interests at heart. The bigger it's got over the years, they don't treat me any different. Well, they actually treat me worse. They give it me more.

* * * * *

Another late February day in Gloves Gym in Bolton and another Anthony has been drafted into work. Anto 'The Apache' Cacace has flown over from his Belfast home to help Crolla prepare. A wiry, tall super-featherweight with heavy hands, Anto cuts a similar-looking figure to Linares, his sunken face decorated with a heavy dark beard. More importantly, he's capable of replicating the Venezuelan's style.

Undefeated in 15 fights, the Celtic titlist is exactly the kind of ambitious sparring partner Crolla wants and needs. Cacace's own fighting plans are wrapped up in the Crolla vs Linares event at the arena. The man from Andersonstown is due to face the winner of the Martin J Ward vs Maxi Hughes British title fight on the undercard.

'It's great to be mixing in this company ahead of me having that fight. It's great for my confidence,' said Anto. 'I've sparred a couple of world champions, I've been away sparring Carl Frampton, but this is the best experience so far. Everyone's been great. Anthony's a real good lad, he's easy-going and even if I wasn't getting paid for this, I'd be here. I'm sure anyone would be like that, too.'

Anto's a man in a hurry. He's had a frustrating career, with overseas moves that didn't quite work out. Since hooking up with trainer Sean McCullough, who's accompanied him to Bolton, he feels his career is back on track.

'I went to Philadelphia and it proved to be a disaster. I was going to go to America and make all this money and have a happy life. It's a dream. I'm happy at home now with my coach. I tried going away. I was away with the McGuigans and with my amateur career and I felt I'd been away my whole life. I don't need it any more. I'm 28 with two kids. I don't want to go anywhere else.'

At times during sparring, Joe steps in the ring to stop the action and give Anto instructions to throw certain combinations, the kind of snappy shots he knows Crolla can expect come fight night.

'I'm trying to work as much like Linares as possible. People say I box a bit like him, so that's good for Anthony hopefully. I try all different shots.

'Linares' movement was the difference in the first fight. I've tried to move like him and believe I have. Anthony's been catching me with shots. He's got the heart, the fitness and I believe he can take Linares apart. He [Linares] blows hot and cold and he's not always on top of his game.

'Anthony's an inspiration. He came back from what happened to him [burglary incident] and went straight into world title fights. He beat Barrosa. I look up to Crolla big time. It may sound cheesy, but it's dreamlike being here.'

I feel like I'm better – Anto mentioned it to me and it's the little things. I've always been dedicated but I'm relaxing more away from training. I'm not running about here, there and everywhere. I'm training smarter, more yoga, I'm more flexible than I've ever been. I feel younger and still feel like I'm improving.

Anto's replicated Linares well. Touching, throwing combinations that he throws. He's very skilful and it's great to have him over. He's coming back next week as well and I think he'll be there on fight night because he's going to fight the winner of Martin J Ward and Maxi Hughes.

Because he's had to come over, there's no chance of sparring falling through. He's back to the hotel then back in the gym. He's sort of in camp with me.

As much as he's enjoying his time with Team Crolla, there appears to be no chance of him uprooting from Belfast despite the current strength of British boxing, particularly in the North West of England. Anto thinks the sport on the island of Ireland is a sleeping giant that's about to awaken.

'At the moment, we have Carl [Frampton], who's a step above everybody, maybe a couple of steps. But the whole of Ireland is full of pros that are good lads. I believe Irish boxing is going to be as big as British boxing.

'We need big promoters to come and sign fighters in Ireland. Not enough people take Irish boxing seriously, but it is serious. The talent is serious.'

Sheldan Keay from the *Manchester Evening News* has arrived at the gym. Despite Joe's protestations about everyone staying away, the paper is an old friend of Team Gallagher and a big supporter of Crolla. Like every other visitor to the gym, Sheldan's struggling to cope with the blasting heat pumping out of the unit above the ring.

Anthony's finished his session but heads over to chat before his shower. His kit is damp with sweat but, of course, everything still matches. It's all grey.

I've had a big sparring week and I'm feeling in a very good place. Bit by bit, it's starting to come. Joe's happy and he's not easy to please. If Joe's happy, I'm happy. Barcelona was great, as much as anything just talking and going through things. We were thinking of going back for a week, but I don't think it's going to work out now. It's a great set-up out there, though, and we'll definitely do it again.

It's been a strange few days for Anthony and everyone else at the gym following news of Scott Quigg's departure. After six hugely successful years with Joe, he's off to the States to work with Freddie Roach.

Me and Scott are big mates. It's bitter-sweet because I think now is the right time. Scott's always wanted to go over to America. I've spoken to him since and I think it'll be a success out there for him. Listen, even if is isn't, he'll have no regrets.

It was amicable; him and Joe shook hands and wished each other the best. I'll miss training with Scott; we trained alongside each other very well. I know he'll miss training alongside me and he's said that. I wish him all the best and, as I always say about Scott Quigg, he deserves everything he gets out of boxing because of how dedicated he is.

I'm very happy for him, a new chapter of his career. He's living the dream out in LA and I know if ever there's a week I want a holiday out there, I'll have a place to stop.

I've told him to take some of those thousands, no those millions, that he's got and get some of it spent in Beverly Hills. I've told him he'll have to go and speak to someone on Rodeo Drive to sort him out and dress him – just like in Pretty Woman! *If I see him in a tracksuit in Beverly Hills, I won't be happy!*

* * * * *

Three weeks out. Crolla's in good form, although he didn't have the best of nights. Sleep was disrupted due to his son Jesse's eczema flaring up and he only managed about five hours.

I'm not crying or owt like that, but it's not easy sparring 12 rounds when you haven't had a good night's sleep. I'm doing 12 rounds with two different lads, but hopefully next week on my sparring days, my little boy will be right. If there's a risk of him being unsettled, I'll stay in a hotel. It's a big week next week. It has to be right.

Anto Cacace's been back from Belfast all week. Joe's been mixing sparring up with other boxers coming to help out, including young Failsworth prospect Danny Wright.

'It's been a great experience, I've loved it. He's a hero of mine, from my local area. I've known him for a good few years and I've

135

been trying to get that spar for a while now. I've wanted to get in with someone who's world class and I've really enjoyed it.

'I did five rounds with him last week and an eight-rounder on Monday. That was a good test for me.

'I had 70 amateur fights, two national titles, one junior and a senior national title. I won a silver and gold in the GBs. I boxed for England a good few times but the reason I turned over is that the lad I beat as an amateur, I didn't want to play second fiddle to. My style's professional and even though I'm only 20 I can mix it with the men, so I may as well get in there and do it.

'Obviously I tried to use my size the best way I can, but Crolla's a strong guy even though he's a lightweight. He's a class above lads I'm going to be mixing with in fights, so I've got to use my head and manipulate my shots to land them.

'His guard is brilliant. He's so tight; it's hard to land any power shots, so you're just wasting energy trying to land them. You try and throw when he throws and find angles. I try and hold ground, edge in and I'm physically strong. I try and use that to draw mistakes out.

'I used to box at Boarshaw [ABC] and go up to Fox [ABC] and do loads of sparring with the boys there, so I've always seen Ant knocking about. I've seen him in Tesco's, too! He's a normal guy, that's the best thing about him; he's the nicest guy in the world. But there's some spite in the ring. When he wants to hit you, he hits you!

'No one round our way has ever said anything bad about Crolla. He's not fake. Some people are fake-nice. He's not – he's genuine.'

The music's been pumped up – by Joe presumably. Ed Sheeran's belting out 'Shape of You'. Two lads are doing their particular dance in the ring. Liam Smith's sparring Mason 'Nutty' Cartwright. Crolla's watching on. It's a good, lively spar, with Mason applying pressure, undeterred by some of Liam's best work. Beefy's landing beautifully with uppercuts and Crolla nods his head in admiration.

He's so relaxed, doesn't waste much.

Ed sings, 'I'm in love with your body' as Liam lands a left hook to the torso. Mason grins, Crolla winces.

He's spiteful too. Very spiteful!

As sparring continues, Crolla's talking through United's EFL Cup win at Wembley.

I watched it at home. My little boy didn't have a clue what was going on when Zlatan got the first goal, but I enjoyed it! We got a bit lucky, but I'll take it.

For Crolla, the training week is nearly at an end. It's been a big sparring week with all the usual extras thrown in – S&C, tactics, swim sprints and bikram yoga.

Because I'd had a really hard week, Joe wanted me to rest on Tuesday – a rare day off. Nice bit of family time, so I took my little boy bowling. No chance of my back going, by the way. My technique's too good!

I was back sparring Wednesday with a bit of technique. I've also done the swimming, strength work and then today finished it off with 12 rounds with Anto [Cacace].

I'm heading over to Media City now to go on the radio. Joe's letting me do it as I've got a few hours spare before I go and see Martin [Cullen]. I've been on it a few times. It's about all issues of the day. I've got to be there at 12.30pm.

It's the eve of the Haye vs Bellew fight. The press conference in Liverpool was an unedifying spectacle. In front of a public audience, the two fighters traded playground insults that threatened to get out of hand.

Just like one of my press conferences! Security in between me and my opponent! Look, I'll be asked on the radio later, but the way I see it is that it's good and bad. It's getting a bit circus-like with all the security and that, but at the same time, the amount of people that are talking about it, the amount of people that'll tune in to watch it, that's what it does, so it works both ways.

There are better fights this weekend. There's Thurman vs Garcia [in Vegas] and if somebody said to me that I can have a ringside ticket for that or Haye vs Bellew, I'd be at Thurman vs Garcia.

You know what? I really hope Bellew does it, but it's a tough ask, do you know what I mean? It's going to be very hard for him and I think Tony has to get past six or seven rounds to give himself a good chance of winning.

I'm going to watch it at home with my family, my brothers. It's me mam's birthday on Sunday as well, so I'll be taking her out for some food. Other than that, I won't be doing much this weekend.

Joe's walking around the gym, checking his stopwatch and making sure everybody's doing as they should be. In the corner of the room, former Team GB boxer Natasha Jonas is hammering away on the heavy bag. Well known to the Smith brothers from her time at Rotunda ABC, Natasha's become a gym regular. She hasn't boxed since the Commonwealth Games in 2014 and has since become a mother.

It's a curious sight, particularly in light of Katie Taylor's recent foray into the pro game. The pair share a special memory from London 2012, the quarter-final that registered the loudest arena noise of the Olympics and the biggest interest as Ireland edged GB.

Joe was asked to have a look at Tash a few weeks ago. She's been in the gym and appears to have her focus back following her time out due to injury and motherhood. So is there another pro set for Team Gallagher?

'I've made a decision, yes. She's up before the board [British Boxing Board of Control] on Saturday, so she's still got all that to do, but when we can we'll do a press conference in a few weeks or whenever.

'She's had a two- or three-week trial and I've said I'll take her on. She wants to give it a go. Obviously people will talk about Katie and it is what it is for the next couple of years.'

For Natasha, joining the gym seems an obvious move.

'There are more Scousers in here than Mancs now – I've tipped it over the edge! We'll have to include Paul Butler as well [from Ellesmere Port]. He hasn't got a purple bin but we have to count him, too.

'Me and Hosea Burton had the same sponsor, so I knew him anyway as we'd meet at sponsors' events. Obviously Scott Cardle used to be on the GB squad and I knew the Smiths from way back. It was only Marcus that I really didn't know.

'Boxing, once you're there, it's like a family. There are little things that the guys have had to change, like not coming out of the changing room naked! Little things! I hate to say it, but I'm just one of the lads now!

'I've always had a good rapport with Joe. I used to see him at shows when I used to be there supporting the Smiths. He'd always say, 'Well done' or 'Good luck', so when it came to making the decision to go pro, he was the top of me list, to be honest. I think he's a brilliant trainer and he's done amazing things.

'I thought that if there was anyone who could take me from being this overweight mum, who pretends to be a keep-fitter two or three times a week, to a world champion, it's going to be Joe.'

Tash goes back to the bag. The music's still blaring – some kind of dance track that's hard to decipher, it's so loud. Joe shouts to Tash to move on to the angle bag.

In between barking instructions to the newest member of his team, Joe's giving snippets of insight into how things are progressing for Crolla and his readiness for the task ahead.

'Anto's more like Linares and looks like him too with the beard. Danny was bringing it hard and fast, which I think Linares will.

'They've done 12 rounds of sparring …' At this point Crolla, now changed into his matching tracksuit, hat and trainers, wanders over as Joe's in full flow.

'I'm trying to do a fucking interview here,' Joe snarls towards Crolla.

'I didn't interrupt you, did I?'

He turns back and smiles. Crolla takes no heed, smiling, and says, *'See you later'* before wandering out of the back door of the gym.

From the dirty pumping heat of the gym to the cold, misty Bolton rain. As the door shuts behind him, a gust of that precious damp air blows through the building, giving temporary relief from the equatorial climate within.

Crolla's gone, but Joe carries on. 'He didn't sleep well last night but he still got 12 rounds at the end of a tough week, so I'm happy at three weeks out. This week in the gym, it's serious now. The amount of bollocking and effing and jeffing. I've been picking him up on every mistake in sparring.

'There's a lot of pressure on sparring now. Next week we're bringing Zelfa Barrett in, another kid to change it up and make sure complacency doesn't set in. It's the big week of sparring next week then we'll start tapering down.

'Anthony's bang on his weight. He's eight pounds over [the 9st 9lbs limit], so he's sparring at the weight he'll be fighting at on the night.

139

* * * * *

Anthony's sat in his car, 20 feet from the back door of the gym. Before setting off for Salford, he sits in the driver's seat and quickly scoffs chicken and roasted vegetables out of his tupperware box. Nutrition taken care of, he sets off on the 12-mile journey to the BBC. He's meant to be there by 12.30pm.

He arrives at Media City and parks in the multi-story car park attached to Booths supermarket. Luckily, he knows where he's going – it's the same building as BBC Manchester, where he's been a guest on *Red Wednesday* recently.

This time, he's a guest on Five Live's *Friday Sports Panel*, presented by Eleanor Oldroyd. His fellow panellists are from rugby union, former Sale Sharks and England winger Mark Cueto, and swimming, Siobhan-Marie O'Connor.

The first subject in this topical sports programme is well within Anthony's comfort zone. In the wake of Zlatan Ibrahimovic claiming his kids forced him to sign for Manchester United, Eleanor is asking, 'When has your family influenced your decisions?'

Some boxers in the build-up to a fight don't want to see their kids because it reminds them they've got a soft side. Some fighters like to lock themselves away from family, it makes them hungrier, but for me personally, it's something I like and something I'd miss.

I've got a little boy, he's three now and I try and use him for motivation. If I do well, it makes his life a bit easier growing up. I can give him some of the things I didn't have as a child.

Obviously I'm glad Zlatan's children sent him to Old Trafford!

My boy's a little young to understand boxing. Don't get me wrong, he knows what daddy does, but it could be Anthony Joshua on the telly and he'd say, 'It's daddy!'

Other topics include man-management (cycling controversies), dodgy tactics (England vs Italy Six Nations) and abuse of referees (amateur football).

Following the break for news and travel, it's on to the weigh-in for Haye vs Bellew. With pictures from the O2 Arena in London on the studio monitors, it's over to Anthony for his thoughts ahead of the big fight – with his own forthcoming night in mind.

I hope I'm as relaxed as these two! One thing you have to remember is that being heavyweights, they're not dry. They're well hydrated and they would've had breakfast this morning [no weight limit].

A lot of fighters at a weigh-in are quiet. They're gaunt and they just want to get on those scales so they can have a drink more than anything.

In three weeks, that'll be us. I've had a long camp and I'll be ready. I'm in a really tough part of camp at the minute, but I wouldn't have it any other way.

Mark Cueto chips in and asks Anthony about the Haye vs Bellew antics in the build-up and what can be expected between now and the first bell.

Some fighters, and I know Tony and he's a bit like this, they need to hate their opponent, even if they don't really hate them. It's the way some people use their training camp. A lot of mind games played.

It's not my style to throw the verbals around and some of the things that have been said have been distasteful, particularly after recent events, with fighters hospitalised.

You saw it with Carl Froch and George Groves; they [fans] love a good grudge match. Listen, there are better fights on this weekend than these two. It's a non-title fight but all eyes will be on it. That's the business side of it and people don't understand.

On Leicester's win over Liverpool in the wake of Claudio Ranieri's sacking…

Beating Liverpool never leaves a bad taste in the mouth! Honestly, I think the treatment of Ranieri was disgusting. He probably had the right to take Leicester down three divisions after what he did last season. It was unbelievable stuff.

* * * * *

It's very much the business end of training now. Day sparring sessions have moved to night to get Anthony's body and mind conditioned to fighting at that time. It co-ordinates sparring with the time Crolla and Linares will meet in the ring.

I didn't finish sparring until 11pm last night. We had Zelfa in, who we've used a lot. He's very sharp on the counter and technically very correct, like Linares. He's got a bit of spite behind his shots as well. He ticks a lot of boxes.

It's nice talking to him afterwards. He was saying he could notice the improvements since we last sparred a few months ago. I know I'm more experienced than him, but it's nice to hear that from him.

With the night sparring, we're getting the body clock right. It's something we've always done. We've started it a little bit further out this time, but it's all specific. It doesn't make any sense to spar in the day and get your head down in the evening – the time you're due in the ring. You want your body awake at the time you're in the ring.

It's the same with training. I've never agreed with the early-morning runs. The odd time we swim at the crack of dawn, but that's just to fit it in. I don't agree with getting out of bed at a stupid time unless it's boxing specific. Some people might say it's soft, and yeah it can give you a bit of mental toughness, but it has to be specific.

As is always the case with rising stars and established fighters, sparring is a win-win situation. Zelfa Barrett is the nephew and protégé of Pat 'Black Flash' Barrett, a former British and European super-lightweight champion.

A popular and exciting unbeaten super-featherweight from Harpurhey, Zelfa's enjoyed every minute of the Crolla camp.

'I was sparring another lad the other day and it was a lot easier than sparring Crolla! The other lad's a good fighter, but he wasn't getting away and doing the sharp movements and I was going through him.

'With Crolla – he's sharp. It's his feet that have surprised me, not his hands, but his footwork. It's really surprised me this camp. Normally I can catch him with certain shots, but not this camp because his footwork's so good, he's gone.

'I've had to up my game and it's been helping bring my game on. I told him how sharp he was. He's been a lot better in this camp. There've been some great spars where he's not even throwing, he's just thinking. It's been good.'

* * * * *

It's Wednesday, another day down and Joe's finished at the gym. His next assignment is to leave Bolton and head south to pick his daughter Sophie up from school in Altrincham. He's happy with the way the day's gone and is still buoyed by last night's sparring session between Anthony and Zelfa Barrett.

'Crolla was brilliant. He sparred brilliantly last night, but Monday was the best I've ever seen him; absolutely class. He was outboxing Zelfa, moving, everything was on-point for three or four rounds. He's got to do 12 rounds of that now.

'I think Anthony's benefited from going to Barcelona, being secluded, being sat down and having things drummed in. It's really fallen into place for him now. Trouble is, when we think we're good, we wake up and watch Jorge Linares and his training [on Instagram] and you feel like turning over and pulling over the duvet!

'But I think Anthony's happier and he knows it's about business. He's such a sociable kid in the gymnasium, but I've cut him down talking to people. Instead of taking 40 minutes to get ready, he's taking 15 or 20. Where he would take ten minutes between sparring and doing the speedball, he's taking one minute. It's all about work ethic and being business minded.

'I feel I've got the nasty Anthony. You can see it in his shots in sparring and he's not throwing single shots, he's throwing combinations. It's his last big, hard week, but the sparring's been good.

'You might get some sparring partners who'd come in and try and beat Anthony Crolla up, but that's not the job when you're coming in to replicate the opponent and throw the shots that we feel the opponent will throw. People like Anthony Cacace – he did everything that you'd want and pay for in a sparring partner. They're not there to try and win a spar, they're trying to implement a style that's best suited to Jorge Linares. Cacace did a very good job at that, as have all the sparring partners.

'We've got Sky coming up now for the next couple of days to do some filming of Ant ahead of the fight. The BBC Premier League predictions are doing something with him on Monday and talkSPORT want him to go to London, but I'm not letting him do that. He's staying where he is and staying focused.

'People don't realise, if he goes to London he's sat on a train for two and a half hours and his diet gets all knocked out of place. Then he gets pulled here and there and he's got to get back and it's tiring, so we can't have that.

'I'm really pleased that I've had no one out this year and the first show is going to be Crolla, whereas last time it was too busy, other fights on and over to Dallas for Liam Smith against Canelo. Anthony lost me for ten days. He hasn't this time, I'm here. I'm not making a big thing of that, but I do think it makes a little difference.'

Joe's on a roll and has a few things to get off his chest. The Haye vs Bellew fight (Bellew won by technical knockout in the 11th round) is believed to have registered huge numbers on pay-per-view. Trash talk certainly helped sell that fight, which is a source of frustration for the trainer.

'There's always room for a nice guy. David Beckham showed that in football and I think with Anthony Crolla that's a story you don't have to sell. His story's crossed over. It's ready made.

'There wasn't much trash talk with Anthony Joshua before his last fight with [Eric] Molina; it was the undercard that sold it. There was Whyte vs Chisora. Why couldn't Whyte and Chisora have fought on the Crolla vs Linares undercard? With Burton vs Buglioni as well, why not have that as the pay-per-view? That's what I don't like. David Haye hadn't beaten anyone of note to get that opportunity. They give it him because he's crossed over and talked well when he was in the jungle [*I'm a Celebrity Get Me Out of Here*].

'You've got hard, proper, solid professionals, fighting men like Anthony Crolla, who's come back [from serious injury] and fought Pérez, Pérez again, Barroso, Linares. He should be getting all the riches and rewards. Anthony Crolla's the story. He's not ducked anyone, he's fought anyone after coming back from head injuries and gone on and gone on and gone on. That's the kid that deserves all the money.

'It pisses me off. That's why I'm getting my promoter's licence now and it'll be a totally different ball game for the new season.'

* * * * *

'Go again,' Joe barks. 'No sloppy shots, don't be square on.' *Bam bam. Bam bam bam. Bam bam. Bam bam bam.* The noise of glove on bag –

the signature tune to Crolla's work. For once, there's no music on in the gym.

In between shots, he moves around the offending object, the touch of a glove manoeuvring the bag back into position like a department store window-dresser angrily turning a disobedient dummy.

Bam bam. Bam bam bam. Bam bam bam. Bam bam.

'Good, good, good, lovely. Feet, slip, roll off as well. More of it. Left hook after that right hook. I told ya!'

Bam bam. Bam bam bam. Bam bam. And so it goes.

The gym is silent apart from the whirr of the evil heater, the hooter that signals the end of a round, the rhythmic thuds and slaps from Crolla's bag work and the squeaks from his shiny trainers on the sticky floor as he pivots and steps away from the bag. And Joe, of course.

'Come on, don't be kiddin' yourself. Hands up. Good. Don't switch off. Roll your head. Return, catch the body shot, return. Catch the head shot, return, roll your head. Good, on your feet.'

The orders are continuous until the hooter signals the end. Anthony lets out an exhausted groan and bends double to allow the sweat to drip off his sodden hair and face and on to the matting.

Sky Sports are in situ filming for their flagship Crolla vs Linares preview programme, hence the lull from the sound system. Producer/reporter Ross Thompson-Jenkins and cameraman Damon Beed are seasoned campaigners. All present are familiar with each other's work and what's required.

Crolla moves around the gym doing a few set-pieces for the camera. Shadow boxing, speedball, a chit-chat on the apron ring. He's comfortable in this habitat.

There's a bond between reporter and fighter – the kind of understanding and familiarity that comes from their respective years working in the sport, getting to know and like the individual, a knowledge of each other's professions.

It's the kind of relationship that's hard, if not impossible, to find in other, more mainstream media-saturated sports. The boxer understands and appreciates the value and need for promotion. The reporter understands the sacrifices, the financial woes, the small halls, the ups and downs and the aches and pains sustained by his subject to get this far.

It's good having the Sky lads in. They're bang on. End of a really good week and now it's three weeks to weigh-in. Good punching session today. Only a few more spars to go and maybe a bit of technique sparring during fight week. Couple more spars and it's a wrap!

* * * * *

There's never a perfect training camp, or so the cliché goes. There'll always be niggles and problems to solve. But this camp has been as near to perfect as Joe could've envisaged. He's happy with the work Anthony is doing and remains sure of his man's impending success – most of the time.

'You're as confident as you can be until you wake up and see Linares doing his work on Instagram and you think "Aaah … fuck's sake, I wish he'd fuck off! Get flu on the way over."'

It's the final leg of training. Next week is fight week – days of media commitments, shake-outs, a bit of boredom, a weigh-in and a lot of tension. It's a pressure every fighter feels, no matter how laid-back. Likewise for the trainer. Crolla is ever the willing student and it's this character trait as much as any other that's helped him to achieve so much, to punch above his weight, so to speak.

Joe Gallagher feels enormous pride in the work the pair have done together and still believes the best is to come.

'There's a sense of maturity about him now, a sense of detail. It's like teaching a child something. Some get it first time while some take five or six times for the penny to drop. I think the penny's dropped with Anthony.

'It's the best I've known him. He was on it again last night. Instead of trying to win the spar he was picking his shots, Linares shots. I want to just wrap him up and take him to a hotel now for a few days to keep him away from everything.

'I say it how it is. If Anthony's shit, he's shit and if he's good, he's good. There's no grey area with me. Sometimes it upsets the kids if they think they've done well and I say, "No, it was shit." But you know, we're fighting for the biggest prizes in the world now.

146

'Anthony doesn't employ me to massage his ego. When I do say he's flying, he knows he must be flying.

'We're turning down a lot of media commitments now. We're too near fight time and I don't need it. I need nasty Anthony. I've said "no" to him doing stuff on his day off. We need to be a bit selfish now. It's about the bigger picture and what happens on Saturday night.

'They [Matchroom] wanted to do a public workout on Saturday but I said "no". It's his day off and if you do a public workout you're switching his brain and his body on. Anthony would then be thinking about the fight for the rest of the day. It's very important that he has those complete days off. Nothing boxing related.

'I've just sent a text to Matchroom to say I want a smaller ring on the night. The ring we had last time, he's fought in that a few times, but I just thought that there were times last time when we could get to Linares, but he used his experience.

'He had a round on, a round off down the straight and he had that bit of space that enabled him to move at distance and have a breather. I feel that a smaller ring will make Linares work a little bit harder and allow Anthony to get into him more often.

'At the same time, Anthony will be in the line of fire more, he won't be able to go for a walk, but I just think it didn't work in the big ring last time and Linares shoe-shined us with his feet. We can't have him dancing and running down the straight. We need him penned in with Anthony getting stuck in.'

Penned in is where the trainer wants his fighter now. Happy that most of his pleas to stay away from Crolla have been adhered to, Joe's conscious all could go off track at the worst possible time. As intrigue in the fight grows the closer it gets, more people will be sniffing around, looking for tickets or favours. Joe's not having it.

'He's had to make sacrifices. He's missed a lot of United games, but we've got to have it right. I know people are going to try and get close to him now so close to fight week, but I'm going to have to kidnap him. I want him to be a little bit further out from home, maybe in Hale, where he can walk into the village and have a coffee and it's all nice and quiet. We can travel anywhere together then and he can cut out the driving.

'But look, he's had a tough training camp with me and he can't wait for the fight to be over so he can get away from me, know what I mean? He won't say it, but I'm sure he's had enough of me shouting and bollocking him for the last few weeks.

'He's done so well up to now. I can't allow it to go pear-shaped with one weekend to go. I mean, fucking hell, imagine if we pull this off? Crolla the *Ring* magazine champion! If he wins this, I think I'll burst out laughing in the ring! I was laughing with him in the gym yesterday saying, "You, the *Ring* champion? It's proper fucking smash and grab stuff!" Well, we'll see!'

Therapy

Abbas Mhar is a musculoskeletal consultant and founder of Complemed Therapy, a practice located on the ground floor of a converted house on Manchester Road, just outside Altrincham town centre.

A former mixed martial artist, Abbas is well placed to work through the various aches and pains picked up during Anthony's training camp.

The treatment room is not unlike a doctor's surgery but with the addition of a massage bed in the centre and some odd, space age-looking machinery.

Anthony's stripped to his underwear (grey with red trim, to match his tracksuit, trainers and baseball cap) and is sprawled on the bed. He's chatting football to Carly, an intern on a placement from the University of Central Lancashire. Monaco's 3-1 victory over Manchester City the previous night is mentioned. Anthony's opinions on the match suggest a great affection for the men from Monte Carlo. Funny that.

Abbas moves a piece of machinery towards the bed. It's a cross between an upright vacuum cleaner and R2-D2, with a long pipe and a pad attached at the end. There's a steady beep as he uses the pad to work on the blisters on Anthony's feet.

He's very pleased with the healing process. 'Miracles happen here, mate,' he smiles. Next, the blisters on the hands are analysed with the same happy verdict.

'What we're doing here is using cryo-stimulation,' Abbas explains. 'We use dry nitrogen vapour at minus 180 degrees. It facilitates structural repair and changes to the skin, muscle, tendons and bone tissue … anything I can get this vapour on. We have a nice little session on the face as well. He needs a lot of work!'

It's cold. I'd love one of these, me. I'd look 25 for the next 50 years! When Stephen [Smith] boxed in November [against Jason Sosa], his face was pretty banged up. He got on this and you should've seen his face in the space of about five days. Unbelievable!

'As he goes into camp and as his activity starts to increase with the different types of training, he's losing his body fat. He loses water so the tissue gets under more stress. It's a critical period with any boxer. They're at their most vulnerable at this stage.

'In the last camp, the blisters were horrendous. What have you done different to not get as many blisters? These are nowhere near as bad this time.'

I don't know, to be honest. They're going to happen because of the workload, aren't they? But everything's been similar, maybe just a bit better.

'Probably because you're not wearing the high-heeled shoes any more. That makes a difference, you know?'

True … I'll stop wearing them. Only at the weekend!

Abbas asks Anthony to flip on to his front and starts manipulating his back, working energetically while all the time chatting away.

'I enjoy working with boxers because they listen. I love boxing anyway and I fought and competed professionally in martial arts – kick-boxing. I took early retirement because I snapped both the anterior and posterior cruciate ligament in my knee. That was my career over, but I was about 28 at the time.

'I went into this area of medicine and it was wonderful because I could empathise with the boxers and kick-boxers that were coming in. I've had some of the injuries myself, the little niggles.'

Crolla's left shoulder has been a source of discomfort of late. The area is getting particular attention from Abbas. It's wear and tear and very much the kind of problem every fighter will have during a camp.

'It's got to the stage where there's hardly any body fat on him, so there's no cushioning. He's like a highly tuned racehorse. It's a fine balance with keeping himself fully hydrated to keep the muscles elastic. Where Anthony is now, at this stage, he's as good physically and mentally as he was going into the last fight. It's all up to him now. It's been a slightly longer camp, so it's been really good.'

Abbas hits a nerve, in the literal sense. 'Feels tight there?'

Yeah ... ha ha, aaagh!

It's not a laugh that suggests fun. It's the kind of grimace and sound you'd hear from somebody stepping into an ice-cold bath.

'He had a very slight tear in the teres minor muscle. That normally would take around two and a half weeks to heal, but it's not hurting really at all now and it's been less than a week.'

It wasn't hurting me when I punched or anything like that, it was just stiff. It was affecting certain exercises and I didn't want it to become more of an issue, which it probably could've done. Then it might have started slowing down me [when I was] letting my shots go. You always get little things. They're expected.

'The great thing about Joe Gallagher, you've got to give credit to him, he's on it. It's the level of attention to detail. He's on the phone to me whenever there are any issues. He doesn't take any chances.' Abbas then laughs. 'He can be a bit of an old woman, though! He texted me last night at 12.30am! I think he had to send me that text to tell me his concerns, just so he could actually go to sleep! He's thinking, "What I'll do now is make sure Abbas can't sleep!"'

R2-D2 has been wheeled back to its resting place and another piece of fancy kit moved into position.

'It's a G5, a piece of physio equipment that vibrates the head of the device at different cycles per second. I'm on 70 cycles per second because I want to get into the ligaments and the tendons. The lower cycles, say 50, I use to work on more superficial injuries.'

Abbas continues to work away as the pair chat about all manner of topics ... more football, boxing and gentle nonsense. All part of the fight routine, a very therapeutic therapy.

Fight week

Just a few days to go before the biggest night of Anthony's career. This is when promoters make the final push. The public workout is usually the first formal engagement for a fighter taking part in a high-profile event. It's mainly for the cameras, although fight fans can always get close to their heroes – particularly if it's Crolla, who'll spend half the day having selfies taken and signing gloves.

The National Football Museum in Manchester city centre has been a favoured Matchroom venue for events such as this when Anthony's the headline act. Based in the unique Urbis building – a huge sloping glass structure next to Victoria station – the ground-floor atrium is taken over by a boxing ring, with spectators vying for a good spot behind the security rope. Others are hanging over the first-floor balcony to get a bird's eye view.

The undercard is represented, too. First in the ring is Jack Arnfield with his trainer Mike Jennings, quickly followed by his opponent Brian Rose and Bobby Rimmer. Next, it's the turn of Marcus Morrison with Joe on the pads. Marcus has brought a few supporters down from Hattersley by the sound of things. Rival Jason Welborn hasn't travelled up from his West Midlands home.

Then it's showtime. A chorus of panto jeers greet the first sight of Linares, who makes his way from the makeshift dressing room at the side of the atrium, decked out in a black shiny tracksuit with a thick white stripe on the arms and legs. He smiles, takes his aviators off, ducks through the ropes and casually springs around the ring, flicking out combinations.

The champion isn't keen on hanging around, it seems. His trainer Ismael Salas is stood in the corner of the ring, but there's no instruction, his fighter's hands aren't wrapped, so no pad work will be happening today. Jorge has a brief skip and without getting anywhere near breaking sweat, he waves to the crowd, flashes his matinee idol smile and effortlessly glides through the ropes and out. The 200-strong crowd boo again, a few verbals are shouted, but it's all done the right way and all those assembled, whether they'll admit it or not, are a bit impressed with this cool operator.

As Linares leaves, Crolla enters. There's a warm handshake and embrace as the pair cross paths. Anthony, all smiles, then jumps up on to the ring apron and waves. The atmosphere's ramped up for the local hero, the 'Pride of Manchester' as so proclaimed on the digital advertising board positioned on the wall to the left of the ring. The Crolla song kicks in.

Watching ringside is Martin Cullen, Anthony's strength and conditioning man. With more than 30 years' experience in his field of expertise, Martin's worked with athletes across sports including rugby league, kick-boxing, MMA, motorsport, football and, of course, boxing.

'I originally started with Martin Murray. His manager brought him to me and I did every fight with him until Argentina [Sergio Martinez v Murray].

'With Anthony, I'm trying to improve everything in his performance – his speed, his body movement, his reactions, his power, his ability to absorb punishment, mental toughness. Everything.

'At the beginning, he was like Ground Zero. It was starting from nothing. Because of the incident [burglary] and what had happened, he'd been dieting forever and he'd lost everything. He was very low level. It took a while to get going. In fact, about three or four weeks into it, I was thinking, "Oh my God, this is going to be a lot harder than I thought!"'

A bespectacled middle-aged man with short salt-and-pepper hair, Martin cuts an impressive physical figure, not surprising given his life's work. He's in demand, largely due to his ambition and attention to detail.

'I remember at our first meeting with Anthony and Joe, I said to them that I wouldn't be happy until I'd made him, physically, the best lightweight in the world. I don't think they believed it at the time, when he was lying on the couch with his crutches. But I knew that if he stuck with it, I'd do it. I think now, physically, he's the best lightweight in the world.

'Everything's in balance and proportion. What you see with a lot of boxers is their bodies out of balance. Certain muscles are over-developed and other muscles are under-developed. That affects performance. It makes them slower and less powerful. When every muscle is in balance, the body works more effectively.

'Anthony is now totally confident in absorbing anyone's punishment. That shot in the sixth round in the last fight? He absorbed it and came back and won the seventh.

'Five years ago, not many people were doing strength and conditioning. There's a right way and a wrong way. If you do it incorrectly, it'll slow a boxer down and their power will go. Look at Anthony: he's improving a little bit for every fight. I'm really happy where he is. His genetics are for endurance, so I've come along to try and put more speed and power in there.

'Mentally, I'm taking him to places he's never been before. Pushing yourself beyond what you've done before, that makes you mentally strong. Anthony's up there with the best I've ever trained. He's got that mental ability where he wants to be the best.

'I used to train Andrew Farrell [ex-rugby league and union player, now union coach]. Nobody would beat him, but Anthony's on a par with Andrew at his best. He wants to get better. He's a dream to work with. I think he's the perfect role model, for young lads especially. You'd want your son to grow up like Anthony. You'd be proud. The only thing is, he's always late!'

Anthony's finished showing off his shadow boxing skills and, unlike Linares, is happy to do the pads for the punters. It's all for show. Joe's not going to give anything away in a public workout, so the pair bang out some simple combinations.

Now changed back into his grey tracksuit, Marcus Morrison is ringside to catch the last few minutes of his friend's exercise. He too is counting down the days until he can get in the ring and fight.

'Everything's perfect. I've had a good ten weeks, a hard training camp. I'm peaking now and ready for Saturday.

'Welborn's shorter than me, stocky, and I can imagine quite bull strong. We've mimicked that in sparring. I've been doing 12 rounds comfortably in the gym. If everything goes to plan, and I'm sure it will, it'll be a comfortable night.

'I've been on Quigg and Crolla undercards a few times. Obviously the focus is on the big night Crolla's got ahead of him, but we all work hard. It's a similar feeling every time. Everyone's pushing each other in the gym. It brings out the best in us.

'I'm fighting for the WBC international, so in terms of a big fight, I'm going into a fight where I know I'm in for a fight and it'll bring out the best in me.'

Routine over, Crolla takes the mic and thanks the crowd for coming. He leaves the ring, smiling, to another chorus of 'ooooooh Anthony Crolla'.

I'm settled into the hotel [Radisson Blu]. Moved in Monday morning and I'm enjoying it all. I'm enjoying fight week – I'm relaxed. I honestly feel better than ever. I'll watch a few box sets and chill out.

I had my last spar on Sunday night and we had Zelfa in the gym last night doing a bit of technique work. It was a nice way to finish off. Camp's more or less done now, I might do some pads to stay sharp, plenty of stretching and staying loose.

I'm locked away from Fran and Jesse now. I got a good luck card off him that he made in nursery, so that's brilliant – it's up in my room now. I'm going to keep looking at it to remind myself why I'm doing all this. It's all the motivation I need. I'm going to get in there on Saturday and push myself to the absolute limits.

You're not showing your hand in a public workout. With me and Joe then, we were hitting pads but we weren't throwing the specific shots we've been working on in the gym. We're not going to give anything away.

I saw Jorge before, shook his hand and asked him if he's OK. That was it. People talk about mind games and all that – I can't be bothered. I just look at it as a job. If I saw him on Saturday morning, Saturday afternoon or on the way to the arena, it wouldn't bother me. Once it's game time, that's it.

There is still a shake-out at the gym to be done and other fight formalities. Time's against them and Joe wants them to leave in ten minutes. That was never going to happen. Thirty minutes later and Crolla's still signing whatever's put in front of him and having photos done with just about everyone who turned up.

'You don't read anything into the public workout; it just gets the fighter in the right mode. They see the fans, you get to see Linares shadow boxing, looking the part. Forgot how good he is!' Joe laughs.

'I think his missus got more of a sweat on stood under the lights! I was just talking to her before, asking her if she's been enjoying the shopping. I think she's spending Jorge's purse from the first fight here in Manchester.

'He's [Linares] a good fighter. I think it's lost on a lot of the British public just what a great talent he is. I think fans that've bought tickets for this fight, and the first fight, I think they'll look back in years to come and say, "I've seen him fight." Jorge Linares won fans here after that first fight. There's huge respect.

'I think a lot of people here have come to watch him as well as Crolla. Four-time world champion at three different weights. Let that sink in. He's a modern-day great in my opinion. He's in the top ten pound-for-pound fighters in the world.

'Both fighters know there's so much on the line. That's why I think it'll be a miles better fight than the first fight. I think there'll be more chances taken and both fighters will look for the knockout. After this fight, there's a multi-million pound fight waiting to happen with Mikey Garcia. That fight would set up Anthony or Jorge for life. It would set up their family, their kids, their future. That's what they're fighting for on Saturday night.'

In an ideal world, Joe would be shadowing Anthony all day, making sure he's turning his phone off, getting rest away from any well-meaning but draining encounters with friends and acquaintances. It's not possible with a busy gym with the schedule of fights so relentless.

'I'm kept busy on fight week. I've got sparring for Liam Smith, Paul Butler and Scott Cardle tomorrow. I'm occupied to an extent. I enjoy it. I get a bit giddy today with the workout. I get nervous away from Anthony. How can you not get nervous? It's someone's child. Doesn't matter how old they are, you're responsible for their health and safety.

'You just think, "Imagine if we do this?" You're visualising the event and all the build-up. Obviously we've still got the press conference. Get that out of the way and we've got MUTV on Thursday night. Friday it's the weigh-in, fuelling up, rules meetings, sorting out gloves, changing rooms, ring-walks, timings, music. There are loads of things that go on in the background.

'He's got nothing serious left to do training-wise, just a shake-out on Thursday. He's done. He's got no problem with the weight. He's a model pro; you never have to worry about him crashing weight as he's never out of shape. You're dealing with a professional so he can have days off. I'm only bringing him into the gym on Thursday so he can visualise and so his body doesn't shut down.'

Locked away

Anthony's settled well into his temporary home. Joe's here too now, intent on making sure the whole point of his man being here – to avoid distractions – isn't a pointless exercise.

It's just after 8pm, the hotel is quiet and Anthony can be heard before he's seen. He's shouting in broad north Mancunian, '*See you in a bit*' to someone on the first floor mezzanine, before he comes into view in his dark blue trainers, dark jeans, dark grey T-shirt and dark blue baseball cap. He bounds down the glass and chrome stairs into the reception area and stops next to the huge statue of Buddha's head in the lobby.

After an earnest apology, Anthony says he'll be back in a few minutes – he's got to chat to someone in the bar. In the meantime Joe appears, still in his training uniform of black T-shirt, black shorts and black trainers. He's looking forward to getting another of the fight week obligations out of the way – the final press conference taking place the following day.

And he wants to hear more from Team Linares. 'I have asked to have his trainer up. He can speak English very well, Ismael Salas. Robert Diaz is doing what I do. He's doing all the talking. Jorge and Anthony aren't going to talk shite, so Robert does it all for him. Jorge Linares can speak English, good English.

'It takes pressure of him, no mithering, and the coach is sat there with no stress, so I've asked to get him up on the big stage.

'The only other thing about tomorrow is that I've asked all the main broadcasters to get there early because Anthony will be there early and we've got to get to MUTV.

'We'll knock out the TV interviews and then it's the top table, so any questions, ask them. Anthony isn't going to hang around until 4pm to answer the same questions over and over. Once the presser ends, we're done.'

Joe suddenly loses his train of thought as he realises he hasn't booked a table for San Carlo on Friday evening. It's something of a pre-fight tradition. He gets on the phone and makes the booking for five: Joe, Anthony, Marcus Morrison, Hosea Burton and Martin Cullen.

The Germany v England friendly international is on in the background. Anthony's arrived at the table and turns to see what the score is. He can't properly see the screen but he's not concerned.

Not one bit bothered. It's not United.

He turns back and takes a cautious sip of his steaming green tea.

Final press conference

The two tables at the top of the Halle Suite function room fill up with the undercard and main event fighters. Eddie Hearn and Sky Sports head of boxing Adam Smith open up the press conference. The support fighters get their chance to speak first before Golden Boy's Robert Diaz is called upon to say a few words.

He speaks of the pressure Anthony is under to win a title for the UK and tells the room Jorge has trained three times as hard.

'In the press conference prior to the first fight, I said you'd see the best Jorge Linares you have ever seen. I think a lot of people agreed that this Jorge Linares was much better than we've seen in the past.

'Well, I'm going to take it a little step further. On Saturday night, you will see a better Jorge Linares than you did in September. I want to give a big round of applause to the man who's behind that – Ismael Salas. Thank you coach!'

A ripple of polite applause spreads throughout the room.

Eddie turns his attention to the champion and asks him about fighting in Manchester again. Jorge, dressed smartly in a grey jacket and black shirt complete with shades, doesn't need the question translated and immediately thunders away in rapid Spanish. Robert turns his thoughts into English.

'Thank you to all the people of Manchester. I'm back and I know once again I have everyone against me in the backyard of my opponent, but look, that's why I trained hard. That's why I'm prepared.

'We respect Anthony tremendously, but I'm not coming here feeling like the champion. I'm coming in here feeling like the challenger because I know I have to win very clear to go back home with my belts.

'I had a tremendous camp. I started my camp at the end of December in Japan – condition and strength. From there, I had eight great weeks, one of the best camps ever, in Vegas. Great training, no injuries.

'I'm anxious. I just can't wait to show you on Saturday night, put it all together and return home with my belts.'

Eddie thanks Robert and Jorge, calling the fighter 'a class act'. Next up is Joe.

'Thanks for everyone coming out and thanks to everyone who's left Anthony alone, like I asked.

'Robert's a great talker – he's as good as you, Eddie – but we know we will get the best Linares. I knew last time. We know what we're dealing with. He's got a world-class coach in Ismael Salas. I'm surprised Ismael isn't up here today to speak. A coach with his credibility, it's not often he comes to this country.

'Last time he was in Manchester I didn't speak one word to him, but we met last weekend and sat there talking for half an hour. After I've finished speaking, I think Ismael should come up and speak a few words. It'd be really good to hear what he has to say about the fight.'

Ismael is sat comfortably in his seat among the press pack, next to Michelle, Jorge's wife. He smiles at Joe's invitation, but it's clear he's not going anywhere near the top table. Joe picks up his thread and continues.

'I took Anthony away. He's in great shape, more mentally than physically.

'Last time the preparations weren't good. I was in Dallas the week before for Liam Smith v Canelo, so Anthony was left alone. The week before that I was in London with the Smiths for the GGG fight, so the last key couple of weeks I wasn't around Anthony.

'All focus has been on Anthony Crolla and he's done what I asked of him. This is the seventh time Anthony's headlined at the Manchester Arena. That hasn't happened since the days of Ricky Hatton. We want to get to ten.

'It's going to be a great event as well as a great fight on the night. Can Anthony Crolla be better? Yes he can. Can Jorge Linares be better? Yes he can. That's why this fight is going to bring pure excitement. Will it go to points? I don't think so.'

When Joe finishes, boxing manager Brian Peters – sitting alongside Katie Taylor, who's also on the undercard – applauds. 'I'm exhausted, Joe!' he shouts. Eddie Hearn chips in too. 'We did want to bring Mr Salas up here but we didn't have time.'

Last up is Anthony, who's dressed down in a green T-shirt littered with sponsors' logos. He's introduced as the underdog, and looks happy with that.

I've always been better going in as the underdog. I know on Saturday night I'm going to need to be the very best Anthony Crolla to beat Jorge Linares. Honestly, I've worked smart these last ten, 12 weeks and I really believe that if I show the improvements that I've made in the gym then I'll get my belts back.

I'm a fan of Jorge Linares; in the first fight I knew he was going to be tough. I came up short last time. It was close, but the right man won. I made mistakes and I believe I've had more room for improvement.

I'm the lucky one. I get to dance under those lights. It might not look it in rounds eight, nine or ten, when you've got to dig deep, but I'm the luckiest person in there. I'll be centre stage with my opponent and I want to take those belts back to my little boy.

I hope he comes in looking for the knockout. If Jorge comes looking for the knockout, he breaks away from what he's best at. And, if he does so, I believe it falls right into my hands.

I've got to be cutting off the ring quicker this time. I've got to respond in bunches a little bit more. There are so many obstacles that are going to be put in front of me from Jorge Linares, but I believe I will have an answer for every one of them.

It was one of the fights of the year last time. I can certainly see us both being even better this time. There's a lot of people out there who think there is no way I can beat Jorge Linares, but I believe on Saturday night I'll prove an awful lot of people wrong.

After the press conference is over, Anthony's had a little time to reflect on what was said and how everyone handled the occasion. There have been suggestions Linares, in his aviators throughout, was looking a little washed out. Anthony's not sure.

It's a possibility but listen, tomorrow we'll both look a little bit gaunt but be in great shape. He's a cool guy, isn't he? He throws his shades on with his suit and he pulls it off. Fair play to him.

The other day he looked more gaunt than me but he was three pounds lighter than me at the check weight. I don't look into all that. I'm just focused on being the best me and I believe that'll be enough on the night to get my belts back.

This is now very much the business end of fight week. We've had the fun of the public workout and the press conference. Now it's weigh-in and then showtime.

I'll hit a few pads tonight with Joe ahead of the weigh-in tomorrow. Otherwise, it's just about getting rest and fuelling up correctly after the weigh-in.

I've gone over the fight in my head over and over and I'm expecting a tough, tough fight, but all I can envisage is an Anthony Crolla win. I'm more confident going into this fight than I was the last one. I really believe there'll be a new world champion.

The crowd is brilliant. They really lift me and I feed off their energy. It's going to be better than it's ever been before for me. I'm absolutely blessed – the proudest Manc there could be in that arena. Winning is something, but winning in front of all them is very special.

Weigh-in

Everyone's back to the Radisson for the weigh-in. The Halle Suite is packed with press seated at the front of the room, with standing room only for members of the public. It's stuffy and noisy and it's fair to assume that a lunchtime drink has been taken by more than a few.

There's a bit of argy bargy between Brian Rose and Jack Arnfield during their face-off, with heads leaning in a little then a push and a shove. Rose's trainer Bobby Rimmer, who used to train Arnfield too, makes a bee line for his former charge. Security steps in to calm things down as tempers fray.

No such drama when it's the turn of Linares and Crolla. It just couldn't happen. Both men strip to their underwear and weigh in the same, 9st 8lbs 4oz. Anthony takes the mic off MC John McDonald.

Your support is absolutely awesome – thank you for getting behind me. I appreciate it from youse all. I hope you have a good night tomorrow and a safe night.

There's huge applause followed by *that* song.

Seated at the front of the room enjoying the show is long-time Crolla pal and stablemate Paul Smith – the eldest of the fighting brothers.

'I'm going to Berlin tomorrow so I'm going to miss this again. I missed the last one coz I was fishing on the Amazon, filming a TV show for ITV. It was good, but we didn't have phones or a signal. We did have a satphone so two days later I found out how he'd got on. I was gutted for him.

'This time, I've got to fly to Berlin because the fella I'm fighting for the world title in May [Tyron Zeuge] is fighting. It's his mandatory, so fingers crossed it's a routine win for him. I'll be there to watch the fight then get in the ring with him afterwards and have a chat, get the ball rolling.'

Smith, like his brothers and the rest of the gym, are either in the corner or ringside normally. It's one of those things, but unlike last time he can at least follow the fight. A respected pundit with Sky Sports, Paul is realistic with regards to his friend. He thinks he can do it, but isn't getting carried away.

'You never get what you deserve in boxing; you get what's on the cards. It's a mad one with boxing. You'll see fighters who work so hard fall short, like Anthony last time. He's come back, corrected a lot of things in the gym and he's worked twice as hard for this one, so maybe that's the reason he lost the last fight. This can catapult him to all the marbles. There's a massive pay day if he wins and fingers crossed.

'That's what the life of a sportsman's about. You've got to earn as much as you can because you can retire at 32 or 33 and you're retired a long time.

'If you look at him [Crolla] when he left Anthony Farnell, and no disrespect to Anthony Farnell, but he came to Joe Gallagher and not many people would've said he could've improved then. He's so hungry and so determined that he's listened to every word Joe's said and he's gone and got help elsewhere, from yoga and strength trainers – everything he could possibly do to improve, he's done.

'He's gone from losing fights to Gary Sykes – and no disrespect to Gary – to beating Pérez for the title and Barroso to having this rematch with Linares. If that doesn't show his willingness to better himself, then nothing will. He's always trying to improve – right down to the bad clobber he wears!'

Eddie Hearn's done his bit for the day and is heading away from the hotel. Matchroom has been a steady visitor to Manchester over the years, a second home for the Essex-based crew. It's a good city for the fight business. North West fighters like Crolla do good numbers. Not Hatton numbers, but great ticket sales all the same. Anthony's been a success story for himself and for Matchroom, a fact not lost on Eddie.

'Anthony's a phenomenal guy, really, when you look at his run. The first Darleys Pérez fight, which he won; everyone said he won. He got a draw so he had to come back again and he demolished him, knocked him out.

'Then he gets Barroso in a mandatory, to which everyone said, "What are you doing?" but he knocks him out, so he gets Linares in a unification and for the *Ring* magazine belt. And then he fights him again. That's five fights against proper elite lightweights, and back to back. No warm-up fights, no tune-up fights or easy defences.

'Whenever a fighter loses, they always want a rematch straight away. We had that opportunity in the contract. But then, sometimes a week or two weeks later, they watch the fight back, talk to their trainer, but there was never any of that. Never any talk of other options, or who else can I fight? The only fight he wanted was the rematch and I think you have to take your hat off to him.'

The Fight

It's been a leisurely day for Anthony. A good night's sleep at the hotel, a long lie-in and then downstairs for a hearty breakfast – you can eat what you like, within reason, once you've made the weight. With plenty of time to kill, he decides to have a stroll and indulges in a bit of shopping on King Street – a haven of banks and boutiques.

Back to the room with some new gear – trainers and a couple of tops – lunch follows then back to bed for more sleep. It's mid-afternoon, snack time then final preparations and kit bag packing for the arena. There's time for some TV before he has to go to work.

Meanwhile, a mile down the road, Joe's already in the dressing room at the venue – he arrived there at around 3.30pm. It's a busy night with three of his fighters in action, but not as hectic as previous nights, when he's had five of his lads on the same bill.

Boxers and their teams arrive via the loading bay entrance of the arena before making their way through a warren of corridors to the dressing rooms. The home changing area consists of two large rooms. The first is mainly empty but for a couple of sofas. Through a connecting door and into another square room with sofas down two sides, a large mirror at one end with toilet and showers to the left. There's a flat screen TV on a wall above one of the sofas. The sound is turned down – Ant and Dec are doing their *Saturday Night Takeaway* thing.

The action at the arena starts early – tea-time. So many local fighters get a chance to fight at these events and even when the crowd is sparse, it's a valuable experience to be a part of the show. Hosea Burton – normally high up the order – is one of the first in the ring. He gets the job done against Tamak Kozma in an eight-rounder to help banish some of the demons from his last-gasp light-heavyweight British title defeat to Frank Buglioni last time out. He's handily outpointed the Hungarian – not the greatest opponent but one with ambition and a winning record.

'Good to get it out of the way but I boxed shite, like. He was tough but not much good.'

As the action warms up and the crowd builds, Martin J Ward gets the decision in his third fight with Maxi Hughes. Crolla sparring partner Anto Cacace now knows his next opponent.

With Hosea home and hosed, Joe's focus is now Marcus Morrison, who's prepared well for his toughest challenge to date, a defence of his WBC international middleweight belt against the rugged Jason Welborn.

It's 6.50pm. Hands wrapped, Morrison has changed into his white silky shorts with gold trim, complete with matching white and gold boots. Crolla would approve. He's moving around the room, shadow boxing and mouthing the words to 'Ain't No Stopping Us Now', which is pumping from the iPod deck on a small table next to a drinks fridge. It's one of Joe's fight-night playlists.

Marcus is relaxed and feels good. 'I can't wait now. I'm looking forward to it.'

Joe pulls his pads on to his hands and ushers Marcus into the middle of the room. There's the familiar sound of glove smashing into pad as Joe orders the combinations – *bam bam, bam bam bam*. ...

Team-mate Paul Butler and Richard Thomas from the BBB of C are watching, sunken, almost fully reclined into the soft brown leather sofa. Cutsman Mick Williamson is leaning against the wall next to the mirror, arms folded.

At 8pm, word reaches the room that Welborn has made his ring walk. Five minutes later, Marcus is on the move. The team filter out of the room and head for the ring.

As expected, Welborn starts at a frenetic pace, cutting the distance that would allow the rangier Marcus to show off his skills. It's relentless from the challenger, wave after wave of attacks, with Marcus landing the odd clever counter before a big left hook puts Welborn on the canvas.

The man from Dudley is undeterred. He gets to his feet and continues his frenzied bombardment – he has the look of a man who's never been given a chance in his life and can't let the opportunity slip.

In the mid-stages of the fight, Marcus is on the ropes again as Welborn's aggression continues. For Morrison fans, any ideas of an easy night for their man have long been forgotten. There's damage to Marcus's nose and swelling to his left eye as Welborn unloads hooks and uppercuts in round seven. It's the first crisis of the Hattersley man's career.

Welborn's fury recedes in round eight but is back in the ninth despite Marcus having some success with the jab. Into the final round, Marcus is still there, gamely throwing back as Welborn seeks to end the fight as he began it – not giving Marcus a second's peace.

End of the tenth, contest over. Marcus bravely stuck in there until the bell, but it's been a very difficult night and there's no doubt where the decision is going. It's unanimous in favour of Welborn, who is ecstatic.

Marcus respectfully applauds, while his face, battered and bruised, tells the story of his first professional loss.

Back in the dressing room, Marcus is comforted by family and friends and there's a hug from Joe. The young fighter is inconsolable. The physical pain isn't the problem, although he'll have to head to hospital for a check-up once showered and changed.

Anthony arrived at the venue during the fight. He's made himself at home, sorting clothes out, hanging T-shirts on a rack, unpacking his kit. Naturally, he's concerned for Marcus, who's changed now, but is still in tears. Ant walks over and gives him a hug without saying anything. He knows how his friend is feeling, but equally he can't let it bother him.

Scott Cardle has turned up; he's telling Marcus that the defeat will make him a better fighter. He then moves over to Anthony, embraces him and gives him a kiss on the cheek.

Marcus is leaving now. Nothing will make him feel better tonight. 'I'm heartbroken. I think my nose is broken. It's so tough [losing].' He heads away for A&E.

Joe's feeling it too. He's running the fight through his head. Already he's been getting grief on social media – many armchair punters of the view Joe should've thrown in the towel. 'I should've pulled him. I said to Mick [Williamson] in the eighth to give me the towel. Then he came back in the ninth. He [Marcus] wanted to see it out. I'm gutted, but I've got to switch on with Crolla now.'

The dressing room is now a hive of activity. Zelfa Barrett arrives and is trying to get his head around the Morrison fight.

'I thought Marcus was going to breeze through the guy [Welborn] but he wasn't coming to play, was he? He'd prepped very well and it showed in the fight that he was in great condition. But Marcus will come again and I can see the rematch happening. He's a winner.

'Maybe it was a lack of experience. He would have learned a lot from that but unfortunately he has to take a loss. It's boxing. It can

165

make or break you and that will make him a totally different fighter. He's a strong guy, he'll get through it.'

Zelfa's sparring work with Crolla will continue right up until the ring walk. He's been brought in to help Anthony switch on as the fight approaches. Barrett will be back at the arena in a fortnight to box on the undercard of Terry Flanagan's WBO title defence against Petr Petrov.

'I'm excited to be fighting at the arena, always wanted to. I'm on a good show in a couple of weeks with Turbo [Terry]. Camp's gone well with Crolla. We've been training in the evening and I'm getting good sparring. He's a world-class operator and very underrated.

'Crolla trains very hard all the time, but this is the best I've seen him. I hope he can do it. Linares is a world-class hall of famer. With what he's been doing in training, he has the attributes to do it.

'Linares is the whole thing, he is unreal. You tell any kid who wants to fight, watch Linares. Crolla has to think about being sharp because people like Linares are special fighters. He makes you miss then makes you pay in a devastating way. You know that Anthony has to be on his game.

'He's so relaxed. He's had time to mentally prepare. In his mind, he would've already been here ten weeks ago. I'm like that so when I get to the venue I don't need to be nervous. I've already been here. I prepare when I'm running, sleeping, on the toilet, eating, talking – I'm thinking about my next opponent now and it's the same with Anthony. He's ready.'

Anthony's hands are wrapped and he's changed into his fightwear for his evening's work. The shorts are white with green, yellow and black trim – a nod to Manchester United's Newton Heath colours – with a green T-shirt littered with sponsors' logos. Zelfa's peeled off the skinny white jeans and cast aside the white T-shirt and sleeveless grey hoodie. He's put on his all-black training gear and is moving around with Crolla, both taking turns to defend and attack light combinations.

Joe, glasses on with notebook in hand, is calling out the instructions to a backing track of 'Playing in the Shadows' by Example. Liam, Stephen and Callum Smith are bobbing in and out of the room.

Callum settles in, sits on the drinks fridge and takes in the scene. Crolla's still smiling, still joking. The switch hasn't yet been flicked. Callum understands. He's the quiet brother, the laid-back one. He doesn't need to rant and rave to get in the zone either.

'Anthony's very mentally strong and I think he's had tunnel vision for the last ten or 12 weeks. Nothing will take his mind off it. He's a good person to be around. He brings out the best in other people. He's a good trainer and I've benefited a lot from training alongside him.

'He's like the fifth Smith brother. I get nearly as much nerves watching him as I do me brothers, so fingers crossed he can pull it off. I've had bad nerves watching him – going back to the Derry Mathews fights. I don't get those kind of nerves with anyone else other than me brothers. It's weird. It's good to sometimes see good people who work hard get the results. He's shown he's worked hard over the years. I think he'd be the first to tell you he's not the most talented or the most skilful, but he works hard and he's become a world champion because of it.

'There's not many more determined than him and I'd back him over anyone to last 12 rounds. He's a Duracell bunny.'

The volume has been ramped up by DJ Joe. It's an eclectic mix, tunes ranging from his favoured old house music to Dizzee Rascal to Tina Turner and 70s disco. Out in the arena, Katie Taylor has beaten Bulgarian Milena Koleva in an eight-round shutout. Next, it's the chief support, the battle of Blackpool, Brian Rose v Jack Arnfield. After 12 rounds, Arnfield has his hand raised as the unanimous winner following a technical fight that failed to ignite. There was more heat at the weigh-in.

The undercard is over. There are still a couple of floater fights to fit in after the main event, but with the knowledge the chief support is finished the mood in the dressingroom changes. The music quietens, voices lower, chatter begins to cease. There's a last visit to the toilet for Anthony – accompanied by a drug testing official.

The laid-back vibe is gone. Anthony's still flashing a smile, but it looks a little forced now. The tension in the room is unnerving. Will Crolla, a constant by his older brother's side during every fight week, is now feeling sick.

'I hate this bit now. I'm fine when he's in there but building up to it I get very nervous because at this level anything can happen. When he's in there it's all right.

'I've watched him since I was about eight. I watched him in the amateurs, when he won the ABAs. I've been to every one of his professional fights other than one when he boxed in Vegas.

'I've been there every time he's lost and every time he's drawn. I remember the first defeat to Youssef Al-Hamidi. I was thinking, "It's a journeyman, he'll beat him easy!" Ant walked into the ring and it didn't look like him. It wasn't nice to see him after the fight. It was the first time I'd seen him cut as well.

'I don't worry about him getting hurt because he's got a top defence. I worry about him losing and how disappointed he'd be and how he'd think he let everyone down.

'He's calm before every fight, then he feeds off the atmosphere. It's a mad feeling when you walk out of here into the arena. I don't know how he must feel. He'll enjoy every minute of it.

'It makes me proud. I think, "Wow, he's just a normal person."'

The Sky Sports camera crew are outside the door – poised to scurry backwards all the way to the ring, bringing the ring walk to life on the big screens in the arena and the small screens all over the world.

There's a cry of 'Let's go' from somewhere as the entourage begins to move. There's a final word from Joe to his fighter as they leave the dressing room.

'No sloppy right hands. Don't be a brave, tough man. Move your feet. This is your chance to make history, son!'

Through the corridor maze, the group marches on through a huge set of double doors and into the corner of the arena. Burley security men now surround them as they wait for the TV cue. There's a burst of 'Hometown Glory' before 'Million Dollar Bill' kicks in and the march to the ring begins in earnest. The crowd erupts as the challenger enters, the familiar smiling face beaming on the big screens.

Anthony is busy fist-pumping punters who are hanging over barriers, desperate to wish him luck. The noise is extraordinary.

These days, it's not a familiar feeling for Anthony to be called first to the ring, but it's a very familiar welcome.

The volume reaches its crescendo as Anthony stoops through the ropes to take the ovation under the burning ring lights amid the strains of 'ooooh …'

The Crolla song continues as Linares is announced by MC John McDonald. The Venezuelan and his team stand waiting as Eminem's 'Guess Who's Back' turns into 'Back in Black' by AC/DC and he moves quickly towards the ring dressed in his black sleeveless tunic and maroon baseball cap.

McDonald completes the announcement formalities as Anthony stretches and throws a flurry of uppercuts while Linares punches the ropes. Both men strip off the excess clothing and meet in the middle of the ring for final instructions from referee Howard Foster.

From the first bell, the crowd do their bit to help the local hero push himself that little bit further. Naturally, he gives it everything, but whereas the first fight had been intriguing with Crolla asking questions, weathering storms and regaining momentum, Linares looks like a man even more on a mission this time.

A cagey opening session is followed by Linares establishing snappy combinations – his calling card. More of the same follow in the early rounds and by the fourth round, it's hard to envisage a happy outcome for 'Million Dollar'. The Venezuelan is measuring distance masterfully as Anthony attempts to assert authority.

There's a moment in the seventh when Linares beautifully engineers a left uppercut that, with a slightly delayed reaction, has Crolla stumbling to the deck. He takes the count, and rises to see out the round. It's typically stubborn from Crolla, but it's sublime from the champion.

Anthony was still trying to make things happen, force a mistake, drag Jorge into a trap. He did so in the eighth with some success and in the ninth too, getting the crowd on its feet, daring to believe. In the tenth, Linares went back to work with the combinations, stinging attacks, after downing tools for a couple of rounds.

Linares is in control in the 11th. He fires in shots as the fistic New Moston version of 'Seven Nation Army' continues to reverberate

169

around the arena. At the end of the round, Joe's seen enough. He wants his man to take no further part and gestures to the referee. Crolla protests. He's desperate to hear the final bell, even though he knows only a miracle can turn this one around.

Trainer relents. His fighter goes out for the 12th and final round, embraces his opponent and gives it another go. It's not enough, Jorge's too cute and when the bell tolls for the end of the contest, respect is shown once more, but nobody is in doubt.

The ring is hectic with the respective teams congregating. The body language from Crolla says everything. The official verdict is handed to the MC, who invites the crowd to acknowledge two great fighters, which they do.

The scorecards are unanimously in favour of the man from Barinas, all 118-109 for the winner and still...

Sky Sports are swiftly in the ring to get the reaction from both men. Linares, with Robert Diaz of course by his side, sends a message to the crowd.

'Thank you everybody, thank you Manchester. Everybody, I love you!'

The arena applauds. It was never quite going to be a Drago vs Balboa kind of night. Any pre-fight booing was purely panto, with the vociferous pro-Crolla crowd only ever full of respect for Linares from the start. The champion knew that and those few words, in English, only emphasised the burgeoning bond.

With Robert Diaz now back on translation duties, his interview continued.

'I respect and admire all of you, Manchester. I didn't feel the pressure this time like last time because I know; out there I have admiration from you too. I want to tell everyone in Manchester; Anthony Crolla has some big balls. He had a lot of heart and that's why he made it to the 12th round with me.

'Anthony and I are both warriors and we fight our hearts out for you. I did what I had to. Now I want to go back to the United States and get the biggest and best opponents. I'm ready to fight everybody.'

Crolla gets hold of the mic..... 'Ooooooh Anthony Crolla' is still being belted out in the background.

Jorge Linares is a great fighter, a great champion and he proved it again tonight. Manchester, I'm so sorry. Thank you for your support. Honestly, I'm taken aback by it, time after time. It means so much to me and I'm sorry I couldn't do it for youse tonight.

He caught me with a great shot and before that I was trying to close the distance. I thought I was going to get to him but I got beat by the better man. No excuses, Jorge Linares is a fantastic fighter. I'm just sorry I couldn't do it.

I'm 30 years old and I'm just going to rest. I've had some tough fights but I believe I can come again. I lost to a very good fighter tonight. I'm going to go away and spend some time with family and friends, rebuild and take it from there.

After the interview in the ring, Anthony's ushered to a neutral corner to talk with Mike Costello from BBC Five Live. He echoes his sentiments about Linares and the fight, before climbing through the ropes and out of the ring.

There's confusion and a little chaos around the press seats near the ring as other broadcasters scramble to grab a word with Anthony. There are still two fights on the card remaining involving recently turned Olympian Lawrence Okolie vs Geoffrey Cave and local lad Tomi Tatham vs Kerel Horejsek. Their teams are trying to fight their way to the ring amid punters, press and the departing Team Crolla.

Hundreds of fans have gathered to get a glimpse or a word and Anthony waves and flashes a dejected smile at those trying to gee him up. Security surrounds him and the team as they start the forlorn journey back to the inner sanctum of the arena.

It was a slow, deliberate ring walk from dressing room to the bright lights, but a quick one in reverse. Supporters are shouting encouragement along the route. They don't feel let down, just sorry that Crolla didn't get his night.

A quick detour to the doctor's room for five stitches in his eye wound, and Anthony's back in the dressing room. He perches on a small coffee table next to the drinks fridge. There's no music playing now but the TV is still on. It's on mute, but quiz show *The Chase* is clearly on repeat. Anthony guested on a celebrity version, which aired shortly after his first fight with Linares. The man himself is quiet too.

Have I got a presser?

Joe confirms that there is a press conference arranged.

Oh right. Do you know what? I don't want to start weeing in case I can't in a bit [drug testing]. Might as well do the presser first.

Joe looks up. 'Any update on Morrison?' he asks, his eyes darting around as he looks at the few bodies left in the dressing room. 'Has he been to hospital?' No one knows for sure, but all presume he did as intended.

The door in the corner of the room opens once more. Eddie Hearn wanders in and grabs a bottle of water from the fridge, opens it, and takes a swig before asking Crolla how he's doing. The pair talk through the fight while Joe continues to walk around the room, picking up bits of kit – wraps, tape, pads – and putting the items in his gym bag. He's reflecting on events as he paces around the room.

'I don't think Anthony could've done any more. I just think about where he's come from in the last three years and the last five fights he's had. It's an awful hard ask. We thought, "Could Linares get better?" Yeah he could. He's peaking now. A very special talent and you just have to acknowledge it.'

But what about the confusion before the start of the 12th round? What was really going on in the corner?

'Linares caught him a couple of times in the 11th and I thought, "We're well behind here." I pulled over Howard Foster and said, "Listen, that's it." But Crolla was giving it, "No Joe, I'm all right. No Joe, don't, please! I don't want to go out like this." He twisted me arm, so I told Howard we'd give it a go for the last round.'

They left the dressing room as a team not two hours previously – full of hope, tension, excitement, adrenaline surging through their veins. They leave the room as a team again to face the post-fight press. Cuts, bruises, bone and muscle injuries have replaced the hope, tension, excitement and adrenaline. As they make their way through the door towards the main arena and a warren of corridors with off-shoot rooms, Joe turns to Anthony with a half-smile and asks, 'How're your ribs, are they sore?'

Yeah. Really sore.

* * * * *

The clocks have gone forward for British summertime. Everyone has lost an hour. Joe, Anthony, Eddie and Will make their way down the corridor and head in the direction of the main arena before darting off to the right, down another alley, and arriving at the room that will host the post-fight press conference.

The makeshift press room operates as a canteen by day and is positioned close to the loading bay area in the bowels of the arena on the Great Ducie Street side of the building. It's cracking on for 1am as Eddie Hearn opens the first door into a small and pokey kitchen area before a second door opens up to the side of the assembled press.

He takes his seat and pulls his chair closer to what looks like a light wooden table but is probably MDF. Anthony and Joe, in matching black hoodies, stroll in seconds later and take their seats. Will stands by the wall. The fight poster 'Repeat or Revenge', with the action images of Linares and Crolla, is positioned behind them. There are two TV mics on the table along with an array of phones and dictaphones belonging to the attending press – written and broadcast all in together.

Eddie Hearn kicks things off by asking for questions from the floor. James Robson from the *Manchester Evening News* opens things up with a straightforward question about Anthony's thoughts on how the fight went.

I thought early on I was landing a few shots to the body and I thought he'd slow down. He didn't! Absolutely gutted but I give it everything. I've got to thank Joe for the amount of work he put in with me. I was flying in the gym, so no excuses whatsoever. I lost to the better man, but me ribs are in bits. From around four, my right side was pretty sore.

He was sharp and accurate. I tried to force it but lost to the better man. His movement was very good, his variety was good. He came back better in most departments. I was very confident going in, the way we'd prepared, the opening few minutes, but I lost to a top fighter. He's been around a long time and I was a fan of his. If it wasn't me taking the punches tonight, I'd probably have been admiring what he was doing. When the cuts heal up and my pride, I'll probably watch it back.

Joe wanted to pull me out but I was pleading for him to let me go on. No lies, I was all right. I think Joe thought he was in his rhythm, I had to stop him and it was very unlikely it was going to come. You ask any fighter, it's not me being brave. Any fighter would want to carry on and not be stopped with a round to go. In the 12th round, I was never in danger of getting stopped. I'm very thankful Joe didn't pull me out.

The left uppercut put me over, but after he put me over he threw a lot of shots but I recovered. I thought I came back pretty well. I know it sounds stupid, but I wouldn't have minded that round going on a bit longer. I think the bell was better for him than me, if that makes sense? But it was a lovely shot he picked out and put me over with.

I'm going to have a little break with my family. I felt I was improving in camp still. Listen, I'll be back. I believe there'll be plenty of options and fights out there for us. I've had a pretty tough two years fight-wise and all the stuff that comes with it, so I'll look after myself and have a few weeks away from boxing and not think about it.

There's a question about a potential Terry Flanagan fight. Could that be an option? Joe, with his eyes downward looking at the table, gently shakes his head as Anthony answers enthusiastically.

He's certainly an option but he's got his own fight on April 8 and I don't know what his plans are going to be. I think there are plenty of options and Eddie's probably best at answering that.

I've got no problem fighting any fighter in the division. If it makes sense, I'll fight anyone to be in the big fights.

Joe speaks up. 'I just want him to have a good break. He's had five hard fights. We kept going with the momentum. He's done 24 rounds with Jorge Linares and I think everyone in Manchester tonight will look back on this and say, "I was there." Jorge Linares was class tonight; he was just on another level. You've got to take your hat off.'

Eddie Hearn plays the promoter's role with a dig at the Flanagan suggestion. 'That's a fight that could be an option down the line, but you saw the crowd and the atmosphere here tonight. Terry Flanagan sold 400 tickets with two weeks to go. He's a lovely guy but it's not the same level of draw. He is the champion, we're currently not the champion, but there are other options as well.

'There's Ricky Burns unifying the division on April 15. I wouldn't rule out moving up to light-welterweight to fight the winner of that fight. I just put the options in front of Joe and Anthony.'

The questions keep coming from the floor. Despite the defeat, it was an impressive showing at the arena – the love from the fans, Crolla the folk hero regardless of the result. How does that feel?

It means so much to me. I was walking around town today and there was a buzz around the town. You've got to remember I'm a Manchester lad who saw it all happen before with Ricky Hatton. Winning those belts would've been an absolute dream come true, but the support I get can't be matched. There's no feeling like it and I'm just absolutely gutted I couldn't do it for them. I just wanted to do them proud and win the title.

A few more queries from the floor taken care of, Anthony thanks everyone for staying behind. He gingerly lifts his weary body out of the chair, smiles and heads back to the dressing room.

CHAPTER 6

Down Time

ANTHONY'S had a few days to get his head around defeat. Mentally, he's in a good place and is now just waiting for the physical issues to heal.

The atmosphere was brilliant, just gutted I couldn't do it for the supporters. Everyone's been saying they had a great night and that's good to hear. Just wish I could've done it. I suppose just walking out in front of that crowd was a success in a way. As I thought, I've got a fracture to the rib. I knew there was summat up. It's been getting better over the last 24 hours or so. It was really painful for a few days – I couldn't drive.

I've been thinking about the fight and I am gutted. I'd worked so hard [that] I really believed I was going to win but I gave it everything. There's no point in me lying and saying I could have done this or that. On the night, I lost to the better man. I could say, 'If my ribs hadn't gone in round four, I could've moved better, done this or that,' but he hit me there and he meant to hit me there. He inflicted the damage, know what I mean? He hit me with a good shot and fractured the rib, so...

After the fight I went back to the hotel, got showered, went to see a few friends and family in a bar. I was getting hugged a lot, which was sore, and came back and had a bit of room service. I then got a few hours' sleep, which normally doesn't happen. I'm getting the urge to get back in the gym but I know I have to rest. When I can, I'm going to do some yoga and swimming to tick over – just to stay healthy, really. I've got a two-pack left – the other four have gone into hibernation!

Jorge's been in contact with Anthony since the fight and is keen to keep in touch. He left Manchester for London and has been enjoying the capital with his wife Michelle.

I saw him in the drug testing room after the fight and he asked me if I wanted to go for some food. It was nice of him but it's a hard thing to do when there are so many people who want to see you. Do I go and see friends and family or go out for food with a guy who's just snotted me! Ha ha …

I did say to him that at some point I'll be in Vegas and we'll catch up. Our paths will cross. He's sound.

Anthony's not the only Crolla to have been charmed by Team Linares. While New Moston's finest was preparing for the biggest fight of his life, his opponent was dining with his mother.

Me mam saw him Saturday morning. Jorge told me after the fight, although me mam had already told me obviously. She loves the boxing – she doesn't like me boxing – but she loves boxing. She went for breakfast with me auntie to San Carlo's in Selfridges. Me auntie said to me mam, 'Look who's at the table next to us? It's Linares and his wife!' Me mam goes over to the table to say hello and Michelle [Linares] goes, 'Hi, can we order…' She thought me mam was a waitress! Mam laughed and explained she wasn't the waitress and Michelle was dead apologetic. Me mam said, 'I've just come over to say hello because I'm Anthony's mother!' Then they were like, 'Oh my God, how crazy!' Jorge put some nice stuff on Instagram about families.

There's still been no break – apart from the rib – for the Crolla family. He's not got around to sorting the promised trip to Dubai. He will, but for the time being, he's been busy. Along with various TV and media commitments, the talks regarding his next opponent have seemingly gathered momentum.

A sixth Manchester derby, at this stage, looks unlikely due to promotional difficulties. Another name that won't go away is WBA super-lightweight champion Ricky Burns. The affable Scot has a unification fight with Julius Indongo in the diary and, regardless of the weight disparity, a domestic clash would be easy to make as both fight under the Matchroom banner.

I think my conditioning on fight night, how I got up after the knockdown, it shows I'm a lightweight. If a Ricky Burns fight makes sense, then obviously it's something I'd seriously consider. It's not like I'd be getting in with a giant light-welterweight. It's an option if it's a huge domestic showdown.

It's been a long time since we sparred, but I'd be confident. When we sparred, I wasn't half the fighter I am now. Personally, I think he was better under Billy Nelson. I don't know whether they'd bring the fight here or we'd go to the Hydro, but they'd turn it into the old England vs Scotland.

Obviously the Flanagan fight gets mentioned but his team have said a few silly things. His team put something out the other day about Manchester backing the wrong horse. I'm not going to bite back. If you think that's the classy thing to do, then do it. I don't want to lower myself to that level.

When Terry fights in a few weeks, I'll wish him all the best. I like his trainer Steve Maylett – I've known him a long time. I heard at a Conor McGregor thing that 'I'm not the kind of man who gets joy from another man's downfall.' I really like that. Why would I want another Manchester fighter to get beaten?

* * * * *

Joe's finished his first week back in the gym following the fight. In the wake of defeat to Linares, rumours have been flying around social media that Anthony's set to leave Joe. Callum Smith's been quick to respond to the claim on Twitter by accusing the person that posted it of simply fishing for retweets. Joe's not taken the bait.

'There are people who'd wish that [Crolla leaving], but there's not a cat in hell's chance. He's in good spirits, having a good laugh. He was out with his friends last night, his face has healed up.

'He'll have a couple of weeks off now but he won't totally switch off. A lot of fighters used to go away and do nothing, like Ricky [Hatton], but you can't do that. Crolla will keep his body switched on with yoga and strength and conditioning.

'I'm not too keen on him having too many more big, hard fights. But he's never going to go back to four- or six-rounders. Listen, I had a load of shit on Twitter after the fight. My missus Michelle told me not to look at it and a mate told me I was trending – all for the wrong reasons! I was shit this, shit that. But when people put that up, it doesn't bother me really. It's more the children and family seeing that crap.

'I don't take much heed of it. The way I look at it is this; if I send out a tweet now and make 20 grown men reply within five minutes, I think, "Wow! I've just affected your day. I control you without you even knowing."

A lot of the online criticism aimed at Joe was in relation to the Marcus Morrison fight. Many are accusing the trainer of allowing his fighter to take an unnecessary beating. Joe was grappling with his decision to keep him in the fight immediately afterwards. Had he done the right thing? With time to consider his actions, Joe's satisfied.

'I said to Mick [Williamson] in round eight, "Pass me the towel, but I might give him one more," but look, Marcus sent me a text the next day saying how gutted he was but that he didn't blame me one bit and if I'd stopped it he'd be feeling worse.

'Welborn was just as knackered as Marcus and Marcus carries the power to turn a fight around. Just because things don't go your own way, you don't just throw in the towel. Sometimes you need to see a bit of gut and as Marcus has said, it might be the best thing that's happened to him. He hasn't been through that experience before. He'll come back, have a couple of warm-ups and then we'll get the rematch on again.

'But that wasn't Marcus in there that night. Looking back, it was a bold move, a calculated risk that didn't quite work out.'

The Morrison and Crolla defeats on the same night have again left Joe a target for online critics.

'A lot of people like to say we've had a bad year. How's it a bad year when three of my kids have become millionaires this year? That's a success story. What you want for fighters when they come into the sport is to come, go out, and not be a slave to the mortgage.

'I think coaches have a hard time. They have their moments but it does get to you. I really do think with the mental health issues and everything, that it is something that we all need to talk about.

'It's very much like I was thinking with Crolla, when I was thinking of stopping it last week, I was thinking, "Do you know what? We've done well, we're not going to catch him, he's going to try and close the show here." So I said to Anthony, "Look, you've been dropped, you're behind here, why do you want to go and get punched in the head for another three minutes?" But you know, at the end of the 12 rounds, Crolla wasn't shattered. He could've done another three rounds, do you know what I mean?'

* * * * *

Anthony's not been able to train or even tick over due to the rib injury. He's not comfortable being away from the gym but he knows he needs a complete rest anyway and should be downing tools.

He's sat in his favourite café in Manchester's Northern Quarter – North Tea Power. It's next door to his yoga place, so he's a regular face for a post-stretch brew. He's discussing his leisure plans, which include a weekend in London to see West End show *Dreamgirls*, as he shovels down avocado and fried egg on brown toast.

As a result, he's missing United's trip to Sunderland and their forthcoming Europa League semi-final tie with Anderlecht. He's planning his trip to the final even though United are only at the quarter-final stage.

I might book Stockholm this week, just in case. Loads have done it. The flights are about 90-odd quid. Not the cheapest of places. It'll cost a fortune.

Talk switches to how hectic it's been in the days since the fight. Despite losing, his phone hasn't stopped with requests for media interviews and other demands on his time, including an invitation to visit his old school.

This is mad, but [points to a picture on his phone] he was the year below me. He's the PE teacher now and his dad was my PE teacher. They're both called John Rodgers. I went to the sports hall for the first time since 2003.

Mr Rodgers retired a little while ago but I gave him tickets for my [first] fight with Pérez. He said it'd be the best retirement present ever if I won. Obviously I bloody drew, but …

I was looking at my form picture from '98 and I was going through everyone. It was mad. There's such-a-body, and those two have got a kid together now. It was mad going through it all.

I wasn't a bad kid at school. I messed about a bit but all the teachers seemed to like me. Miss Ager, though, sometimes she used to give it me. I saw her for the first time since leaving and it was good to see her. I remember when she first came to the school, she knew I used to box a bit and she'd just come from a school in Liverpool [Archbishop Beck]. I remember her telling me how there was a family of boxing brothers in her old school called the Smiths!

The aim was to get five high passes back then and I got six. I was probably average or just above. I could've done so much better. I didn't revise or anything because all I was thinking about was boxing. It's paid off because boxing's been good to me, but I was one of the lucky ones. For 90 per cent of the lads not paying attention, it hasn't worked out for them.

But I had a focus. For example, at dinner, I used to pass out and say I was eating at home because I wanted to eat something healthy. I never ate at school – stupid really. Back then, I thought it was healthy to just eat a little bit of jacket potato. I'd be starving myself at school. Stupid.

After I'd finished at school, I went to Hopwood Hall College [Middleton], where they had a boxing academy. That made sense to me, but to be honest, I wasn't doing my course work. I was doing a bricklaying course and I'd come in every day dressed up – matching jeans and trainers and all that – while the other kids were coming in with their work-gear on looking for a day on the trowel.

The teacher said to me, 'This ain't for you, is it? You don't want to be a bricklayer, come in here,' so I'd just be in the office putting things in folders! He'd always say, 'If boxing doesn't work out, you should be running a bar on the beach – you're kidding no one!'

You got more hours in the gym if you did a bricklaying course rather than sport. Every day I was late for the class. But the teacher – and I can't remember his name – used to change the register for me every day so I got my education maintenance allowance. I passed me first year as a bricklayer but I never went into the second year. At that point, I was just doing bits of coaching – I've got my England boxing level 1 and a second's licence. I was in the corner for our William a few times.

* * * * *

Back from a weekend in London with friends, Crolla's buzzing about *Dreamgirls'*

I was watching the girl off Glee. Ah, what's she called? Not joking, she was unbelievable. The voice on her! She's a big name, ahh what is it! Amber Riley, that's it. She's amazing.

I thought I was going there undercover but some girl came up to me and said, 'Can I have a picture – my dad won't believe me that you're here!' She'd just phoned her dad to say I was there, but he didn't believe her! He said, 'Why would he be watching Dreamgirls?' *I love that kind of stuff, though.*

* * * * *

A new member of Team Gallagher has been officially announced. Natasha Jonas has held a press conference at the Hilton Hotel in Liverpool to confirm her plans to turn pro and train in Bolton.

She's already bedded into the gym on the quiet and admits she enjoys training with Crolla, for one reason or another.

'He's brilliant. He's a good lad, a good laugh and a good motivator. He keeps the gym smiling and always has some gossip to tell you. He keeps me up to date with all the reality TV shows. He loves it. His playlist with all the pop songs keeps me going.'

* * * * *

It's back to work for Anthony, but not in the gym. He's been booked by Sky Sports for punditry duty at the Burns vs Indongo fight in Glasgow. Friend and colleague Scott Cardle defends his British lightweight title on the undercard.

I had to get someone to do me tie. I'm 30 years of age and I had to get someone to make my tie! I get quite a bit of attention up here. Went out for a few drinks with the Matchroom lot and Adam Booth was there with Dave Coldwell. It was good, talking about boxing and hearing some funny stories. We were in this bar and quite a few people were coming up to us, a lot asking about a Burns fight.

Hopefully, Scottie can do this tonight. I know he's favourite, but it'll be a tricky fight. He's [Robbie Barrett] in good form, southpaw and tricky. It'll be interesting, but I think he can win tonight and get that Lonsdale Belt. No one's seen half of what Scottie Cardle can do.

I enjoy sparring him – apart from once when his bloody elbow went through me head guard! It was a weird one and it was the only time I've ever had to pull out of a fight. I was due to fight John Simpson, so John Murray stepped in at short notice and won – which paved the way for me and John [Murray] to fight.

The night at the SSE Hydro doesn't go as planned. There's disappointment for Scott, who loses a points decision and his belt to Robbie Barrett from Barnsley. It gets worse for the home crowd when Ricky Burns is outpointed by the awkward and largely unknown Namibian Julius Indongo.

Along with the results on the night, Anthony's choice of suit was eye-catching and set social media alight. A navy number with an almost tartan white fleck throughout.

I was winding me mates up. I was saying, 'Lads, I don't care what you say; I know it looks the bollocks!' They were all biting, know what I mean. I should've got a free suit off Hugo Boss with all the attention on that suit.

The man behind that suit was friend, sponsor and Morson CEO Ged Mason.

'After the Linares fight, I knew how upset he was so when I was in the Hugo Boss store in Manchester, there was this rascal of a suit, dark blue with a white pattern through it. The manager showed me a picture of Mayweather wearing it.

'I couldn't resist it, so I bought him this suit to cheer him up. I sent him down, saying I had a suit for him. I said if it's good enough for Mayweather, it's good enough for you. Lo and behold, he liked it and he wore it on Sky. He thinks I've set him up. He'll probably batter me now, but I think he looked cool. Only him and Mayweather could carry that suit off.'

* * * * *

It's the end of April and Crolla's back in the gym after a week-long holiday in Dubai. As is the norm, he's popped in to sign some gloves and assorted bits and pieces for the other fighters at the gym. Favours are asked from friends for items to auction for charity, so they all do their bit.

Looking refreshed and without a pound of weight added, Crolla bounces around the gym, smiling and chatting to the grafters.

It was good to get away and get some quality time with the family, which we rarely get. Jesse was an absolute rascal. He loved every minute of it. I don't know where he gets his energy from. He was running up sand dunes. All these other families with their kids [were] falling asleep and he's running

183

up steep dunes constantly. I think people were looking at us thinking, 'What are you giving him?' I think he might be a little runner.

It was good, though. It gave me a bit of time to reflect but mainly to switch off and recharge. I did think about the fight, but I've accepted it. I got beat off the better man. Sometimes you envisage things and think, 'What if I did this or that?' But it didn't happen, so I'll take my time and work at coming back better. I believe I will do.

He says his goodbyes to his pals before leaving through the back door. He jumps into his car and sets off for Bolton town centre, just a few minutes' drive away.

He's in good form, particularly as he was at the Etihad the previous night – 24 hours after arriving back from holiday – to watch United frustrate City in the Manchester derby. The match ended goalless with the City fans letting their feelings known about Jose Mourinho's tactics at the end of the 90 minutes.

I was in the seat next to the home fans. They were going ballistic. At the end, me mate Shaun was giving it 'Yes, yes!' just to wind them up. They were giving him loads back, shouting: 'You're celebrating a fucking draw! It's embarrassing!'

Anthony pulls into a pay and display on the edge of town and heads to the precinct. Costa Coffee, not his favourite, but the nearest, is the venue. He sits with a latte, a hot cross bun and strawberry jam.

Talk turns to Joshua vs Klitschko. He's heading down to Wembley to take in the fight, along with making an appearance at a pre-fight event.

I'm not sitting on the fence. If I'm really pushed, the timing might be right and Joshua wins. But, if Klitschko's got anything left, then I think he wins. The more I see of Klitschko, the more I'm going with him. He seems very relaxed.

With Fury, he lost that fight before he got in the ring. I remember watching it in my house with my mate and I said, 'He does not want to be there.' They were showing Klitschko wrapping his hands on his own. He's a really intelligent man and I think the build-up got to him.

In the build-up, he was watching his 6ft 9in opponent rolling around the floor dressed as Batman. Klitschko's thinking, 'What the ... ?' He couldn't get his head around it. When Fury came in a few minutes later pretending he was late because of the traffic, Klitschko must have thought, 'Get me out of here!' I don't think it's like that with Joshua.

Talk of big fights inevitably leads Crolla to thoughts of a return and he can't help but itch to get back in the gym. He has no choice but to stay rested for the time being, though.

When I was in the gym before, I just wanted to start shadow boxing. I know I can't go back to the gym yet, but even when I was over there in Dubai I wanted to do a bit [of training]. It's been four weeks and the rib isn't 100 per cent, but I need a shoulder X-ray now. It's been a niggle for a while – it's the injury Abbas was working on before the fight. We'll see what the X-ray shows. There are certain movements I can't do. In terms of the next fight, it's all up in the air. I wouldn't say no to Vegas and there's been talk of Monaco. I don't know, but I'm planning to stay at lightweight.

A move to super-lightweight was mooted as a quick route to another world title and the kudos of potentially winning a belt in a different division. That only made sense if Ricky Burns could claim victory over Julius Indongo. That didn't happen.

I was only thinking of stepping up if the Burns fight was an option, but obviously that isn't now. When I was in Scotland, before the fight, everyone was asking me about me and Ricky.

Anthony's been in touch with Joe while he's been away from the team, but a break following an intensive training camp is no bad thing.

At the moment we can kind of be mates, that sort of thing. Towards the end of the camp and when it's all finished, you don't want to speak to each other for a while. Not in any bad sense, but he's also probably thinking he doesn't have to babysit me for a bit – I'm a bit laid-back!

It was funny, though. Rumours started after the fight that I was leaving Joe. Someone asked me. I just said no, not at all, but people just like to talk. But that's rumours. I've heard some whoppers!

I've been knocked out in sparring; I've knocked people out in sparring. I remember once being asked about chinning Stephen Smith? Apparently Scottie Cardle chinned me in sparring yet we hadn't even sparred. These things do the rounds. Who would start these? There are some sad people. For a gladiator sport, the amount of bitching and gossip that goes on is embarrassing.

The next opponent is still up in the air. Joe's busy in the gym with the other fighters, but talks have started and names suggested.

'We're still looking at Vegas in September or Monaco in November. It depends what the Vegas one is. If it's a six- or eight-rounder, we might have both. The Burns fight is still there. But I want him to take his fans to Vegas. I think Golden Boy could shove him on an undercard. They know he brings fans, which would help to pay for his purse. It'd be good.'

Flanagan?

'That won't happen. It'll never, ever happen. After the last fight [Crolla vs Linares II] they made it clear that Crolla isn't on their agenda. They say Crolla's just there for popularity stakes while they're about winning fights and titles. All right then, off you go!

'At the end of the day, Terry Flanagan still needs Crolla for his money fight, but they've binned the fight off, so great!'

* * * * *

Anthony's enjoyed another weekend in London, not for a musical this time, but the big heavyweight clash at Wembley Stadium. It was a chance to catch up with his old mate Scott Quigg, who was having his first fight with Freddie Roach on the undercard. Crolla walked out as part of Team Quigg, Scott winning on points against Viorel Simion.

His old foe Jorge Linares was also present and he had been trying to organise a reunion that was proving tricky.

We were meant to be meeting up but it was madness at Wembley. He'd been moved from where he was when he was watching the Luke Campbell vs Darleys Pérez fight. I couldn't get up to where he was.

I also just missed him at the hotel – the Hilton next door. I'd been in there after the fight but I wasn't stopping over. I was driving home. He wanted to meet the next day but obviously I couldn't.

I ended up watching the main event with Freddie [Roach]. He said to me that Linares was in the top three fighters he'd trained. That was a big thing for me for him to say that. It was good talking to him and he was really complimentary about me.

What a main event, though? What a fight! Joshua let a few shots go and he was exhausted. I was watching, thinking, 'There's no way he can win this!' But for him to pull it around and do what he did – all credit. You know the way this country is – he was one or two shots away from everyone mocking him on social media.

I think Klitschko's dominated so many fights behind the jab and it was comfortable for him. But he got caught – and what a shot! It was better than any other result. If Joshua had blown him away, then Klitschko would've been an old man. But as it was, Klitschko looked great and for Anthony to show that heart ... wow! I've had situations where I've found a second wind, but nothing like that. He was gone, hurt, exhausted. Fair play to him.

* * * * *

It's the middle of May and Crolla's first official day back in the gym. The rib now fully healed, he's back in amongst it and Joe's happy to have him back.

'Butler's in, Natasha's in, the Smiths are in – Beefy [Liam] showed his face today as well – and Marcus had his first day back a couple of days ago.

'Marcus is all right; hopefully we'll get him out on the show in Newcastle in June. I don't want him sitting around and dwelling on it [defeat], I want him to get out, get on the horse and get a win. He's had a little break with the missus and I just want him to get a win before the end of the season. I want him going into the new season talking about a win as his last fight. We'll see how he comes back now.'

Joe's particularly pleased today because his recent recruit Natasha has been featured prominently in *The Times*. The piece by Sarah Shephard details the boxer's life, balancing training with being a mum along with all the other hopes and fears every fighter deals with.

'For *The Times* do a full page on her is unbelievable. Natasha's on fire, she's lost a load of weight and looks a million dollars. She can't wait to get going.'

It was good to get back in and catch up with the lads – and the girls! Natasha's looking great. I was in there looking round and thinking, 'Ahh, I've missed this place! I've missed sunny Bolton!' It's really good to be back. It sounds daft, but I can't wait to get back in camp.

I've been doing bits, ticking over, but the rib injury restricted me. I can punch now, although certain shots trouble me. I can't wait to get the shoulder sorted.

CHAPTER 7

I Love Manchester

22.05.17

It's late on a Monday night in May. News is filtering through of an explosion following an Ariana Grande concert at the Manchester Arena. Social media goes into overdrive as more details of the devastation are revealed.

Manchester-born Salman Abedi, 22, detonated a suicide bomb as people were leaving the concert shortly after 10.30pm. There were 20,000 gathered for the gig – many of them children – with the explosion taking place as people streamed into the arena foyer.

Everyone who was awake and following the horrific events on phones and TV can recall the moment they realised this was a terrible point in the city's history. A sort of JFK moment for Manchester.

I was on social media and saw reports of an explosion, then I put Sky News on and it came on across the bottom of the screen. I just thought, 'Shit, I hope everyone's OK.' Then I remembered that I had cousins at the concert.

I rang my cousin, Leanne, because I knew she was there with her little girl. She said they were OK and she told me she'd seen my other cousin Leah, who's from the other side of the family. She'd spotted Leah in a car as they were driving away from the arena, so they were all OK.

Our Will then phoned me to see if I'd heard about Leah. She's 17 and there's only about six months between Leah and Will, so they're very close. Thankfully, she was OK but she was so lucky. On her way out of the arena, she was knocked over by a body. A body flew into her. When she was on the floor, she looked to her right and there was another body split in half. There were limbs everywhere. She heard a bang and was then knocked to the floor. I can't get me head round it.

Will went straight round to see her. She was covered in blood and very shook up. It'll never leave her. She's our Darren's [uncle] daughter. I went round to see her the day after. Her mum called me into another room and was telling me how they'd had to clean her up when she got home. She had to see a doctor and get tested for hepatitis and all that.

She showed me her studded leather jacket. It had human flesh all over it. It was like something out of a horror story. Fucking hell, you can't imagine it. She was literally five seconds from dying.

I was telling Leah that her and her mate were the luckiest people in the world. They could very easily be dead. What a week they had, though. On the Friday [before Monday's concert], Darren's wife, Jane, found out she had throat cancer. It's like, fuck me! It's positive and treatable but what a few days they had. It's was Darren's 50th as well.

I just can't work it out. I've had so many fights there but where the bomb went off, I don't go in or out that way. It feels weird because I know all my mates go in that way. I go in the delivery side of the arena. It's madness what's happened.

* * * * *

Manchester was in a state of shock. Vigils were held; Tony Walsh recited his emotive poem 'This is the Place' as everybody stood together in defiance. Mancunians tried to go about their business as normally as possible.

Every facet of society was affected, even football. Less than two days after the attack, Manchester United were taking on Ajax in the Europa League Final in Stockholm. There was debate as to whether it should go ahead, but UEFA gave it the green light, so with heavy hearts the show went on.

Anthony's gamble on cheap flights to the Swedish capital had worked out well, but his excitement had diminished.

It was quiet in the airport and getting on the plane. Normally, everyone's on the beer and it's all mad and giddy. The day was subdued after what had happened. I saw loads of people I knew, but it was a strange day. It seemed weird. I'd been really looking forward to it but when I was getting on the plane I was thinking, 'I'm not arsed.'

We had a good day and a good walk around Stockholm – went off to some areas away from the crowds. Some random stuff going on. But I didn't let me hair down, didn't have a drink.

When we got into the stadium, it was brilliant with all the Manchester chants and everything. The singing for Manchester – it gave you goosebumps. We all knew even the blues were up for us, just to give Manchester something to smile about. It was one of those times when we could all put football aside.

Obviously we won and there was a big celebration, but it was a strange one. It was for Manchester and there's no prouder Mancunian than me.

* * * * *

It's nearly 3.30pm on Friday afternoon and Anthony's parked on Liverpool Road, Castlefield in Manchester city centre. It's that rare thing – a blisteringly hot Manchester spring day.

He's sat chatting in his car when he takes a call from a BBC Five Live producer. He's been asked to do an interview and needs to get to Albert Square to meet up with their drive team. The area is extra busy with road closures due to the Great CityGames, so a short distance has become something of a headache. He fiddles with the satnav to work out how best to solve the problem. Northern Quarter car park is a bit round the houses but his favourite tea shop is there. He'll still have time for a pre-interview brew, so he heads towards the Mancunian Way.

The interview has been set up to cover Anthony's involvement in the Great Manchester Run, which takes place on Sunday, but also his cousin's traumatic experience at the arena.

Walking through Piccadilly Gardens en route to Albert Square and his media commitments, a tall lad with a dark brown beard almost staggers into Crolla. He's younger than the straggly facial hair and haunted expression would suggest – maybe 20 – and wearing an adidas black tracksuit top with black jeans halfway down his legs. It's a sad sight.

Bad news that 'spice', innit? Very sad. Horrible stuff.

On arrival at the square, Crolla makes contact with the BBC and waits by an impressive pole vault – part of the Great CityGames – which has been set up directly outside the town hall. Local people have come out to support the event. It's been that way on each day since Monday night – Mancunians turning up for vigils, or any other gathering, to show togetherness and defiance.

Before competition begins, there's a call from the MC for a minute's silence to remember those who died in the arena atrocity. After a round of applause, the athletics get under way and Anna Foster from Five Live turns up to interview Anthony live for their drive programme. Recent events naturally dominate the conversation.

It's heartbreaking; the only positive really is the goodness that's come out of it. The city's showed its strength since the tragic event. Honestly, I'm the proudest Mancunian there is, but even more so now. You know the poem [Tony Walsh – 'This is the Place'], people coming from all over to show support?

I was in Stockholm and there were messages from our rivals Manchester City and Liverpool, who wanted us to win. Just because it might bring a little bit of joy.

The interview turns to Anthony's involvement in the Great Manchester Run – a 10km race around the city – and an event he's been a big supporter of. As usual, he'll be heading up a Team Crolla select band of participants, raising money for autism and victims of the bomb. The fundraising effort has been cranked up a notch.

I know I'll be putting more of my gear up for auction over the internet and social media and I know a few of the other fighters will do the same. I'm hopeful we can raise some good money because there are some great people out there who want to buy sweaty shorts and sweaty gloves! It's crazy! It's stuff that's been worn in world title fights. There are some very keen collectors out there and what better causes could it go to?

BBC done, it's on to Key 103 and reporter Justin Mottershead, who's been waiting patiently to grab a few minutes with Crolla.

All media interviews done, all requests taken care of, now it's on to his friend and former foe John Murray's gym in Reddish to sign some gloves for a charity event. Just part of the gig.

* * * * *

It's the summer silly season and the Twitter world has been alive with news of an imminent deal for an Anthony Crolla vs Ricky Burns fight. Burns has tweeted his approval, Anthony's responded in similar fashion – if the deal is right. There are still plenty of issues to sort out, but it's a proposition that appeals to both men and fight fans reckon it'd be a classic.

The fight was previously mooted ahead of the Burns vs Indongo clash. That didn't go to script so no world titles on the line, but no belts would be needed for a domestic clash involving two extremely popular characters.

There'd be no needle whatsoever, more love than war during any press build-up, but the endearing, smiley nature of both lads would give it a certain unique selling point. When all's said and done, it's two former world champions, England vs Scotland, both Matchroom fighters who fight on Sky Sports. No barriers.

Look, it's a fight I'd like if it all makes sense. I won't be moving up and I think he'll be happy to come down to lightweight so that's OK. Whether it's Manchester or Glasgow, it'll sell out. I reckon it'll be Manchester because you can get more in. He'll bring a right few fans down so it'll be a great atmosphere.

It's a hard fight obviously, a 50/50, but I'd rather have a good fight like that than do a ten-rounder against someone I'm supposed to beat up.

You could say he was cold last time out against Indongo, who was awkward and better than anyone thought he was going to be. It's hard to know if it was an off-night or if Ricky's lost form.

It's the night before Ohara Davies takes on Josh Taylor, two good super-lightweight prospects putting their '0' on the line. Davies has also had his say about the prospective Crolla vs Burns bout – a contest he'd like to see. The occasionally brash Londoner is respectful to both men, but Crolla's also seen Josh at close quarters and fancies the Scot to do the job.

It's a close call – Ohara has deceivingly long arms. I remember when I first sparred him, I came out of my corner and he hit me with a jab and I was thinking, 'How's he hit me from there?' Eddie Hearn asked me what I thought of him and I said I thought he had real potential. He was a bit raw back then, but he spends his life in the gym and fighters like that can only get better.

I watched Josh spar in the Wild Card in LA. He was with his club team ahead of the Commonwealth Games in Glasgow. I remember he handled a kid who'd been giving everyone real trouble. He did very well and I thought he was a very smart and skilled lad. He has that GB pedigree and obviously he fought in the World Series of Boxing so had that kind of pro education before turning over. I like him and I just give him the edge over Davies.

Whoever loses, though, they can of course come back, it's not the end of the world. Two good kids, so it's a great fight from that point of view.

* * * * *

While Crolla's been training in the miserable Manchester weather, Joe Gallagher's in Monaco with Callum Smith, who's signed up for the World Boxing Super Series in the super-middleweight division.

Joe Facetimed me, you know, by mistake! That's what he said. He meant to phone but Facetimed instead. Funny that, as he was sat by a pool in some kind of beach club. Four days he's there! All expenses paid!

Eddie Hearn's already said that if they do a lightweight version, I'm in it, if only for the trip!

It's not all been doom and gloom for Anthony. He's still buzzing after getting the chance to take on a legend in one of his favourite sports.

It was at the Airport Inn in Wilmslow. I was asked to do a fundraiser for autism and throw a few darts with Phil Taylor. John [Murray] was there, Phil Bardsley [footballer] and Al Foran [impressionist] – he's a really good lad and a Red as well.

I beat the Power! Well, I got a bit of help with about 100 knocked off my score. I got a go at the double – you've got to take your chances, haven't you? Phil was just laughing his head off. I love the darts, me. When I was a little kid, me grandad would have us all playing a game of darts on a Sunday.

I've watched the darts for years and not many people get the chance to play against a legend. Then [they] knocked a few hundred off John's score as well, but I was the only one who beat him!

* * * * *

It's a grey and miserable Monday morning in Bolton. There are fewer cars and vans than normal parked in the small industrial estate. Joe's Audi's parked right outside the back door of the gym.

Through the first door and into the 'community' gym – there's no sign of life, although the same cannot be said of the adjoining room. The distinctive cry of men grunting and yelling whilst hitting heavy bags, the bags swinging, causing the chains that hold them to creak and squeak.

Inside the second door, working those bags, is the tall, topless Callum Smith, black cap turned backwards. Next in sight is Anthony Crolla alongside Paul Butler and Scott Cardle – the latter's first day back in the gym following his Easter weekend loss to Robbie Barrett three months ago. Joe's there too, of course, shouting instructions. 'Jab! One-twos! Come on! Liven it up!' All this played out to a musical backdrop of Gabrielle's 90s hit 'Dreams' – a seemingly never-ending remix dance version.

For once, the huge heater that normally pumps out mercilessly hot air is switched off. It makes for a more pleasant environment, although there's still plenty of sweat dripping from the fighters to the matted floor.

Every three minutes, Joe shouts 'change' and they move around the bags. So it goes on until the routines change to (JCB) tyre flips, sledgehammer on tyre and medicine ball throws in the ring.

Joe pipes up: 'Hope you appreciate you're watching four former British champions and two former world champions train!'

Floor work follows, with the session ending with chin-ups, sit-ups and press-ups. Cardle is last on the mat, his soaking black T-shirt clinging to his now slightly fuller figure. Butler and Smith sit in the ring, laughing down at him as he grunts and strains to complete his reps. Callum shouts, 'Welcome back' as Paul chuckles again.

Natasha Jonas, Marcus Morrison and Callum Johnson are officially in camp but not in Bolton today. Callum and Marcus have a confirmed date in the diary – Saturday, 29 July at Bowlers Exhibition Centre against opponents to be arranged.

It's just ten days since Marcus suffered his second career defeat on the bounce in what should've been a fairly straightforward contest against Tyan Booth in Derby. The idea was to get the Welborn defeat out his system and finish the season with a win. It didn't work out that way, as Joe explained.

'Just got nicked on the scorecards on the night. We got let down in Newcastle the week before [fight cancelled], so we got this fight. We thought he'd nick it, but he didn't, so there it is, night night. I said to Marcus, "Don't worry about it, it's four rounds and we crack on to the next one."

'I said, "Listen, you can sit and sulk about it, but it doesn't matter. Look at Crolla!" It doesn't mean anything. He got nicked on points, he's got to work on it, and it's all part of learning.'

At this point, Scott Cardle walks out of the changing room with just a beige towel around his waist. He's trying to locate the scales. They're in a black bag next to the static bikes on the right-hand side of the ring. He quickly sets up the kit as Joe makes his way over.

'Shall we have a guess?' says Joe. Cardle drops the towel while Joe predicts 11st 3lbs. A brief pause, the digital screen settles at the weight. It's just shy of 11st 4lbs. Scott's a pound lighter than when he went on holiday. He's happy enough with that.

Cardle heads back to the changing room while talk turns to Crolla's next move. A fight with Burns has been on the cards for a while, but Josh Taylor's very impressive demolition of Ohara Davies may have added a different dimension.

As I thought, Taylor was just too complete for Davies. He's a very good fighter. He moved well, worked well on the inside, can whip the body shots in and counters well. The knockdown was a belter.

It's a weird one with Davies. He did sort of quit in a way but he give it a right go as well. But I was really impressed with Taylor – and he now wants the Burns fight!

Taylor made it clear he wants an all-Scottish affair, but Ricky was non-committal ringside after the fight. Joe has his own thoughts on the whole situation.

'Ricky Burns walked into Eddie Hearn's office two months ago and said, "I want to fight Anthony Crolla." They were talking about it back then, but let's not forget the history in this. Twice we wanted a world title fight with him [Burns] and they said we're not world class.

They want a pension fight now and I don't feel Anthony has to be in that type of do-or-die fight. There's plenty of mileage still on the clock for Anthony, there's not for Ricky Burns. Why do we want to put ourselves in that position? His career's finished. He'll never fight for a world title again, but Anthony's career isn't finished.

'I've said, "Here's an amount, here's a figure." Pay that and I can't stop Anthony going and earning that. I've told Eddie that if we can't do that purse, then there's no fight.

'Last year we were in Monte Carlo and Eddie was saying that if Anthony lost to Linares, then this would be ideal to bring Anthony back. He said it again this year that we'd get Anthony somebody in Monte Carlo. Golovkin's fought there a few times, there's good money there and it doesn't have to be a name.

'If you look at it, Scott Quigg fought in a big fight and lost, Martin Murray fought in a big fight and lost – all the headline acts lost, but they all come back with a touch-up. Anthony Crolla, after his last five hard fights, they're on about throwing him into another life or death. Why? If there's any kid that deserves a touch-up coming back, then it's Anthony.

'I don't think it necessarily has to be a name for the Manchester Arena. Anthony could do six or seven thousand [tickets] against an also-ran. But I'd like Anthony to fight in Monte Carlo, no pressure selling tickets, just train then go over there with a few of his fans – 20, 50 or 100. It is what it is. He goes there, gets a win and we come back to the arena in March next year.

'That lightweight title, by the end of the year, the divisions are all going to be mixed up. I think Linares will move up, Garcia will move up, so it's just a case of getting Anthony a win so we can push him up the ratings. When titles then become vacant, he's in position. Anthony needs a win.'

Crolla's showered and changed into standard post-training gear of trainers, jeans, T-shirt, bomber jacket and the obligatory baseball cap. He's ready for a brew, so it's off to Starbucks in the Bolton Arndale.

He climbs into his Merc, which is parked close to the door. With the ignition on, the radio blares 'Human' by Rag 'n' Bone Man. He turns it down and sets off on the short drive, reflecting on another session in the bag.

I feel good. It's good to be in there [gym]. I've lost a bit of weight, but for a few weeks there I went a bit soft, a bit tubby. I wasn't bad, but just a bit heavy. I'll go to the gym near us later and then I'll go to Martin tomorrow.

Joe's put across his views about the next challenge – but is it an opinion Anthony shares?

I do get Joe's point. Lose that fight [Ricky Burns] and it's a long old road back. Listen, I don't think I would lose that fight but you have to be a realist and anything can happen in a fight.

At the same time, and I will be sitting down and chatting more with Joe, I think about the Monaco route and I don't think I can be arsed fighting there. I like being in meaningful fights. Do I want to just beat someone up for ten rounds, fighting in front of a few hundred people? Look, if they can match the figure for Burns, then sound.

Once parked in the multi-storey – and it takes a while – it's a short walk, a couple of flights of stairs and a stride through the mall to the venue. When the drinks arrive, Crolla leans back and stirs his latte as talk drifts to other bits of gossip and boxing news.

His long-touted Manchester rival Terry Flanagan was a guest at the recent centenary celebrations at Collyhurst and Moston Boxing Club – an event Crolla missed due to being on Stephen Smith's stag do in Ibiza.

I was the only Manc out of 28! Jamie Carragher was on the do as well – proper sound lad. He had a right go at it and was putting the bottles of lager away!

Flanagan, like Crolla, is constantly asked about their potential match-up. Like Anthony, he's not keen on getting involved in any chit-chat. He's been using his energy to try and land a unification fight with Jorge Linares.

I saw a picture of Terry with his belt at the event. I was sorry I couldn't make it – Tommy [McDonagh] had been on to me. I can understand Terry wanting to fight Jorge – if they can make that happen. Actually, I'm going to be seeing Jorge this weekend. I need to text him.

I'm working the Eubank vs Abraham fight for ITV on Saturday, and Jorge's living down there now for a few months. Ismael Salas is going to train

David Haye so Linares is over too and living in the Park Plaza. I wouldn't mind going in the gym, not sparring, but just going in there for a few days. Joe would be cool with it. It's not like I'd be going down there to train with Salas, who I do think is a great coach, by the way.

I'm looking forward to going down there to work on the TV anyway. Doing ITV is new for me – it was Richard Poxon who got me involved. He's always been really sound with me.

When I had the accident [burglary incident], I remember he sorted a Watt bike to be dropped at my house. I thought that was a nice touch. He told me the bike would do me the world of good but that if I didn't want to use it, just let him know and he'd come and get it. I just thought, 'fair play'.

Working on the ITV show will also put Anthony ringside to analyse his recent sparring partner Anto Cacace. The Belfast man is challenging Martin J Ward for his British super-featherweight belt.

Carl Frampton said Anto's the most talented kid he's ever trained with. He is very talented but I don't think he was that fit when he came over and was sparring me. He's a great lad as well.

He deserves his chance. He used to work weekends at a pizza place, driving around delivering pizzas on a Friday and a Saturday night. Martin Ward seems sound too, but Anto's a great lad and I really hope he does it.

I nearly boxed Martin's brother when I was 16 or 17. Bobby beat Amir [Khan] in a schoolboy final. He was good, Bobby. I was going to box him in a quarter-final. I knew that if I beat him, I was either going to go to the world juniors or the European juniors – can't remember which one. But anyway, I'd never been as fit in all my life. I was confident I was going to beat him. I felt brilliant and as I was putting my boots on, the officials called me over to tell me my medical card had run out!

My old amateur coach at the time was recovering from cancer and he'd just taken his eye off the ball and that was it. I was heartbroken, devastated for days. Bobby went on to beat Liam Walsh in the final.

Anthony's scrolling down on his phone in between sips of his coffee. He's looking for bits of United news on Twitter. There's a link to a piece about Wayne Rooney leaving Old Trafford for his boyhood club Everton.

Wayne's sound. He's a really good lad. I knew he was going, but I was half-gutted when he went. I am happy with Lukaku [new United signing], though. He's a big powerhouse, a big, strong centre-forward who's done it in the Premier League. I think he'll be a success. He's young as well.

People argue about the fee, but it doesn't really matter. He's going to be successful and that's the main thing. But him and Pogba and the daft handshakes! When do you get a bit old to be doing that? Can you imagine Roy Keane if they were doing that in front of him? He'd clout them. It'd be brilliant!

Brew time over, Anthony heads back to his car and on to the second training session of the day. The work is monotonous, the routine tedious, but luckily there's always a bright light on the horizon.

It's all training for me now at the minute, but I do have the theatre to look forward to. I'm going to see Sister Act *at the Palace next week. Alexandra Burke's in it – looking forward to it. She was in The Bodyguard and I went to watch that. It's me favourite, that one, I loved it. More theatre for me! I worry about myself at times! I'm not going to lie, though, I proper enjoy it!*

The only other thing I do is watch reality TV! I watch utter shite. I watch terrible, terrible television like Ex on the beach. *I laugh and cringe, but I love it. I watch* Made in Chelsea *all of that. I'm shocking, absolutely shocking.*

* * * * *

Ahead of his TV obligations at the Eubank vs Abraham fight, Anthony has an eye on attending the Mayweather vs McGregor, London leg of the world tour to promote their forthcoming fight in Las Vegas. The rights and wrongs of the MMA vs boxing hybrid fight have inspired debate throughout combat sport and beyond. There has largely been negativity with a sprinkling of curiosity from the boxing community. Some have argued it puts boxing in the media spotlight and therefore it's a good thing. Very few, though, have given it any credence whatsoever as a contest. Many MMA fans think their man can pull off the impossible.

On the Friday, I ended up front row for the Mayweather vs McGregor presser. I got given a ticket and then ITV, who were filming it, said they wanted to interview me at the venue, so I got a better seat. Then, the MC was speaking to people from the MMA world and the boxing world in the ring, and he wanted to speak to me in the ring, so I got upgraded to front row. I was sat there next to Chase & Status [drum and bass duo].

It was mad. I was stopping in the hotel where Mayweather was staying. A few of his girls were staying on my floor! McGregor was meant to be in the hotel but I didn't see him.

Security was mental. It's turned into a big circus but then, sitting front row, it was a good laugh. I was staying right next door to Wembley, so it would've been daft not to go.

I caught up with Jorge at the Eubank fight on Saturday night. He's looking well. He was there with his missus. It was good and it was a decent show. Abraham was the perfect opponent – very smart matchmaking. Eubank on points was just buying money! I've heard this Turk [Avni Yildirim] he's got next is decent.

Anthony's immediate fight future still hasn't been settled. A Burns fight still seems to have momentum and all should become clear very soon.

Meeting Eddie [Hearn] on Monday, so should know what's happening next week. He's not mega-pushing me against Burns, but you can see that that's the fight he wants.

Nothing's changed from my point of view. October 7 in Manchester would be the date. There are still options with Monaco or Vegas in November. Vegas would be on the Joshua v Klitschko undercard and it'd be great to fight in Vegas, but if it's for less than half the money, what do you do? I've got to weigh it up.

* * * * *

Regardless of the next opponent, Anthony has settled into a training regime and is living the life, a life he rarely slips out of in any case. He even stayed in bed and didn't get up in the early hours to watch the first ever overseas Manchester derby. United and City met in a pre-season friendly in Houston, Texas.

He's recorded the game and intends to watch it after returning home from his first gym session of the day. This afternoon, he'll head to Wigan to do a session with Martin Cullen. He's not going straight home afterwards; he's accepted an offer to take in Wigan Warriors vs Leeds Rhinos.

Tough sport, rugby league. Union is as well. Tough. If Jesse goes to an Oldham school, he'll play rugby there. I wouldn't mind getting him into rugby. He'll be a little whippet. We'll have to get some beef on his legs, though!

A few of the Wigan lads invited me down to watch in the hospitality – some of them train in the gym with Martin and they're good lads. I thought I should go before I get into camp. I asked Martin if he'd like to.

I'm in a good place to start camp – it wouldn't take me ten or 12 weeks to get fit. I'm a little bit soft but I'm within a stone.

Conditioning session at the gym completed, Anthony's sat in the viewing area above the main gym. There's a young work experience lad here to interview him. Ray Davidson, 15, is a keen amateur boxer from Timperley ABC. Anthony knows his dad Mark, who's head coach at the club. Ray wants to know if Anthony would like Jesse to follow his path into the sport.

You know what? A lot of people would think I'm like, 'Yeah, get him into boxing; he'll be a little champ!' Nah, it'd be my worst nightmare. I really hope he doesn't. He's only three, so of course it's way too early, but when I'm training the kids sometimes [at Fox ABC] he loves coming in. He runs up to the bags, and all that. Look, I certainly won't encourage it, but if he wants to do it, then I'll let him.

I just wouldn't want all the pressure and expectations on him. I've seen it with my little brother [Will]. When he was younger, he had a lot of pressure. Jesse would have it worse. Look at Ricky Hatton's son [Campbell]. He's doing well, but when he first came into boxing I remember him fighting some lad in his second fight and this lad brought two coaches [of fans] down with him! It's probably quite intimidating for a 12-year-old kid when there are 100 people to watch him.

Listen, boxing's been very good to me but I'd much rather Jesse made his own way in a different sport. Hopefully it's in sport, but if not, in whatever he wants to do. Fran doesn't mind me boxing, but she wouldn't be mad on him boxing. She'd probably like him to do the training for confidence. I'd like him to do the training for that myself, but then my worry is that he'll end up OK at it. If he stands out a bit, then all of sudden he wants to box and, bang, it's too late.

I'd like him to do a bit. You don't want him getting knocked around at school. You've got to stand up for yourself, but that's the dilemma.

CHAPTER 8

Date in the Diary

T HE future is clear: the next Crolla fight has been announced. Any ideas of fighting in Vegas were ended following Wladimir Klitschko's retirement. There won't be a rematch with Anthony Joshua and so no place on an undercard for Anthony. Monaco was still an option, but after prolonged negotiations, a clash with Ricky Burns has now been signed and sealed. In what's being labelled a 'must-win' all-British showdown, the fight is set for Manchester on Saturday, 7 October.

The winner will get back in line for another shot at a world title, but the loser faces a long road back or, potentially, nowhere to go.

Matchroom has called a press conference to announce the fight, with the favoured Halle Suite at the Radisson Blu once again playing host. Eddie Hearn chairs the meeting and after a brief scene-setter he throws to Charlie Sims, Ricky's manager and son of his trainer Tony Sims.

Charlie talks of a potential 'fight of the year' and again refers to it as a must-win bout.

Ricky Burns, in black training gear with matching baseball cap, is sat to Hearn's left and gives his thoughts on the fight.

'It's the first time I'll be fighting in Manchester and I'm sure it'll be a great night for the fans. I've so much respect for Anthony, he's a great fighter, but this is going to be a great fight. I'm really looking forward to getting in there.

'Obviously it's back down at lightweight. I'd been speaking about it before – Tony wasn't too keen on it, but I know I can do it properly and this fight can lead to bigger things.

'This fight was even spoken about when we were both competing at super-feather. We're both coming back after a loss, so this is the perfect fight for us.

'I know I'll have a good crowd coming down – the boxing fans are going to win with this. The two of us are going to lay it all on the line and the best man will win.'

Hearn picks up again and speaks of the two similar characters on the top table. Crolla, flanked on the right and smartly turned out in dark three-piece suit, concurs with his rival.

It's a no-brainer. I think me and Ricky are cut from the same cloth and we both fought the top fighters in the world for the last few years. We probably could have had a nice easy fight, a bit of a touch, but we're real fighters and this is what we want. There's so much on the line. The winner is almost guaranteed a world title fight.

There's not going to be too much trash-talking, A Gloves Are Off *would be pretty painful with us both! This doesn't need that. Everyone in boxing knows this will be a proper fight. We both have the best fans in British boxing and Ricky will bring huge support, as will the lads on the undercard.*

The amount of people who come up to me in the street and ask, 'When are we back at the arena?' There was no way it was going to be anywhere else and I'm just glad it can be against a great fighter like Ricky, who'll bring the best out of us. It's a fight I can't wait for.

Both of us have never been lacking in digging deep. The winner will have to dig deep, something I'm prepared to do and Ricky will too. At some point, we'll meet in the middle of the ring, exchange blows and that's when the roof on that arena will come off. We'll go to war and I'm very confident it will be tough, but it will be a fight I'll win and move on.

Scott Quigg is standing at the back of the room, behind the line of TV crews. He's there to support his old gym pal and is standing alone in his grey adidas tracksuit, minding his own business. He's due to fight again in November and is back in the UK due to visa stipulations.

'It's about sorting my visa out. If I get it sorted, I can be there [USA] for three years at a time. At the minute, I can go there for three months but then I have to leave for three months. That's why I'm back here now. Being in and around that gym and that environment, you're learning so much. That's where I want to be, especially at this stage of my career with two or three years left. We've got to give it everything and make the most of it.

'I'm going back to LA in a couple of weeks for ten weeks. The date I've been given provisionally is November 4 in Monte Carlo. There's another option, depending on where Joshua fights, but it'd be a week later. Either way, that's when I'm going to be fighting.

'Obviously, I want the biggest fights possible. Santa Cruz is fighting Mares, Frampton's just had a fight fall through, there's Valdez or Selby. They're the fights we want to make, but at the minute they're not available. For Selby, that's a fight that can be made depending on where he wants to go next. I'm not being forced upon him as a mandatory, but these are the kind of fights I want. I want to stay active, keep improving under Freddie [Roach], so if I have to have another fight before a big fight, the way I look at it is it's just giving us more time to gel.

'I don't know if Frampton has to take care of an obligation to fight Gutierrez [the original contest was cancelled due to a freak Gutierrez shower injury] – I'm not sure about the contract – but it's a fight I've always wanted. I believe I can beat him [Frampton] and while I don't think it'll happen this year, it could definitely happen next year. Hopefully that fight can be made, so we can settle the score once and for all.

'The [featherweight] division's packed. I'm lucky to be around at this time. If you look at the top five in all the governing bodies, all the top names, there are great fights to be made. Moving to train with Freddie, the excitement is all new and fresh. I can't wait to get back out there. The last camp was one of the best camps I've had. I was happy to be in a different environment, [a] different part of the world to train in and [have] different people around you. Sometimes they say [a] change is as good as a rest and it definitely rejuvenated me. The quality of sparring in the gym. I was sparring Valdez and other Mexican kids, and just being around them and the ring knowledge Freddie can pass on, I've just been soaking it up like a sponge.'

Being back in the UK doesn't mean holiday time for Scott. He hasn't let up on his own gruelling training sessions despite trainer Freddie Roach being more than 5,000 miles away in California. In fact, he's so pleased with his morning's efforts that he's arrived at the Radisson with treat in hand – a white coffee, no sugar. That's living.

'Over here, I'm still working on the stuff I was doing over there. I'm working with Darren Phillips. Everything's ticking over nicely, so when I go over there, I'll have ten weeks where I'm not having to get fit. I'm in shape now. I'll be going straight into learning and absorbing everything I've been taught.

'I'm still in the transition period. I've had one fight with Freddie, so everything we've been working on didn't necessarily come out in that fight; there were some bad habits in that fight. In the next fight, you'll see the improvements that I've been showing in the gym. It's something that excites me because I know that when I do take that form into the ring, people will see a miles-improved Scott Quigg.'

Ricky and Anthony have completed the formalities; they've done a head-to-head for the cameras, both flashing their pearly whites. They've stepped down from the top table now to give one-to-one interviews.

'These are two of the nicest fellas you could meet in boxing,' Quigg continues. 'There's no trash talk but when they step in the ring, they'll both give it everything. It has got [the] potential to be fight of the year because they're both at the stage of their careers where it's must-win. They always give it everything anyway, but where does the loser go from here?

'I think Anthony's the fresher of the two and I believe that from when Ricky had his jaw broken, he doesn't exchange as much and fights in spurts. I think Anthony will be too sharp, too busy and have too much variety when they do come to the exchanges. Anthony's got more confidence with letting his hands go than Ricky. I see Anthony winning by three or four rounds.'

Ricky Burns is sat in the front row, ahead of the top table, finishing off an interview with BBC Sport. As polite and courteous as his counterpart, he has time for everyone and does all that's asked of him with a smile. He's enjoying the occasion and can't wait to fight in Manchester for the first time.

'I've been in the Manchester Arena to watch a few fights before but I've never actually boxed here myself. I know what to expect. Anthony's got a great following and I know a good crowd's gonna come down from Glasgow.

'I was talking to a few of the boys before the press conference and I was saying that this is one fight where in the build-up you're not going to get anybody kicking off, no trash talk. I like to do my talking in the ring. I've had 48 professional fights and I've always been the same – same as Anthony said, people know what they're going to get in the ring.

'After my last fight, I had a wee break. Obviously being based down in London, they were giving me different options with a few names I could fight. Rather than messing about, why not just jump straight back in with a big name? We're in the same boat; we've both lost our world titles and are looking for a big fight to get our name back up there.'

Much has been made of the size difference. Anthony was always adamant that he didn't need to step up. Lightweight has always been a comfortable limit for him to make. As a three-weight world champion, Burns knows all about stepping up divisions, but doesn't believe dropping down is a problem.

'Moving to lightweight's always been an option for me. The last three fights – obviously I was a light-welter – the week before the fight I've been hovering around 9st 12lbs or 9st 13lbs, so I've always been slightly under. I've always said, I even said this to Tony [Sims], that I'm too small for light-welter but it was just getting the last couple of pounds off for lightweight that was the problem. I've spoken to my team. We've worked out a plan and brought a dietician on board, so I'm sure we can get the weight down properly. I don't see it being a problem.'

Any casual boxing fans hoping for pre-fight histrionics will be sorely disappointed, with both men focusing solely on the battle in the ring. No pushing and shoving and no psychology either, despite the fact both have met before as sparring partners.

'I don't look too much into the sparring side of things. When you're in fights, that's when it really matters. Me and Tony will sit back and watch of few of Crolla's fights. We've already been speaking about what we'll be working on for this fight, but like I said, we're expecting a very hard fight. Myself, as much as him, I tend to get carried away when I'm in there. It'll only be a matter of time before we're both going at it and the best man will win.

'As Eddie said, the winner of this could possibly go into a world title fight. That was the best news I've heard in a bit. If I get the win, which I'm confident I will do, then I could fight for a world title and it doesn't get any better than that. I don't need any more incentive than that. I've still got a few big nights left in me.'

Anthony, meanwhile, is stood at the side of the room posing for a photographer who wants the traditional fists-up shot. He's being asked to turn this way and that all the time, a huge grin across his face.

There was never going to be any tables being thrown up there, was there? It's a genuine fight and it doesn't need that. I believe we'll go to war and I'll come out on top. Camp carries on now [and] I'm in a good place for the hard work to start. I've been in the gym a month already and October 7 works well for me. It's now about getting the right sparring in at the right time.

I'm waiting for Joe to decide what to do. It's [a] busy time for him with Callum fighting three weeks before me, Paul Butler on the week before, as well as lads on the undercards on those shows. It's a very busy time for Joe. I wouldn't mind going away for a week or two, but I'll see how it fits in with the other lads. I can't be selfish even though boxing's a selfish sport. It's got to work for the whole team.

There are two months until fight night. The event at the arena will bring back many traumatic memories for the crowd that night – and Anthony's family.

I want everyone to come to the arena, have a great time, then go home that night after a local lad's had one of the great nights of his career. I want to give them something to cheer about and that's just added motivation. People say that it's added pressure to fight at the arena, but I just use it as motivation. It's going to be a very special night with a special atmosphere and I'm sure we can deliver a fight to match it.

Three hours after he arrived at the hotel, Crolla is still doing interviews with boxing websites. Even in a media-friendly boxing world, this kind of interaction is unusual. Anthony doesn't use any excuses about having to be here or there (even though he should be elsewhere by now). Not until every picture has been taken and every quote recorded does he take his leave.

* * * * *

The next day, all is back to normal. Anthony's feeling good despite his tiring media day.

You don't wanna be rude, you've got to do the interviews. You've got to be thankful for it, but I was exhausted afterwards. I went off to Wigan to do strength and conditioning with Martin [Cullen] and surprisingly, I had a really good session.

I've had a good session today as well – first spar with Scottie Cardle for a while this morning and I've just done a big swim with Sam [Hyde], who can shift in the pool for a big lump! Fair play to him; he's come into our gym after being the big fish elsewhere and he's given it a real go.

Unbeaten Sale cruiserweight Sam 'Nowhere2' Hyde is another new edition to Team Gallagher. He was formerly trained and managed by Ensley Bingham at Champs Camp, Moss Side. When Sam's pad man Dan Murray left for pastures new, Sam looked for a change. According to Anthony, he's fitting in well with his new surroundings.

I asked him how his swimming was and he said, 'Yeah, I'm mint!' and we were all laughing, giving it, 'Oh, are you now?', but he's not bad, to be fair.

He's done everything that's been asked of him and he seems to be enjoying it. He sparred today – Steve Collins Jr. He didn't look bad.

* * * * *

Joe Gallagher's finished gym and swim work for the day. The second part of his routine is under way, catching up with e-mails and getting stuck into a bit of social media. He regularly posts updates and photos from the gym to keep fans and critics alike up to date with his fighters' progress.

Work with Crolla is going well – as a couple of Instagram shots would suggest – and despite his earlier reservations, he's feeling confident about his man and the challenge ahead.

'I said to Anthony in the gym the other day that he looked like he'd been in a time tardis – he's looking younger! He looks happy, fresh and full of enthusiasm and he's got the bit between his teeth. He looks like a kid who's just turned professional and is about to have his first fight on a big show. It's good to see a fighter who's been so long in the game still so excited.

'Anthony started sparring on Wednesday, he sparred very well, and he's going to have to develop a new set of tools for this job. Burns is a kid we know and we've looked at him a few times over the years. We've been ringside and watched him and it's very much the same for him. He knows Anthony.

'Money-wise, the fight is a good deal and once [the] Joshua vs Klitschko [rematch] got cancelled, then a Vegas night was dead in the water, so with the money on offer it was too good a payday to turn down. Fighting at the arena as well, it's all worked out all right.

'Crolla's got a good profile in America now – his last fight with Linares was on Showtime – so to fight in Vegas against an American in some sort of eliminator would've been good. But obviously with the arena repaired and them wanting boxing back again, Crolla wants to fight there again. We win, then who's to say we won't get an away-day next year?'

One of the key issues in getting the deal done was settled as soon as Burns agreed to fight at lightweight. With Anthony comfortably making weight and in no hurry to step up, that situation could add an interesting dynamic to proceedings. At 34, will Burns struggle to drop down? Not according to Gallagher.

'He was a lightweight, he's been a world champion at three different weights and he knows how to make weight. I don't expect that to take any toll whatsoever. He's a fit kid and a young 34 who's been in the mix with all the good world fighters.

'Also, when he's in domestic fights, he raises his game even more. There's a warning there that Ricky Burns isn't finished yet and we're not going to take heed of people who say he is finished.'

* * * * *

Another Monday morning in Bolton. It's a sparring day for several members of the team, so the heater's on full Saharan setting as incoming fighters and their teams gather around the ring in the north-east corner of the room, next to the speedball. Hosea Burton, Paul Butler, Callum Smith, Liam Smith, Marcus Morrison and Sam Hyde are all pairing up on bags as Joe shouts above the music.

'Come on! Left hook to the body, there you go, good! Neat and tidy, go again, better, sit, drop to the body, back to the head, catch the shot, nearly there, come on, roll your head after the shot, come on! Hands up as you move, think … time.' It's a rhythmic outpouring from the trainer, almost in time to the beats from the racket on the playlist.

Natasha Jonas is already done for the day and is sat ringside in her civvies, taking it all in. Anthony's getting ready to spar while Will Crolla's turned up to do a bit of work too.

'I've got to lose a bit of weight because I want to fight again soon. I'm going to give it a go as a professional next year, but I want to compete in an amateur tournament in December. For my last fight, I was 58kg (9st 2lbs) but I'm 12st 7lbs now, so I've got a lot to lose!'

The autumn will be one of the busiest periods Joe's encountered. He's stood at the corner of the ring in his all-black uniform of trainers, shorts and T-shirt, with his glasses sliding slightly down his nose. He's looking at notes for the day's hectic training schedule. Over the next three months, he expects to have ten fighters out on shows, starting with Callum Smith on Saturday, 16 September in Liverpool.

'Callum's four weeks out, so he's stepped up to eight rounds now, which means we're using two sparring partners for him. We're getting different kids in at the moment to just figure out sparring partners for Anthony's fight with Burns.

'The gym's going to be very busy from now on, but you wouldn't want it any other way. It's stressful, though. Driving in this morning, I had a right fucking pain in me chest and I'm thinking, "Oh fucking hell!" Nobody would be surprised if I had one [heart attack]. I was up this morning at seven, on the phone to Eddie Hearn at quarter past, and then at half past I get a text from the World Boxing Super

Series. I've done two hours' work before I get in here and then I train the lads and again tonight. You've got to then organise sparring and watch fights, so it's relentless.'

Anthony climbs into the ring to do a few rounds with Kane Gardner, a Beswick lad who's preparing for his professional debut. Joe's looking for fighters who can replicate some of the specific threats Burns will pose.

'Ricky's orthodox, upright, he has a good jab and a good left hook to the body. He does the basics quite well. He doesn't have loads of tools in the box, but those he does have, have served him well. It's a tough night's work for Anthony. Just look who he's been up against – Beltran, Crawford, Indongo and he hasn't disgraced himself, he's pushed them close. This is a hard fight.'

Anthony touches gloves with Kane at the end of their spar. There's blood on Crolla's white T-shirt, but it's not from his face. He's irritated a blister on his chest. He gets out of the ring, changes into a black T-shirt and starts on his chin-ups and push-ups. It's a tough start to the week and he admits to feeling a bit tired.

Kane, on the other hand, has a big smile on his face after doing six rounds with a former world champion. A good amateur, the 22-year-old won 55 of 88 bouts and is working towards his first fight in the paid ranks on Steve Wood's ViP show at the Victoria Warehouse on Friday, 2 September. Anthony's dad Wayne goes back a long way with Kane's trainer Ian Harrison, with the pair coming through the boxing ranks together.

While Anthony's spar is over, Joe's busy overseeing some of his other fighters in the ring.

The Army have brought a few fighters in for some work and there's a big Canadian heavyweight called Simon Kean, who's lined up to do a few rounds with Sam Hyde. Just as the pair get going, Kean is cut above his left eye and while it's just a small nick, it's enough to bring the spar to an end.

Anthony finishes off his chin-ups, press-ups and stretches and disappears into the changing area. Joe's eyes are darting around the room as he oversees the final minutes of the morning session, still vocally harassing the remaining fighters to put in maximum effort.

The music is silenced and the gym voices quieten down. A busy morning of sparring is over; Joe looks again at his notes to work out who's doing what and where. With so many fights on the horizon, it's all about organisation – who's building up and who's tapering down.

For Crolla's preparations, Joe's at the stage where the serious work has only just begun. So with the date in the diary, is the fighter now focused and switched on?

'Not today, he was shit. He came in last Wednesday and sparred brilliant. He's sparred again today and he's been shit. He was exhausted and I'm thinking, "What have you been doing all weekend?" He was at Old Trafford yesterday [United beat West Ham 4-0], but I don't know what else he's doing. I don't know whether he's been here and there, being a social animal.

'I took him to Barcelona [last camp] to get him away from all that. You forget how tiring it is just travelling around, meeting people, all that type of stuff. You can't have two days off and then on Monday be bolloxed. He can't be the social butterfly any more, nipping here, nipping there.

'I can't have days like today, when he comes in and gets snotted by a kid who hasn't had a pro fight yet. You do have days like that, but it shouldn't be on a Monday when you've had the weekend at home. He knows. He's got to think about himself and boxing.'

I was a little bit tired today, which is surprising for a Monday, but it's getting used to being sparring-fit again. I'll be all right. I'm getting the rounds in.

Kane's a good, young, hungry kid who wants to make an impression and that's what we want. He has similarities with Burns and we'll use a few people like that. We'll bring in some quality, well-schooled fighters as well.

Ricky's going to be big on the night. He was a big lightweight and as he's coming back down, some people are saying it's in my favour. Well, maybe, but we won't be relying on that. He's got a great engine, so we're not relying on him losing anything. He says he only moved up to light-welter for the opportunities. Tony Sims said he didn't want him to move down, but I don't know, maybe he was playing mind games. We'll see.

Both Crolla boys are showered and changed and about to head into Bolton town centre for a coffee and a snack. With Will's renewed dedication to the sport, it's put to Anthony whether he'd fancy doing a few rounds with his younger brother.

He's probably too big now. He's soft, though, so if he didn't get me out of there early, I'd give him a good hiding.

Will smiles and Anthony flashes him a look that suggests he might be joking. Maybe.

He's talented. He got to the national semi-finals a couple of times. Once he lost to a Rotunda kid by a point. It could have gone either way; he was a real good kid who boxed for England. Another time, he was robbed blind. He should've had a national title. That bit of luck might have pushed him on.

Even when he was doing all that, though, he's probably only been fit for a handful of fights. He was playing at it. He's young enough, he's only 18. There's never been any pressure from me. I used to hate the pressure he had because he's my brother. People expect things.

If he had my work ethic, he'd have been a good fighter. If he decides he wants to come back, I'll support and help him in every possible way, but he's got to want to do it himself. He'd need to do a good year in the amateurs and assess it from there. To be honest, though, I don't want him to box.

* * * * *

Training takes a twist as boxing merges with the world of athletics. Anthony's been asked to take part in a unique 'Golden Relay' event at Manchester's Regional Arena. The World Championships have recently come to an end in London, with Usain Bolt pulling his hamstring in his last final, while Mo Farah retired from the track with silver to add to his astonishing collection.

Meanwhile, preparations were in full swing for the England Athletics International meeting featuring all the home nations, along with Ireland and Denmark. The event has been bolstered this year by the reforming of Great Britain's 2004 Olympic gold medal-winning 4x100m relay team. They're competing again for one night only to raise money for the 'We Love Manchester Emergency Fund'. The catalyst is Sale's Darren Campbell, who despite being expatriated in south Wales for decades cannot fail to hear his city's call.

'My father-in-law passed away the same week as the Manchester bomb. I didn't really do anything for Manchester at the time because

I was trying to heal my family, so then I thought, "Let's run and try and raise a bit of money!"

'I phoned the guys [Jason Gardener, Marlon Devonish and Mark Lewis-Francis] and asked them if they'd support this and, fair play, they didn't even hesitate.

'A year ago, we met up for the first time and spoke about what happened that night [Athens 2004]. We've been at functions together and that, but you're never going to talk about that then. The bond was cemented again, so when I said, "Let's do this" [Golden Relay], they were all, "Yeah!" I was hoping they would because I'm the oldest!'

Athletics clubs with competitive teams have been invited to challenge the boys of 2004. Anthony and his pal Scott Quigg – back again from LA – have been asked to do the same. They're in a scratch team that includes personal trainer and TV presenter Richard Callender and Darren's 18-year-old son Aaryn. A big boxing fan, Darren couldn't miss the opportunity to get the fighters involved.

'I was looking to see what other kinds of teams I could get to take part. That's why I love Manchester! You call them [Crolla and Quigg] and they just come out. They'll always do something good. It's totally out of their comfort zone, but they come out and I've so much respect for them.

'Me and Crolla have got a lot of mutual friends. We know how hard life has been at the beginning. I'm no different from him, I appreciate where I'm at and I do little bits that can make a bit of a difference. That's why we're all here. It's great that these guys are here [Crolla and Quigg] because they've helped with all the publicity – although I wouldn't get in a ring with them!'

Crolla and Quigg are in the indoor warm-up area as serious athletes jump, stretch and sprint around them. Both fighters are nervous, but both are dismissing the notion, pretending to take it all in their stride. What's clear is they do not want to disgrace themselves. They try talking tactics, but it just descends into playground abuse.

You go first leg – there's no way you'd be able to take the baton in a proper handover. I can't do second, though. There's no way you'll find me with the baton.

'Fuck off!' Quigg said. 'I'll go first, no problem, but don't give me that. You can't fucking run now anyway. Don't embarrass us!'

Darren Campbell walks over in his royal blue top and black lycra shorts. He turns 44 in a few weeks, but can still carry off the outfit and move quite quickly. His almost ever-present smile fades for a moment as he attempts to impart some wisdom to the bickering boxers. 'Listen lads, come and have a run through with us. No, seriously, come on the track and have a work through with the baton changes. Watch us, it's simple, you just shout, "Hand!" and crack on.'

Crolla and Quigg are still nervously giggling. They're men who've entered arenas and faced elite opponents who would hand them life-altering beatings given half a chance, yet they chuckle and goad each other at the prospect of a fun run.

They've had the run-through from the man in charge. Campbell's ushered the two fighters around the indoor warm-up track, situated adjacent to the outdoor track. It would be fair to say they've not taken the pre-race instructions too seriously. Darren's happy enough, though.

'I think they'll be all right – they've got my son and he's against me on the second leg! The good thing is, there are a lot of different teams here, some younger, but these guys are fit and they're very professional in what they do. Running fast is a different thing, though, so that does give us a slight advantage, although we're not as fast as we used to be!' Darren grew up on the Racecourse estate in Sale, a once-notorious place populated by Ardwick and Ancoats overspill. Sport was the saving grace for Darren. He played football and played it well, but was so fast that he joined Sale Harriers. The rest is history. He continued to try other things, though, such as training at Sale West ABC, where he encountered a young Richard Hatton.

'I went boxing once or twice. I was rubbish. Ricky was there, so I used to see him back in the day. I did pick up things from boxing, though. Our training methods change. Boxers used to just run and run, but now it's high intensity. The long runs – almost a waste of time. I did pad work, lots of pads, speedball with lots of explosive movement. I thought outside the box and because I knew boxing and I'd seen different training methods, during the winter I'd break it up. Otherwise, it was boring, just doing the same things year in year out.

'I've always watched boxing from Ricky Hatton to these guys [Crolla and Quigg] carrying it on. That's what makes Manchester so special. We have different rivalries with United and City, and even though I don't live in Manchester any more, it's why Manchester is the best city.'

Darren moved to Wales to become a sprint legend, but is a regular visitor to the North West and stays in touch with his old mates and colleagues.

'I'll never forget one day I came up from Wales to watch one of Ricky's fights. I got there late, but because he's met my wife and all that, he's in the dressing room getting ready to fight and he's like, "Yeah D, how's it going?" He hits the pads and says, "How's the wife? How're the kids?" He's relaxed as hell!

'I spoke at a boxing dinner in London, not last year, the year before, and I felt confident talking about the sport. Whether you're a boxer or an athlete, it's a lonely game. Don't get me wrong, you have your team-mates and if you've got a good group you'll be working to similar goals – Olympics, world championships etc. But it is a lonely game.

'Those guys [boxers] pound the streets on their own. At times they're in the gym on their own trying to self-motivate or self-heal when things have gone bad. You never lie to yourself or cut corners because they know when they step in the ring that that cut corner will come back to bite you. It was the same for me, but they've got 12 rounds, three minutes [each round] and I've got ten or 20 seconds and I can't get it again for four years. Everything has to be right.

'We're hard-working people and we can get anything done. Anthony showed that. Look what he came back from [burglary] and how he came back? That's an inspiration to all of us because most of us would've given up. When he got his title shot, he took it. That's what it's about. I got my title shot, Olympic gold, and I took it. The key is what you've got up here [points to head].'

Crolla and Quigg have been working through tactics. They've been practising baton changes with their new team-mates while

Darren and his golden comrades effortlessly glide around the indoor track in sync. Preparations over, one of the event organisers comes over to tell everyone it's nearly race time. It's just after 8pm and the crowd in the arena outside are waiting. There's a final word of encouragement from Darren to all those taking part in the race before he turns, smiling, to make his way outside.

'I always try and give back to show people what's possible. Everything I am and everything I learned started here. Good, bad, everything. You have to utilise that and coming from where I come from, been through the things I've been through, you know?

'You have to show the kids success. The fact Anthony's here supporting this shows he hasn't changed. That's always been my biggest battle. How do I achieve the success that I want and then don't change? That's what's expected, but I still go back to Sale because it's no good people being successful and then they don't go back. How can kids think it's possible and believe you're successful if they never see you? Be yourself, that's the secret. Be humble, don't forget where you come from and go back and help when you can.'

The athletes are called into position. Those running the first leg settle into their blocks. The starter's gun fires and Quigg gets out well but struggles to keep pace with Jason Gardener. The baton change between the boxer and Aaryn Campbell is decent enough, but the latter's dad has put a bit more distance between them by the time Crolla takes over for the third leg around the bend.

The crowd is loving the show as Anthony finds the outstretched hand of Richard Callender, who sprints impressively for home. The Olympians have already finished by now in a time of 43.72 seconds, but it's a good effort from the random quartet, who finish in 51.51 seconds, less than a second ahead of an all-girls team and fourth out of eight.

There's a judge's inquiry about some of the baton changes! I missed it first time, got it the second time. You know, when I did get the baton I thought I was going to fly. I got it and I was like … phew! Oh my God! I could see them [Legends] when they were starting off and Marlon was stood in the lane next to me, but then … vrrrroooooooomm!

* * * * *

The press have been invited to Bolton to watch a Callum Smith workout ahead of his forthcoming fight in the World Boxing Super Series against the Swede Erik Skoglund. A couple of camera crews and a few members of the written press are in attendance.

Paul Butler's there, too. He's finished his first session of the day and, as is his wont, he hangs around to watch Callum go through the final stages of his yoga routine. A student of boxing, his appetite for detail is obsessive and since joining forces with Joe, he's taken to learning off all his team-mates.

'A year's flown by. I've really enjoyed it and I'm learning all the time. The gym's constantly buzzing, there's always a big fight around the corner and everyone thrives off each other. Nobody wants to be beaten, whether we're doing track or swimming or bar-bag together. Everyone's constantly pushing each other.

'Since I've been here, I've always finished my sparring then I watch the others. Everyone's got a different style here. You watch Callum and you think he'll just be a long-range counter-punter because of the size of him, but he's not. He's probably one of the best inside fighters in the gym. You look at him and think, "How's he doing that?" It's his feet, the way he shuffles them across. Beefy's the same and when he starts to let them go and let them flow, there's not many better.

'Crolla's another one. Everyone thinks he's just this come-forward fighter, but of late he's been sitting on the back foot and his shot selection on the back foot has been brilliant. Scott Cardle, how loose he is, how he slips his shots and counters. You're learning something new off everyone.

'I help Tash out a lot. We have a few good rounds together. She's southpaw but she's mainly going to be boxing orthodox fighters, so I get in and do some rounds, which is good for the pair of us. Joe brings in good sparring as well.'

The oppressive heat forces the conversation into another room, through the connecting door and into the lesser-used gym that sits adjacent to the home of Team Gallagher. Butler's had three fights with Joe and is now preparing for his rematch with Stuey Hall.

'With the first fight, everyone knew I was a super-flyweight coming up to bantamweight, but now I'm a fully-fledged bantamweight. In the first fight, I won the first five or six rounds then had to pinch rounds. He was at the time bigger than me. This time, he's still going to look bigger than me but I'm going to be as strong as him. Going down the home straight, he's not going to be the bully. If anyone's going to be the bully this time, it's going to be me. I'm younger and fresher.

'We were sparring partners before the first fight. It got a bit heated for that one, a few things got said, but I think there's a mutual respect there. As the fight gets closer, things will get said but we'll be friends afterwards. Beating Stuey Hall will open doors. There's the winner of Jamie McDonnell and [Liborio] Solis. If I was to come through that, then you've got to look possibly at the winner of Ryan Burnett and Zhanat [Zhakiyanov], which would be a massive unification fight.'

Callum's finishing off a yoga session with teacher Raquelle Gracie, before breaking off to speak to the assembled press. He's explaining the format of the World Boxing Super Series, giving his opinion on yoga and, of course, the forthcoming fight. Skogland and Callum share a common opponent in Luke Blackledge, and all the homework has been done.

'I know enough about him [Skogland]. I think all four non-seeds are good fighters, very capable fighters, but we watched him and I think stylistically he's tall, upright and I feel he'll bring out my boxing ability and I'll show my skills more. People know me for power and getting knockouts, but they'll see my boxing skills.

'George Groves' WBA title is also on the line in this competition, so I think if I win the tournament it sets up a unification with any of the other super-middleweight champions. I had a world title shot [Anthony Dirrell for the WBC belt] but it was taking too long. Waiting around wasn't helping me improve and wasn't helping my career. I need fights and I feel I'm ready for the best in the world.'

Is it realistic to have so many fights in the super series in a short space of time?

'Yeah – I've been at me best when I've been active. I've been doing a lot of sparring for this fight for that reason. In my first year as a pro, I had nine fights in nine months. I don't want to be inactive. Fighting brings the best out of me.'

While Callum's been the centre of attention, those assembled at the gym want a word with Joe, too. The addition of yoga to help the fighters with their warm-downs is something of a talking point. Joe's keen to explain the thinking behind the move.

'We have a few in the gym who do yoga and there's some that won't. I understand where they're coming from because they haven't been before and they're uncomfortable going to a class. They don't know positions, dog-down or whatever it is. So I thought I'd bring in a yoga instructor a couple of times a week to warm them down and go through stretches.

'It's like a skinny kid going into a weights gym; it's just giving them the confidence to be able to go to yoga class. Yoga's potentially the reason Ryan Giggs prolonged his career for four or five years, do you know what I mean?

'Sometimes in here, I've told them to warm down after a session and I come back in and they're in the shower! You've got to stretch, warm down and do it proper. It's just as important as the session itself.

'I was getting frustrated with some of the lads not doing it themselves, so everything's done for them now, no excuses.'

* * * * *

Love it or loathe it, it's just a couple of days before Floyd Mayweather takes on Conor McGregor in the fight that has got everyone talking. Anthony's sat on the ring apron discussing the forthcoming event in Las Vegas.

I was asked by Michael Vaughan [former England cricket captain] about the fight the other day. He wanted to know what the equivalent was in football terms. I said it's like Ashton United beating Real Madrid. He thought it was more like his team Sheffield Wednesday, but I told him it was more like semi-professional lads against the best team in the world.

It's a circus. It's strictly business and all about money. As long as people know that, but it's absolutely crazy that anyone's giving Conor any kind of chance.

God forbid if anything went wrong, there'd be a lot of people with a lot of questions to answer. But, of course, money talks. It'd be the biggest sporting upset of all time if Conor was to win this. Floyd wins when he wants to.

DATE IN THE DIARY

Going the distance wouldn't be the best thing. Best-case scenario is Conor comes out of it healthy, with the fight only going a few rounds. It's really bad for boxing if it goes anywhere near the distance.

He won't win the fight but even for him to do well, it will be awful for boxing.

It's going to generate more than a billion dollars. It's almost like a fantasy match, just like Mayweather fighting Conor in the Octagon.

Joe Gallagher said: 'I see a lot of experts asked for a prediction but they don't want to give one. You know what? Conor has you believing. But listen, Floyd's been in the game long enough; he's seen it all before. As big as Conor is in MMA, I fancy Floyd winning in six rounds or it's a success story for Conor McGregor. Actually, it's a success story for McGregor full stop. He's managed to talk the world into believing he can win this fight.

'You can never rule him out, he's got a puncher's chance, he's dedicated and has trained specifically for Mayweather. Will it be a great fight? I can't see it. We've seen it before with Manny [Pacquiao] and Floyd. Everyone got excited and we had a 12-round snoozefest. So yeah, I expect Floyd to prevail. It's Hulk Hogan against Rocky Balboa, isn't it?'

Callum Smith said: 'It is laughable but I'm going to watch, so it can't be that laughable, can it? I don't think it's competitive. Provided Mayweather hasn't aged massively overnight, then he'll be far too good for him [McGregor]. I think Floyd will knock him out. I think McGregor will tire late on because no matter how hard you train, it's hard doing 12 three-minute rounds.'

Paul Butler said: 'It's just a show, isn't it? McGregor's training to learn how to box; Mayweather's training to beat McGregor. I see Mayweather having a look at him for the first two rounds, as he does with everyone, then he'll up the pace in rounds four, five, six and start working the body. I think he'll stop him on his feet around rounds eight or nine.'

Anthony spent a large chunk of the previous evening in Media City recording an episode of *A Question of Sport*. He's been a guest on the long-running BBC programme before and it's something he always enjoys doing.

It was a good laugh. Last time, I was on Phil Tufnell's team and he hadn't had a win in about four or five episodes, but we won. This time, I was on Matt's team. He's a bit sharper, but we lost 29-28. There was me, Matt and the high jumper Morgan Lake.

Years ago, I went on it in me boxing gear, on a conveyer belt. Me and a few other sports people as part of one of the games. I've been on it twice as a panellist. Last time I was on it, the answer to my 'home' question was Ricky Burns. Mad innit, that?

I've done other random TV bits. More than a year ago, me and Callum went on a celebrity version of Pointless *but they haven't shown it yet. There was us and snooker players – Ken Doherty and some others. Don't know when it's going to get shown.*

Local photographer Karen Priestley has been taking some shots in the gym throughout the morning and is now showing Crolla some of the images of the day and also some pictures from years ago. He's identifying the time and place of the images, simply through recognition of his outfit for the evening.

I remember wearing that jacket after I fought Steve Foster Jr. That was taken ringside at Froch vs Groves after I'd had my fight. I'm weird for stuff like that!

My memory's a bit mad like that. I don't know what I had for breakfast this morning, but I can remember anything to do with clothes from years ago. I can remember all of my opponents' outfits. I can describe the shorts and everything of every one of my opponents.

* * * * *

As predicted by Anthony, his trainer and team-mates (and just about everybody else with a passing interest in boxing), Conor McGregor failed in his attempt to inflict a first professional defeat on Floyd Mayweather. The Irish MMA star made it to the tenth round before the referee intervened to stop the fight. Floyd retired (again) immediately after the contest with his now-perfect record of 50-0. The pay-per-view figures and vast sums of cash generated would confirm neither man was a loser.

The acrimonious press tour and hype surrounding the cross-combat fight was like nothing ever previously seen in Las Vegas.

Like nearly every fighter who ever boxed, Anthony Crolla's always dreamed of seeing his name up in lights on the Sin City Strip. No one will ever do a 'Ricky' and take the vast army of thousands of fans repeatedly across the Atlantic, but Anthony has always had a hankering to headline in the neon Mecca of boxing.

He had been due to get a chance to showcase his skills in a high-profile fight on the undercard of Floyd Mayweather vs Victor Ortiz in September 2011. Mexican legend Erik Morales was lined up and the deal was done, only for the fight to be scuppered when Morales was offered an opportunity to face Rodrigo Barrios for the WBC light-welterweight title. The winner of that fight was to get a shot at Amir Khan in December.

So Anthony, and hundreds of his supporters who'd booked flights and accommodation, were left in limbo. Promoter Oscar De La Hoya received a barrage of 'questions' via social media and while it wasn't the Mexican he should've been fighting, Oscar moved swiftly to ensure Anthony was on the bill with an eight-rounder against Juan Montiel.

'He was a decent Mexican,' Joe said. 'He was meant to be shit but then I heard that he had Nacho Beristáin in his corner. I thought, "Yeah, he must be shit!" Nacho doesn't have bums. It was the same night that Stephen Smith lost to Lee Selby. I'd said to Anthony that I really wanted to go, but I knew Stephen had a hard fight and there was no way I could be in Vegas.'

I went out on my own. Mike Marsden was in my corner but he didn't get there until the Thursday night. I had my dad in there and my best mate as well. That was my corner! It was a character-building fight.

Robert Diaz looked after me while I was on my own. He phoned me and said to let him know if I needed anything, if I needed to get to the gym or anywhere else. But I was out there on my own, training on my own. I'd arrived on the Sunday at the MGM and I was just walking up and down the Strip all the time. I did too much walking.

A bit later after the fight, I was watching a Marquez vs Mayweather 24/7 and there was someone in the gym next to Marquez and I thought, 'I know that face' and it was him, Montiel.

CHAPTER 9

Burns Night

Fight week

The sparring and training has finished. It's now just about ticking over and taking care of formalities as the big night approaches. Anthony has left home for his temporary base at the Radisson Blu Hotel. It's a now familiar routine as he leaves nothing to chance.

It's about getting rest now. I'm not switching off but it's just a matter of staying sharp and looking forward to the night. I've got the last few daft things to do, like picking me kit up.

I'll see a little bit of the family this week but it's about not taking risks. You never know if Jesse would have a bad night, which would mean I don't get enough sleep. It's best to make sure I get my sleep in.

The end of training camp is the time that many fighters hate. It can feel like a slow countdown to the fight, with too much time to kill. Crolla takes it all in his stride and never lets boredom get the better of him. The hotel has all he needs and he can watch as many box sets as he likes. Another plus is that he finally got to see that missing episode of *Pointless*.

It was a little bit late going out and having now watched it, I probably shouldn't have bothered going on it with some of my answers! It was hard, but it was a good laugh and I enjoy doing that kind of thing. It's something different.

It's something I watch on a Saturday night at me nanna's, so it's strange to be on it. Surreal but good fun.

It's Wednesday tea time in Manchester city centre and 200 people have packed into the atrium area of the National Football Museum. The venue is only open to the public during office hours but they've made a concession for Anthony's public workout. It's a familiar setting for this activity – the usual pre-fight starting point. It's a chance for fans to have a look at the fighters moving around the ring, doing very little but just enough to satisfy the gathered snappers, camera crews and written press.

It's international week, too, so no Premier League football, and as a result some of the footballers not representing their countries have a bit more free time. United captain Michael Carrick has turned up with his young son to lend Crolla some support. He's stood with the rest of Anthony's fans behind a barrier a metre or so from the boxing ring. One of the Matchroom team spot him and usher him in to the roped off area, so he can watch the workout without the constant selfie requests. Michael had asked for no favours and was happy where he was, but accepts the invite for a better view and a chance to catch up with his pal.

Joe's four undercard fighters are taking part, along with the two main men. First in is Scott Cardle, who gets a good ovation as he flicks out combinations. Shadow boxing is followed by skipping and he's done for the day. He leans on the ropes and does a quick interview for the crowd and reiterates his desire to claw his way back to a British title fight. First stop Lee Connelly on Saturday night.

Sam Hyde jumps in next. He faces Gheorghe Danut and, like Cardle, goes through a swift routine with Joe before addressing the crowd with a few words about his first fight as part of Team Gallagher. He promises to be patient on Saturday and show off his skills.

'Nowhere2' Hyde steps out of the ring and perches on a table in a storage area beneath the stairs, to the side of the ring. He's slowly peeling the white tape from around his knuckles as he assesses the challenge ahead.

'It's my 12th fight but the first with Joe [as trainer]. I don't think there've been any major differences but loads of small changes. One of the things has been the consistency of the training and the confidence that being around top-level fighters can bring. It's just made me step up to the next level.

'I've always pushed myself and trained hard but at Gallagher's gym you're training for 12-round fights all the time. I've never understood the expression "success breeds success" but now I certainly do. It's amazing.

'When I first met up with Joe, he said he'd asked the lads what they thought of me and if they were happy with me joining the gym. He said that if there was one bad apple then it would cause a bad environment, so I'm just glad that everyone's accepted me and let me in. It's like I've been at the gym forever.

'They've all been complimentary of me and what I've been doing well. They've also told me what I can work on and I couldn't be happier. I'm really excited for Saturday night and what I can do in the ring. I'm going to be calm and the longer the fight goes on the better.'

Anthony has arrived with his brother Will. They've been escorted in through a quieter entrance to the holding/storage area. He smiles and fist-pumps all of his team-mates and gives Sam a little slap on the back. When he's out of earshot, Sam waxes lyrical about the help Crolla has given him.

'He's been great. One thing I've learned about him, though, is that you've got to watch where you're walking when he comes into the gym because he's in his own little world! You could be skipping and he'll walk straight in front of you, he won't see you. It's funny and at first I thought he must have loads on his mind or must have a big task in front of him. But it's just that when he's in the gym, it's all about work. Sometimes he doesn't even let on because he hasn't seen you!'

Standing quietly at the back of the holding area is the tall, lean frame of Marcus Morrison. He looks a little pensive, as if the forthcoming weekend is very much in his thoughts. He is desperate to get successive defeats out of his system and waves to the crowd when he's announced as next in the ring. Following his session, he tells those assembled he will get things back on track on Saturday night when he faces Poland's Mariusz Biskupski.

Finally, before the main-event fighters, Hosea Burton climbs through the ropes and does his stuff. Like those before him, he finishes off with a quick interview and repeats his wish that Frank Buglioni has to be next – as soon as he's seen off 'Pitbull' at the arena.

It's rare that a rival to a Manchester fighter, particularly one as popular as Crolla, would ever be greeted by anything other than boos from the locals. It's nearly always knockabout stuff, but there isn't a single jeer for Ricky Burns. He gets a round of applause as he springs into the ring with his ever-present smile. There are no hand wraps around the tools of his trade, so he's clearly decided against even the most basic of pad routines.

On the mic at the end of the swiftest of workouts, he thanks all those who've turned out and promises a top night of action when he goes toe to toe with his former sparring pal.

Then on to the man they've all come to see. It's Crolla time. The huge beaming smile – all shiny white teeth – is there for all to see as he dances around throwing uppercuts. Unlike Burns, he does do a little work on the pads with Joe before taking the mic to thank everybody for coming out to support him.

He clambers through the ropes, sits on the ring apron and begins to tug the tape from his hands.

It's really good of everyone to turn out and it's nice to see Michael [Carrick] here as well. He's a great lad and I really appreciate him coming to see me. He'll be there on Saturday night and it's great to have someone I admire so much support me. There are no airs or graces to him and he does an awful lot for charities and stuff. He's just a good guy. He's going to be treated to a good fight on Saturday, I'm sure about that. I can't let the man down!

I believe I've improved again and had a good camp with good, specific sparring. I feel I've nailed some things down and I look forward to putting it into practice on Saturday night. The gym's bouncing and we're on a good roll at the moment.

I can't read anything into tonight – Ricky's only shadow boxed and touched his toes a few times! It's just a nice thing to hit a few pads and give the fans something to look at, and I suppose I look at Ricky now and it makes it sort of real now.

Thursday is final press conference day at Hotel Football. Former United defender Gary Neville is in the building he part owns and has made a point of tracking down Crolla to wish him well at the weekend. Anthony then makes his way to the first floor, where all the undercard fighters along with himself and Ricky Burns are due to face the press.

Eddie Hearn is in town to promote the fight. He sits at the two-tiered top table to introduce all the boxers and big-up the Battle of Britain clash. A huge promotional banner has been erected behind the tables with images of Crolla on the left, his face painted with the St George's cross, and Burns sporting the Saltire. The event has no gimmicky name, which is apt given the fact the build-up has been bereft of hype. The fight is a no-nonsense trade fight, so the simple 'Crolla vs Burns' billing is fitting.

The undercard lads all get their moment in the spotlight. Hyde, Cardle, Burton and Morrison are introduced in that order, followed by Conor Benn, Lewis Ritson and Robbie Barrett – the latter pair fighting for the British lightweight title. Sam Eggington, who defends his European title, says a few words and then focus switches to the main bout of the night.

Ricky Burns and Anthony Crolla take it in turns to say good things about each other but both stress the fans will get the fight they want, friendship going out of the window at the first bell. Following the head-to-head photos, all break away for individual interviews.

There's been plenty of chat about the loser being left with nowhere to go. Anthony's not been keen on such talk and Ricky Burns has appeared exasperated by that particular question. 'I look at every fight as a must-win fight,' he said. 'The incentive that has been put in front of us, with the possibility of challenging for the world title again, I need to make sure that I go out and win this, which I am confident of doing.

'We're both in the same boat now, coming back after a loss and looking to get our names back amongst the big boys. There were a few names mentioned for my next fight, but this was the only fight that I wanted once I knew it could be made.

'People are saying to me now, "If you lose this, what are you going to do?" That thought hasn't crossed my mind. I know this is a hard fight but the carrot of a possible world title fight means that the rewards are massive. I didn't need any more incentive for this fight. That just topped it off for me.

'I've never thought about what I've done in my career because it's nowhere near finished yet. I'm not retiring until boxing is out of my system. The last thing I want to do is pack it in too early and then, a year down the line, want to come back. I won't be done until I hate training and I am fed up with dieting.'

I don't believe we're putting our legacies on the line. If you look at our records, we've both boxed top fighters and that's why we do this job. When we do retire, we'll have no regrets because we can say we took on the best.

Ricky's a top guy and, as a fighter, I have so much respect for him. When you look through the names he's fought, it's unbelievable. He's had a great career, he's a three-weight world champion and he wants to win another world title, and so do I.

Joe Gallagher used the press conference to praise Ricky Burns and his achievements in a 16-year professional career. He's been playing down Crolla's favoured status with the bookies in a bid to ease any pressure his man might be feeling. He's happy with how everything panned out.

'Everyone's been back-slapping and very complimentary and rightly so. There doesn't need to be any chairs thrown or tables tipped over. It's just two very good fighters that have earned their dues in the game. They've become world champions by fighting at the highest level and they're going to go and do it again against each other. They're ultimate pros.'

The respect shown by all involved in the build-up has been warmly received by boxing fans, the press and certainly the British Boxing Board of Control. It's something Joe would like to see more of, although he recognises the need for needle if the occasion suits.

'If you look at David Haye versus Tony Bellew last time, everyone bought into it and it helped with the pay-per-view buys. As diplomatic as they both were the other day at their presser [rematch set for 17 December 2017], it won't be long before that starts again. Listen, with these two [Crolla and Burns], it's just not in their nature. They're two gentlemen.

'If you were trying to do the trash talk thing, you look at the recent Conor McGregor and Floyd Mayweather fight and how on earth can you compete with that? You've got one of the greatest self-publicists in the world in Conor McGregor and what he's done? What a fantastic story.

'I don't like seeing argy bargy at weigh-ins and press conferences. There's no need. Just like footballers, these [boxers] are role models for children that are in amateur boxing gyms. You see these kids practising an Anthony Crolla body shot or adopting a Naz [Prince Naseem Hamed] style and a Canelo move. You don't see them practising throwing tables or how to throw punches at weigh-ins.'

Another night at the hotel, another night of watching the weight and the telly and the final formality is in sight. The weigh-in is being held just a few floors down from his room in the Halle Suite. As with just about every Crolla event, it's open to the public and by 12.45pm the room is packed. There's a roped-off area at the front of the room for the press, with two rows of TV cameras, one row on a platform, the other lined up directly in front of the scales, which have been placed on a low makeshift stage.

MC Craig Stephen rattles through the undercard, with all making the correct weights. There's a very minor scare for Sam Eggington, who is a fraction over the 10st 7lbs welterweight limit. He whips off his underpants and with a towel strategically held to protect his modesty, he comes in bang on the limit.

It's always a big fight when Michael Buffer's in town and today is no exception. The distinctive silver-haired, navy-suited announcer takes over from Craig for the main event and calls first Burns then Crolla, who weigh in at 9st 8lbs 5oz and 9st 8lbs 9oz respectively. Both men look good at the weight, the heavily tattooed torso of Burns looking healthy and in no way drained and dry. Anthony strikes his best bodybuilding pose, showing off a fine physique, his 'Crolla' tattoo extended down his right side.

Both men smile at the final face-off, which puts an end to the final public formalities of fight week.

The crowd disappears from the room, many now heading back to city centre office desks, while the fighters begin their refuelling process. For Anthony, there is never any drama about making weight. While many fighters take to the scales with horribly sunken faces, craving hydration and food, Anthony tends to hit the target comfortably. His preparations are sensible and his diet is something he's always stuck to. All his meals are prepared by WAM catering, his auntie Pamela and uncle Wayne's business.

I'll always start the day with either oats, fish and greens or some fish with avocado. I don't take loads of supplements or anything like that, but I do have herbs like moringa and sea moss with my breakfast. Some of them taste horrendous.

For lunch, it'll usually be turkey and greens or more fish and greens and possibly some quinoa. For tea, it's fish and vegetables. The fish is seabass, cod or salmon.

I don't eat much meat and if I do it's only white meat. I don't eat pork and rarely eat red meat at all, probably a couple of steaks a year. That'd be about it. My diet is clean, but I do have a thing for protein bars. I have a few too many of them – it takes my chocolate cravings away!

Fight Night

It's the morning of the fight. It'll be a day of food, relaxation, television, tension, tedium and excitement. For the most part, Anthony will be alone.

I've had a good night last night, got a good night's sleep. I didn't watch a box set, I was just watching normal telly in the room; a bit of reality TV. I got in a bit of Cheshire Housewives, *which was good. I missed it on Monday because I was in the gym.*

After breakfast, Anthony heads back to his room for a while before heading out into town for a walk with Martin Cullen and a catch-up over a brew with his mam. After lunch, it's back to the room for a kip before getting his bag ready for the night ahead. Joe, meanwhile, has his hands full with last-minute running around and with half his gym in action in just a matter of hours, he has plenty to do.

It's going to be a busy night for him with five fighters on the bill, but I like that. It's good walking into the dressing room with each win – which I'm confident they will be. It lifts you. Obviously I'm fighting last but I'm sure I'll have four good wins before me and then I'll go out and win.

I'm not superstitious at all, but I'll always pray in the changing room before I go out. I don't go to church anywhere near as much as I should, but

I do go the odd time and before every fight I say a prayer. I never pray that I win; I just pray that we're both all right and we both come out safe.

* * * * *

The arena is sparsely populated. A few early birds are scattered around the vast swathes of empty seats. There are far more press and officials than paying punters inside the venue. The first fight of a busy night of boxing has been and gone and it's not yet 5pm. Macclesfield super-middleweight Jake Haigh outpointed Anthony Fox of Wiltshire over four rounds. Haigh is trained by Ricky Hatton, but tonight it's one of his assistants, Blain Younis, in the corner. The 'Hitman' is in Dublin as one of his other boxers, Chris Blaney, is fighting for a Celtic title.

Next up, there's a routine win for Glasgow's Joe Ham, followed by the return of Marcus 'Sweet M 'n' M' Morrison. He's facing tough Pole Mariusz Biskupski in his latest bid to rid his mind of the Welborn demons. Tall, slick and skilful, Marcus is determined to get the 'W' and goes about his job well, each blow and grunt audible in the cavernous room. After bossing the action from the first bell, he forces a stoppage in the fourth of a scheduled six rounds.

It's a very different walk back to the dressing room than the journey he faced at the end of March. No blood on the pristine white, shiny shorts and just an air of relief as he makes his way from the arena floor, through the double doors into the corridor. He does a right turn and after 50 yards a left into the Team Gallagher dressing room.

'Fighting at this time, you have to make the best of a bad job,' said Marcus. 'These things don't always run smoothly but the important thing was coming here and getting the win. The only thing going through my head when I was walking to the ring was, "I need a win here. I desperately need a win."

'If I'd got clipped – and as we know, anything can happen in boxing – if something had gone wrong, then it would've been curtains. You're going into battle with another man who's going at you. There were a lot of nerves but I've done the job and I can move forward now.

'People have told me in the last few months that my confidence was down. I never wanted to admit that I wasn't confident because

I am confident and I believe in my ability. I'm not a weak-minded person but subconsciously there was a lack of confidence. It's hard to admit these doubts to yourself. It is a big confidence boost to win.

'Last time I was here [after defeat to Welborn], I remember being in the shower thinking my life had fallen through my fingertips. My nose was broken in the second round, my eyes were busted up and my jaw was hurting. It was a nightmare, but those days are gone.'

Hosea Burton is sitting on a chair in the reception room adjacent to the main dressing room. He's sitting opposite corner man Adam Gigli, who's wrapping his hands. Family members and friends are gathered around, with the imposing grey-suited figure of his cousin Tyson Fury standing tallest among them, looking down at the fine work in progress.

In the inner sanctum next door, Joe is fiddling with his iPod dock, which is perched on the table next to the door. Two Smiths – Stephen and Callum – are buzzing around the room, along with Ross Garritty and Paul Ready from Matchroom. Cutsman Mick Williamson is changing T-shirts next to the mirror while Scott Cardle is stretching near the entrance to the shower with yoga teacher Raquelle Gracie.

Sam Hyde heads out to the arena for his six-round cruiserweight contest with Gheorghe Danut of Romania. It proves to be a hard night. Danut is rough and tough and Sam takes a tumble in the third after a tangling of legs and looks to be in trouble. He gets to his feet but is clearly limping and has to climb off the canvas a few more times as his legs are going from under him whenever there's any kind of pressure from Danut. His first fight under Joe's tutelage didn't exactly go to plan, but he sees out the six rounds and has his hand raised as the winner by 58 points to 54.

The injury is not insignificant and the fighter has to wait for a wheelchair to arrive ringside before he can get back to the dressing room. Once there, medics begin assessing him as Sam applies a bag of ice to the huge swelling.

'It's fucked. Have you seen the size of it?' he says, pointing to his right knee. Despite the injury, he's pleased to get his first win and keep momentum going for the gym. His dad arrives to take him to hospital and Sam's wheeled away, scrolling away on his phone, still dressed in his shiny blue shorts.

A photo from the ring apron is quickly doing the rounds. It shows Sam on the ring floor, his face contorted and his right knee bent all out of shape, the kneecap clearly in a place it doesn't belong. Not for the squeamish, but evidence of Sam's intestinal fortitude.

The card is moving along at pace and no time is wasted as Charlie Flynn, the second Scottish fighter to take to the ring, gets a solid job done with a points win over Liam Richards in the fourth fight of the night. Next in is Gavin McDonnell, who is looking to get back to world level following his defeat to Ray Vargas back in February. He has to deal with a change in opponent after Jay Carney's withdrawal on medical grounds. Hungarian Jozsef Ajtai isn't much of a match and as soon as the Doncaster man catches up with Ajtai in the first round, the fight is over.

Back in the Team Gallagher dressing room, Cardle's completed his final preparations and, like Marcus before him, heads towards what he hopes will be a first step to retribution after losing his British lightweight title to Robbie Barrett.

Cardle starts well against the game Lee Connelly and dominates the fight throughout, and although he takes some unnecessary shots late on he's a clear points winner. Another job done for both him and Joe.

As he casually makes his way back into the dressing room for a shower and change, there's another baton change as Hosea 'The Hammer' pulls on his black sponsored T-shirt and leaves for the centre of the arena. He's had to deal with a very late change of opponent, with Edinburgh-based Fijian Ratu Latianara now posing the challenge.

Hosea is going up against a cruiserweight and has given away a significant weight advantage, but he puts the unbeaten 30-year-old on the canvas with a clever uppercut in the first round and doesn't relent until the fight is stopped. It's an impressive count-out victory which may help, or hinder, his chances of a Frank Buglioni rematch.

A section of the vast arena is blocked off but the rest is by now two-thirds full. The acoustics have changed and the temperature in the room has risen. In between bouts, the music's being ramped up. Promoter Eddie Hearn takes advantage of the very brief pause in the action to do an interview with talkSPORT ringside. He then has a word with Luke Campbell, who is part of the radio station's boxing commentary team for the night, before taking his seat for the Barrett vs Ritson scrap.

It's a devastating performance from the challenger – Cardle's sparring partner – who stakes his claim as the new kid on the domestic lightweight block. It's one-way traffic until the seventh round, when Barrett's trainer Stefy Bull throws in the towel to save his man for another day.

Crolla and Burns have by now arrived at the arena and are settled into their respective dressing rooms. Both made their entrances via the loading bay area of the venue looking relaxed, confident and happy. Meanwhile, there's an interesting scene taking shape outside in the corridor, with Joe Gallagher and Ricky's trainer Tony Sims stood with Matchroom head of boxing Frank Smith. A coin toss is to settle the matter of ring walks. Joe had been unhappy at suggestions that Anthony would do anything other than walk second at the arena he calls his 'house'.

In the opposing camp, it was felt many concessions had already been made to help make the fight. The only way to solve the situation was 'heads or tails'. Joe called 'heads' and came up trumps. It's agreed that Crolla will walk second, but is to be the first fighter announced in the ring. The two trainers shake hands and go back into their respective offices for the evening.

Crolla's had his hands wrapped by Adam Gigli and is getting warm, shadow boxing in front of the wide mirror. After initially unpacking his kit bag, he realised he'd left all the corner T-shirts back at the hotel. It's a little brother's job to remedy this kind of problem, so Will has been despatched to retrieve the missing gear.

No drama. Will returns with the required items and Anthony pulls on his red Under Armour T-shirt with sponsors JD and Morson prominent in white. He hasn't put his fight shorts on yet as he moves around laughing and joking with the Smiths, Callum Johnson and the lads that have done their work for the night. Four wins out of four so far for Team Gallagher. Added pressure for Anthony, just in case it's needed.

Inside the arena, the first strains of 'oooooh Anthony Crolla' can be heard. The crowd is getting excited. Not long to go now for the majority of those present, who are only concerned with watching 'Million Dollar'. The concourse bars are still doing a brisk trade but the venue is nearly full as Sam Eggington marches to the ring, his EBU belt held aloft behind him.

French opponent Mohamed Mimoune has been left in the ring for several minutes to gather his thoughts ahead of their welterweight clash. It's another chapter in the astonishing Eggington story. With no amateur pedigree and limited natural ability, he was considered a journeyman at the start of his career. The man himself had only thought of boxing as a means to earn extra income to supplement his wages as a forklift driver. From small hall opponent to elite champion, the man from Birmingham now stood, remarkably, on the cusp of a world title shot should he retain his belt against the mandatory challenger. Unfortunately, on this occasion, the fairy tale had an unsatisfactory ending for Sam. Mimoune was cute and awkward and frustrated 'The Savage' from the off. After 12 tricky rounds, the Frenchman deservedly left the ring as the new European champion. There were no complaints from Sam, just sadness and a realisation that his six-foot frame could no longer boil down to 10st 7lbs.

Back in the dressing room, Anthony is being pulled and stretched all over the place by Raquelle. In between his contortions, he's thanking family and friends who've popped in to wish him luck. Loose-limbed and relaxed, he moves on to pad work with Joe, who shouts out the instructions. Anthony obliges with snappy combinations … *bam bam, bam bam bam, bam bam* …

While Anthony continues to work up a sweat, Conor Benn is called to the ring, with his name greeted by more than a few boos. His dad was always popular in these parts, so the reaction from the crowd is something of a curiosity. All becomes clear when the section of the audience booing Benn go wild for Nathan Clarke. The latter has the support of a small army who've made the relatively short journey from south Cheshire to support their man.

Unfortunately for them, and particularly Nathan, the fight has barely begun before Benn has his rival on the canvas. A heavy knockdown quickly follows and while Clarke is game and insists he is fit to continue, he's quickly pinned to the ropes and under attack from a Benn barrage, forcing referee Darren Sarginson to step in and wave it off. Clarke, a talented boxer and respected amateur coach, is furious, his pride surely dented, but Benn was ruthless and a statement has been made.

With the chief support now over, the crowd's giddiness heightens dramatically. 'Jump Around' by House of Pain is always a good one to get punters, well, jumping around. The arena is bouncing, voices well oiled, as the Crolla song reaches peak volume.

The lights are dimmed further, as anticipation grows. Michael Buffer, just a few weeks away from turning 73, glides through the ropes and takes the centre of the ring. Decked out in a double-breasted black tuxedo, Buffer's working the room, a wink here, a smile there. When Neil Diamond's 'Sweet Caroline' begins, the crowd switch on completely, belting it out with gusto. The MC is playing along, like an orchestra's conductor with mic as baton. The lights from thousands of mobile phones add to the spectacle.

As agreed, Ricky is called first to deafening boos, the first time the Manchester public has turned on him. They have to now, it's just got serious. They have to do all they can to be Crolla's '12th man', as he likes to call them.

Burns, still smiling, makes his way in to a dance tune that's hard to fathom due to the arena noise. He eases himself through the ropes to take the applause of his travelling fans and the continued jeers from the rest. He's chatting to his corner, still wearing his white gown with 'Rickster' in blue emblazoned across it.

Now it's Crolla's turn. Buffer ups the volume to make himself heard as he calls to the ring the 'fighting pride of Man-ches-teeeeeeeer!'

Everybody in the venue is on their feet. 'Oooh Anthony Crolla' is, not surprisingly, competing with Whitney Houston's 'Million Dollar Bill' until the chorus kicks in and everyone joins in with Whitney.

Once in the ring, Anthony raises his fists to the heavens and has a little trot around the canvas before heading to the corner for final instructions. He raises his arms again, this time for Joe to peel off the red T-shirt and fully reveal his special fight shorts. They're black with red trim and a yellow panel down the sides that feature the Manchester worker bee. Across the waistband is written MCROLLA, the MCR in red, the OLLA in yellow. It's a clever play on words combining his surname with the city's abbreviation.

Melissa Anglesea from fightwear designer Suzi Wong is again responsible for the fancy shorts, and not just Crolla's. She's also put together a striking look for Ricky, who's gone for the 'Apollo Creed'-style stars and stripes from the Rocky films.

Michael Buffer goes through the formalities, working through Crolla's vital statistics first before building to the climax. Terry O'Connor calls both men to the centre for final instructions and we're off.

The crowd settles down a little as both men go to work. Crolla's immediately the busier of the two, bouncing around, moving, although tentative and certainly not letting his hands go. Burns is more cautious but tries to use his longer reach to land the jab.

There's nothing between them in the second round either as both show the other plenty of respect. Burns attempts to land a big overhand right, Crolla ducks out of the way and tries to regain the initiative with his jab and solid work to the body.

In rounds three and four, the heavier shots are coming from Burns, with Crolla managing to block or evade mostly while shooting back with the jab and hooks to the body. Burns is upping the tempo and aggressively seeking an opening, but Crolla has the final say in most of the exchanges.

There's more of the same in the fifth and sixth rounds, with Burns looking to land big shots and both men prepared to stand toe-to-toe. Both land low blows but apologise profusely. It's been that kind of week, so of course it had to be that kind of sporting fight.

Round seven and Burns lands the punch of the contest, a right uppercut, through the middle that rocks back the head of Crolla. Damage is immediately obvious as blood splatters across Anthony's face. There's a trickle from both nostrils, with the nose suddenly appearing a little fuller.

The Scot looks to capitalise on a potential injury in the eighth, but Anthony seems unfazed and sticks to his plan, bobbing, weaving, throwing the jab and working the body when in close. Anthony looks wearier in the ninth, blood flowing from his nose, and at times he's happy to hold.

The crowd sense the local man needs a lift and kick into life again. It seems to do the trick as he controls the centre of the ring in round ten with a renewed sense of urgency and workrate. He keeps up the pressure going into the 11th round and asserts himself with body shots, pinning Burns to the ropes.

It's round 12 – the final three minutes. The fighters embrace before continuing where they left off. Both have success with right hands, Burns stinging the widened Crolla nose, while Anthony forces his opponent back with a busy combination that ends with a hefty right hook.

Burns tries one last salvo but the Crolla guard remains tight. When the bell sounds, they embrace in the centre of the ring before their respective corners invade and both men raise their arms in an almost involuntary act of celebration/defiance.

Everybody is on their feet. Crolla's team-mates – the Smiths, Johnson and those who have been in action bar Sam – are applauding and saluting their comrade. Michael Carrick is happy and clapping enthusiastically. Carl Froch, who's on duty for Sky Sports, has it in favour of Crolla by a couple of rounds. Luke Campbell, working for talkSPORT, has struggled to separate them.

The judges' scorecards come in fairly swiftly. Michael Buffer implores the crowd to give the fighters a hand before reading the official verdict. 'Victor Loughlin has it 116-113, Steve Gray 117-112, Michael Alexander 116-114, all three cards to the winner by unanimous decision ... the fighting pride of Manchesteeeeeeeer, Anthony Million Dollaarr Croooollaaaaa!'

The crowd erupts as Crolla's hand is raised. Ricky Burns smiles and congratulates his rival. Anthony jumps up in each corner to salute the crowd, before fist-pumping Carrick, who leans in through the ropes. After a quick interview alongside Ricky Burns for Sky, he makes his way to the ropes for a live chat with talkSPORT.

'It was a great fight. Were the scorecards right?'

Yeah, I thought the right man won. I thought it was quality over quantity. Early on, Joe was saying, 'You're boxing lovely, don't get involved' and I know it's stupid, but I felt I was boring people. But I think we gave each other and the crowd a good fight. I'm glad we didn't disappoint in the end.

'Ricky landed a good uppercut that seemed to damage your nose. Did it affect you in there?'

It didn't bother me but it was just a good shot. Joe got it bang-on in the corner – which unfortunately he nearly always does – and he said to me, 'He's looking for the uppercut' and when I got hit with it, I thought, 'What an idiot!'

'That win now puts you back on track?'

I'm normally calm on fight day but I hated it today, hated every minute of it. I thought, 'I don't want to walk my son to school with everyone talking about me losing and how I'm going to quit.' To get the win I'm absolutely made up. It's one of the biggest wins of my career, that.

Joe's stood next to Anthony and is brought in on the chat. He knows how big a deal it's been for his man to complete the job on an emotional night.

'It's brilliant, and not just for Anthony but for the whole of Manchester with what went on earlier this year. There was pressure, there was an elephant in the room, and there was talk of retirement for the loser, with the winner moving on. Anthony boxed wonderful at times and it was a great performance.'

Final questions are posed to Eddie Hearn.

'They're two cracking guys. I had it close, with Crolla just edging it. He was busier, cleaner and I think that was the general consensus. Maybe we look at the return up in Scotland. Ricky was good enough to come here and I know Anthony will want to go on to challenge for world titles, but both of these two need each other.

'It was a great fight, technically excellent and they're two great men, two great ambassadors. Maybe give them a bit of a rest and a nice Christmas and we'll do it again.'

Back in the dressing room, the mood is more exhausted than exhilarated. There's relief and the realisation of a job well done. Anthony slips his fight shorts off and takes off the T-shirt he'd put on after the fight. Stripped to just his underpants (black to match the shorts, of course), he slumps into a chair next to a partition wall and the large mirror.

Well-wishers are filtering in and out of the dressing room. There's an appearance from Michael Carrick, who congratulates Anthony on a job well done.

Eddie Hearn then walks in for a chat with Anthony before stepping away to conduct an interview with James Helder from iFL TV. Joe moves over to his fighter and tells him he'll have to throw some clothes on as they have to get to the press conference. Both Anthony and Ricky will face the media together.

In the opposing dressing room, Ricky Burns is already showered and changed. He's waiting at the door for the nod from Matchroom to go to the press room. He's chatting to Tony Sims, who's animatedly recreating certain shots from the fight. Burns forces a smile as he talks through what's just happened.

'I need to go home and watch the fight, but I thought I'd done enough to nick it. It was close. Tony was saying to me during the rounds that he felt I was getting outworked, but being in there, he [Crolla] wasn't landing any clean punches. I felt I was picking him off with the jab and landing the cleaner shots. Don't get me wrong, some of the rounds were close and it was a good fight. I know Eddie was talking about doing it again, so fingers crossed it can happen in Glasgow.

'One hundred per cent there's life in me yet! People were writing me off from the start and I showed I've still got a few big nights left in me.'

Both teams make their way to the press room. The long MDF table is set in front of the huge Crolla vs Burns fight poster. Underneath sits Eddie Hearn with Anthony, then Joe to his right. To his left, Ricky and Tony. Eddie thanks the press for being there and Anthony's invited to speak first.

It was good to be involved in a good fight with a top guy like Ricky. It was a great night for me. I thought I'd definitely done enough. It was a tough fight. I look forward to watching it back.

Ricky repeats his thoughts about nicking the fight, but most of the questions are directed Crolla's way, with a couple focusing on the worker bee tribute.

My cousin [Leah] was here tonight and she'll be going home happy. It meant absolutely everything to me to win after everything that's happened. I was here at the re-opening a few weeks back and it was a very special night.

There were people in here for the first time since that horrible night. They came out to support me and it was an emotional night for people, so I had to make sure I got the win.

When I walk out, you get those nerves and I say to myself, 'I'm the luckiest person in the world.' I'm living a childhood dream here. I'm just glad we put on a great fight for everyone.

The arena is more or less empty bar some security staff as Anthony, now showered and changed into grey skinny jeans, white T-shirt and a long black and red lumberjack shirt, makes his way wearily out into the mild Manchester night. He's heading to his after-party at El Diablo on Deansgate Locks with Fran, Will and some other friends and family. It's probably the last thing he wants to do, but his supporters and the bar owner expect. He won't let them down.

* * * * *

It's the day after the night before and Anthony's got a sore head – and nose. The pain isn't drink-related despite his appearance in town in the wee small hours, just the usual post-battle bumps and bruises.

I didn't go mad – I literally had two drinks and only because they were forced down me! The after-party went really well. I got there at just gone 2am and everyone was smashed. It was rammed so everyone was happy, but it can be hard work with everyone talking broken biscuits! I would've rather have done another 12 rounds! Nah, it was good to see so many people that had supported me.

Anthony's had a day to get his head around everything that's happened. The night at the arena had been something that'll live long in his memory – the atmosphere, the emotion, the result. Behind the scenes, pre-fight appearances were deceptive.

On the day of the fight I really was as nervous as anything. I said it straight after the fight, but I was sat in my hotel room, just sitting there feeling more nervous than I had done in years. For the first time before a fight, I was scared. I kept telling myself, 'There are loads of kids who'd love to be in this position, so be grateful for it.' I was proper nervous. I hated it.

Walking around town, everyone was coming up to me saying, 'Do Manchester proud' and all that kind of stuff. I was thinking, 'I cannot get beaten here!'

Your mind starts playing games with you. I was thinking about the school run on Monday morning and I was imagining everyone saying 'Aahh, unlucky on Saturday.' I was sat there with all these crazy thoughts going through me head. I was scared. Everyone had been saying how relaxed I was looking. Well, it's some poker face I've got then!

I don't think I'll ever be nervous like that again. Maybe it was the whole Manchester thing, my cousin Leah being caught up in it all. There was the worker bee, everything. I just had to do it.

Now? It's the greatest thing ever.

It's Tuesday lunchtime and Anthony has a little time to kill before visiting Abbas Mhar at Complemed for a routine post-fight rub-down. He's sat on a long communal dining table sheltered under a lean-to outside Altrincham's Market House. He's sipping a creamy cortado from a glass and hoovering up an impressive-looking mushroom sourdough pizza. He has a couple of chocolate cannolis in a white dish set aside for dessert.

I have been eating since the fight but I've not been an absolute pig. When I change me diet, I get heartburn from the acid. It's horrendous, so I tend to behave myself.

He's dressed as if still in training – red hoodie, grey tracksuit bottoms and dark green trainers – all Under Armour in brand, but less obvious in Crolla colour-co-ordination terms. He's bereft of baseball cap, so the hair is neatly tended, slicked back with a side parting as sharp as the knife that's sliced through the remaining pizza.

I'm just going to take things easy for a bit. I'm going to have a few days away with the family at some point, but not a big holiday. We've put an offer in on a new house, so we'll see what happens there.

In terms of the next fight? I don't know. It'll all become clearer soon enough. I don't think a rematch with Ricky really makes sense. The fight wasn't controversial or anything, so I'm not sure if that could happen.

It's a pleasant enough October day – hence the al fresco dining. The odd passer-by nods in Anthony's direction and a middle-aged man in a suit comes over to shake his hand and congratulate him on his weekend performance. There are few signs he's been in a hard fight. His nose, visibly swollen in the hours after the fight, has calmed down and there's just some minor bruising beneath his left eye. He's feeling good and looking forward to whatever the future holds.

I still wouldn't dismiss the idea of fighting in Vegas or even New York at some point. But the arena is very special. Manchester is very special and I've said it before, but I'm so grateful for the support I get. There is no prouder Mancunian than me.

Future plans

Opportunity knocks. Doors will always open for a winner and that's the case for Anthony. His plan is to continue fighting. For how long is unclear but at present he feels able to compete at the highest level. Promoter Eddie Hearn has been pivotal in helping map out Crolla's route to world honours. There's always a plan, always a strategy when dealing with a fighter's future.

'Anthony's a phenomenal guy, really. When you look at his run – the first Darleys Pérez fight, which he won. Everyone said he won. He got a draw, so he had to come back again and he demolished him, knocked him out.

'Then he gets Barroso in a mandatory, to which everyone said, "What are you doing?" but he knocks *him* out. Then he gets Linares in a unification and for the *Ring* magazine belt – and then he fights him again. That's five fights against proper elite lightweights, and back to back. No warm-up fights, no tune-up fights or easy defences. Then he goes and fights Burns!

'You get to the stage with a fighter when you start looking at the exit. I know the next steps for Anthony Crolla. That's my job. I don't want him fighting until he's 35 or 36 and shopworn. I want him to make his money, achieve his dreams and then get out of the game.'

Joe Gallagher's thoughts echo Hearn's sentiments – he's stressed many times that he doesn't want Anthony fighting for much longer. Regardless of what happens next, Joe has ideas for that time when 'Million Dollar' boxes no more.

'You'd have to speak to Anthony and see what he thinks, but one hundred per cent I'd like to keep working with him. I don't want Anthony to feel pressured with, "You're not fighting for me now but you can work with me." It's whatever he wants to do. He could do punditry work on TV and radio, but I'd like him to be involved when I step back from training. Stephen Smith's another one in the gym that'd be a very good assistant, a very good coach. He's travelled the world and fought at the highest level. They're the type of kids I'd like to integrate into training. Anthony's got his second's licence; he's been in the corner with me and had a great education. Anthony could help keep the Manchester scene going as a trainer.'

Joe has long said that he'll walk away from training when the younger fighters in his stable have done their bit in the game. That still gives him a good few years yet, but another career looks set to complement the coaching.

'I've got my promoter's licence. It's all cleared, so I've just got to see what the landscape is for the kids that at the moment are fighting on undercards. If I can't get them out regularly, then I might put shows on. It'd just be four-rounders for the likes of Burton, Hyde and Morrison. But it's a busy time for me and I can't do that with so much going on.

'I might do a show in conjunction with somebody else or I might go it alone with a little show and test the water. Look, it's great when Matchroom and Sky roll into town but there'll be a day where they may not come to Manchester as often as they are doing and these kids need to fight. It's no different for any other Manchester promoters that are keeping kids busy. Pat [Barrett] is doing it at Collyhurst with young Zelfa [Barrett], Steve Wood keeps his kids busy until the big shows come and he gets them on TV.

'Matchroom can be quite selective. They get the pick of the Olympians, they've got a good association with Robert McCracken at Team GB, so it's a case of keeping them [Gallagher fighters] busy, relevant and not stale by just being in the gym all the time.'

Joe's never spoken to me about his plans for the future. But I'd love to stay working with him when the time comes for me to finish boxing. He's really busy with the gym and he probably will need help. I definitely see myself staying in the sport. Even going back to my amateur gym and seeing Jimmy [Lewis] and the kids. They are buzzing when I go in and I love that. I really enjoy trying to pass on what I've learned over the years.

Look, I've still got lots I want to achieve. I've had 41 fights and I know I won't be having 50, that's for sure. You never know, I don't want to put a number on it, but I do want another world title. That's the plan. I want to earn good money to make life easier after I finish boxing, but I never started boxing for money. I wouldn't do it just for money.

I've got other things I can do even now while I'm still fighting. The media work is something I enjoy. I get paid good money to talk about something I really love. I'm a bit of a boxing anorak, so it's easy in a way. Working on TV and radio is certainly something I'd always be interested in, so I may have options in that area. Obviously I'd like to keep working with the kids and maybe help Joe out down the line.

Whatever happens, one thing's for certain. I won't be leaving the sport, I'll always be involved. In terms of work and what people do with their lives? Well, boxing is all I've ever wanted. That's it.

Team-mates

The gym dynamic has always been a key element in Anthony's success. He thrives working alongside other fighters, pushing himself to be better than everyone else. Boxers of all shapes, sizes and genders, but all with the same goal.

You've always got some kind of competition in the gym. Whether we're in the gym or the pool, there's always competition. As Joe says, this isn't a gym with a jewel in the crown; it's a crown full of jewels.

When it comes to in-house sparring, the bigger lads – Paul Smith, Callum Smith, Hosea Burton and Callum Johnson – tend to stick together. Crolla has plenty of dance partners in and around his weight with Stephen Smith, Scott Cardle and, until recently, Scott Quigg, who's moved on to train with Freddie Roach in California.

There isn't a lad, or girl, in the gym who I don't get on with. That's the good thing about the gym. It has to be a happy gym.

Scott Quigg: 'Anthony has an unbelievable will to win. That's his mentality. What he can do is push himself beyond limits others won't.

When he starts to feel uncomfortable, he keeps going. Same as me, we keep going and that's why we bounce off each other.

'Every aspect of the training; his nutrition, his strength, it's done to perfection. There's a routine there and nothing comes in the way of that. At the end of the day, nothing beats hard work.

'Success breeds success. If someone was taking a rest on the bike and Anthony was giving it his all, that someone will then feed off Anthony. If someone's doing 50 press-ups, he'll do 100. He's set the bar to where he wants to get and he won't accept anything less. It's the mentality of the lad.

'I used to put too much pressure on myself, but he's like, "You're gonna do the work so you might as well do it with a smile on your face instead of frowning." Me? I have many grumpy days, but him? No. For instance, if something's annoyed him, he won't take it out on anyone else. He's always smiling, always polite and always nice. If someone's annoyed me, I can walk round with a miserable face and be off with people.

'He's one of the kindest people outside of the ring. You won't meet a nicer lad; he'd do anything for you. But, believe me, when he's in the ring, his looks are deceiving. He won't give me any fashion tips, though, so I hold that against him.'

Quigg's probably got the best wardrobe out there. I'm talking designer stuff. His wardrobe is worth thousands. He's got a Dolce & Gabbana suit worth more than £3,000 and he's not even worn it – and he won't wear it!

You'd hope he's got a bit better knocking around Beverly Hills, but I doubt it. Scott's happy in his tracksuit with yesterday's dinner over it. He could pull off wearing all the gear, but he's too happy in a trackie. It'd be an easy job to dress him, no budget shop for Quigg. I think he's got half the Montclair collection!

Paul Smith: 'As a lad, you couldn't meet any more loyal a man. He's someone you'd want on your side. Listen, I've been in his corner against a Scouser [Derry Mathews] and I'd be in his corner against anyone.

'He could be a Celtic fan and he'd have Rangers fans following him. That's how nice he is, a nice, likeable lad. He does wear his

United top and he does rub it in people's faces that he's a United fan, but it's just football.

'I've been to United vs Liverpool with Crolla at Old Trafford and I've been to Liverpool vs United at Anfield. I've kicked him up the arse as he's walking in the away end and they've beat us or we've beat them. Football aside, the Manc/Scouse rivalry goes out the window for me.

'He's a mate, a proper friend. He was at me wedding and me kids' Christenings and he's been at funerals for our family. He's a family friend.'

Paul's brothers all give him loads, but they know he's the boss of them. I've had some great trips and great times with Paul.

He's a top bloke all round and probably the most entertaining person on social media! You just know he'll be having a Twitter fight every single day.

Stephen Smith: 'We are a very close unit. A lot of people laugh and say Crolla's the fifth Smith brother. We're really close with Anthony. It's one of them where we know what it's like watching brothers and it's a nightmare. We'd all say the same thing – it's easier fighting than watching your brothers. It's not much different watching Anthony. That's how close we are. He's a very nice lad and when you see someone put in what he puts in, you want him to do well. He deserves everything he gets.

'He's round the bend, though. He comes in and hangs his boxies [underpants] up in the changing room. There's something missing in terms of the way he dresses and that, but it's been a joke from day one. If he's got a grey tracksuit on with a purple T-shirt, he'll have purple boxies on and purple socks with a purple stripe on his grey shoes. He's mad, it's obsessive. He loves his fashion but it's something we just laugh about.'

You wouldn't meet many nicer people than Stephen but he is funny, sharp and witty. He's the hardest grafter out of them all and is very much all about family. If there's anyone who deserves a world title through graft, it's Stephen.

Liam Smith: 'I remember once walking in the gym and having a go at his shorts. "They're snide shorts, them, Crolla!" And he fell out with me! He couldn't believe I'd said his kit's shit! I was laughing and had to say I was only messin'. I mean, a lot of boxers like to have their kit matching, but day to day? He trains like that! Me, I go to a drawer and drag any T-shirt, any pair of shorts and any socks to go training in. No one's looking. There aren't too many times anyone's watching you train, yet he's always matching.

'He's one of the nicest lads I've ever met in me life and he's a good-looking lad as well. But he's a tough bastard. Look at Barroso, John Murray, these hard fights, but he toughs it out then has his say. He's a tough little fucker and he has got that nasty side in there [the ring]. I think that's why he's so liked in boxing; people know he's got that side to him, whereas outside the ring he's a complete gentleman.'

Liam's the easiest to wind up, he'll bite at anything! But anything he does, he's good at. You could give him a tennis racket or a snooker cue and he can just do it.

He frustrates me. I love watching Liam and when people ask me who the best Smith is, I always say Liam's the most talented, without a doubt. Everything's easy to him. I've seen him come in the gym unfit and overweight and he'll spar and his timing is bang-on. It's like he's never been away.

Callum Smith: 'I'm nearly as nervous watching him box as when my brothers fight. I don't get those kind of nerves with anyone else. It's great to see good people who work hard get results. I think he'd be the first to tell you he's not the most talented or the most skilful, but he works hard and he's become a world champion because of it.'

Callum might be the best of the lot of them, he may have the highest career earnings in the end, but he knows he's the little brother and I like that. They all give it to Paul, give him loads of stick, but they respect him as the eldest. The Smiths – every one of them is different. People have said I'm the fifth Smith brother and I'm proud of that. If you could have the best bits of all of them, you'd have the perfect fighter.

Scott Cardle: 'I've been in this gym for six years and I was there when Crolla was trying to get on *Prizefighter* with people saying he's finished. I don't know what changed, maybe him as a person, but he got the world title shot and then more bad luck. It's a mental thing and the psychology of Crolla is incredible. There were times when he was very low, but you'd never say that Crolla was finished; you knew he could come back because I'd seen him in the gym. He had so much more and he got there.

'Everyone says he's the nicest guy in boxing, but nah, I really can't deny that! I'll tell you, when you're weighing in, we all struggle with the last few pounds. Weigh-in day, everyone's in a bad mood, but not him. When you've got fans coming up to you and you've got to get a pound off and you just want to get it over with so you can get a drink in you, but he's like "Hiya!", hugging and kissing people. He'll be having pictures taken and everything. I've never seen anything like it. That's why he's such a popular fella, not just in Manchester, but everyone loves him because he's real. He can't be anything else.

'Listen, in sparring he can land a few dodgy shots, don't get me wrong. But I haven't got a bad word to say about him. His motivation is an inspiration for me.'

Cardle's the joker in the gym. He's hilarious and great company. I don't know what it is about Scottie, but he's a great night out! He's someone that's very good at picking up the team. Maybe it's the accent that kills me!

Hosea Burton: 'One of the only things you can slag him off for is that he likes to sing along to the songs on in the gym. He's not a great singer! You'll be training and he suddenly bursts into song.

'I can't rip him about his clothes because he's always turned out immaculate. He is colour co-ordinated all the time and I think he looks well. Look, I can't call anyone about their clothes because I'm dressed like a scruff all the time! I don't care what the next man thinks. As long as I'm happy, I'm OK.

'He's a great man to have around, but he's a bag hog. We work on the bags together and he will deliberately get in your way. He'll do it so you move out of his way. I've said to him a few times, "Ant, you're going to have to fuck off because you're getting on me nerves!" And he'll just start laughing and stay in your way all the time. It's annoying and he does it just to wind you up. Everyone in the gym that's shared a bag with him will tell you he's horrible. He's great to train with, you just can't share a bag with him!

'Other than that, I can't really fault him. He trains really hard and he's a proper professional.'

Hosea is as dry as anything. He's funny without even knowing. I remember once, when we were going out to LA, I thought he was going to belt me! We got on a plane and he started stripping off. He stripped down to his white vest and I thought he was messing about. I'm going, 'Are you serious?' I was in stitches laughing at him and he was giving it, 'What are you laughing at? It's boiling!' I just couldn't stop laughing at his vest. He's just not one bit arsed! He's a great lad, and a really top lad to have in the gym.

Marcus Morrison: 'The form Anthony's shown over the last couple of years – he's come on massively. He's won titles and defended them. When things get tough, he can slug it out. He's a top bloke and a great fighter.'

Marcus is a talented lad. So talented and I wish I had his genetics! He just needs that bit more self-belief but then I didn't always have confidence in my own ability. He can get that confidence in his ability and he'll be a threat to absolutely anyone.

Callum Johnson: 'He's a dickhead … ha ha! Nah, he's just a smashing lad and he's great to be around. I remember him from years ago in the amateurs and now he fights at the arena. I've watched him walk out in those big fights and I just think, "Wow!" He's an inspiration and he's been there and done it. He deserves everything he gets.

'He comes in the gym in all his matching gear, but to be fair, he's a smart kid and a good-looking lad. He can have a 12-round war and there won't be a hair out of place! I don't understand the reality TV stuff, though. You come in the gym in the morning and they're all talking about *Love Island* or whatever! Actually, I could see Crolla rocking up on *Love Island*! I think he'd go well in that!'

Callum [Johnson] is another very talented lad and again someone that should believe in himself more. Such a talent, but he's had a tough time dealing with his dad's death. His dad was his best mate and a very good man. His dad gave him lots of belief and hopefully he'll get that back. He lives far away, so isn't in the gym all the time, but he very much loves the team and is one of the best fighters in the gym.

Paul Butler: 'You couldn't get a better, more down-to-earth lad than Crolla. He's always in the gym first and mainly out of the gym last. He's constantly working. He's never out of a hard fight, either. Watching him spar, his counter-punching and shot selection is brilliant. His music's not great, though. I try and get in after him, so his music's off!'

Butler is probably the quietest lad in the gym, but great to train alongside. One of the fittest lads in the gym and very professional right from the warm-up all the way through.

Natasha Jonas: 'He's brilliant. He's a good lad, a good laugh and a good motivator. He keeps the gym smiling and always has some gossip to tell you. He keeps me up to date with all the reality TV shows. He loves it. His playlist with all the pop songs keeps me going!'

Forget the girl thing, Tasha trains as hard as anyone. She's an inspiration, you know, she's a mum and she works so hard. We don't treat her any different. She is one of the lads and the only thing we do different now is close the changing room door! She's great.

Sam Hyde: 'Apart from the fact he's always in his own world, he's sound and a great guy to train alongside. He is funny but he has an amazing work ethic and I'm learning so much from him and the other lads in the gym.

Sam's surprised me a lot. He's a grafter and I didn't expect him to work as hard as he does. He's a good addition to the gym and a top lad.

Afters ...
Stevie Bell, Bell's Gym
'Crolla was a young lad and he was really quiet when he first came to the gym [Arnie's]. We had to sort of get him into the feel of the gym. He was, and people say it now, too nice to be a boxer. That is him, a genuinely lovely bloke.

'He's a proper pretty boy. I remember that loads of girls used to love him and he brought the good-looking ladies to the gym. He always loved taking his top off when the girls were there. He thought he was chocolate!

'We did a lot of sparring together and he was dead respectful. I was respectful of him too because he was a good amateur as well. We had some really good spars. Some days he'd get the better of me, other days I'd get the better of him, but there weren't many days I got the better of him! I was a little bit ahead of him in my career, but he was great for me to learn off as well because he had a great style.

'I think he's showed people what he's made of. He's shown a lot of balls to come back from early defeats to Youssef Al-Hamidi and Gary Sykes. I think the move to Joe [Gallagher] did him the world of good. I love Anthony [Farnell] to death, but I think that move was perfect for him. He's come on leaps and bounds. When you watch him, he just looks like he knows exactly what he's doing. He's relaxed and I'd never seen him like that when I was training with him. You can see how he's improved as a fighter and a person as well.

'He listens. If you told him to go and run up some steps a hundred times, he'd do it. You need to be able to do that to be a champ. He'll listen to the trainer, he's not one to think he knows better than everyone else. He does what he's told, so with someone like Joe, who knows the game, seen it, done it, it's perfect for Crolla and Crolla's perfect for him.'

Paulie Malignaggi

'Southern Italians are emotional, shoot from the hip type of people. I think Crolla has that. You see it when he wins a fight, his exuberant reaction. It's part of his genetic code. He likes a good tear-up when he's in the ring as well.

'Crolla is certainly one of the nice guys in boxing. He's a football fan, so we have that in common. Also, when he's in the ring, he wants to win so badly. There is a mean streak. I remember the Barroso fight. It was very, very impressive. Barroso was a guy I'd seen in the States. Scary power, scary guy. He came to the UK and destroyed Kevin Mitchell – he retired him and Kevin was a quality fighter. Crolla's a nice guy but he handled this guy, who's so tough, so rugged, so strong. In a wild tussle of an affair, he stopped him to the body. Remember, this is still a fighter, however nice a guy he is! If you're in the ring with him, you're crossing him. The one thing we're taught as boxers is that even if your mother's opposite you in the ring, you gotta knock her out!'

Jamie Moore

'Crolla could easily be happy with what he's done, but it's testament to his dedication that he still has that ambition. Considering where he was ten years ago, he's over-achieved. He was beaten by Gary Sykes for the English title. Fair play to him.

'He is the nicest lad you'll meet and one of the bravest in the ring – but he's not too brave on planes! I've been on flights with Crolla and he was a mess, absolutely petrified! Even old ladies were telling him to shape up!'

Ged Mason OBE, CEO Morson Group

'A lot of people have approached me asking for help. I can't sponsor every boxer, but I go on a case-by-case basis to see what they're about as a person. I'm very protective of our brand, so I want to make sure the guys that wear the Morson hat conduct themselves in the right manner.

'I met a lad called Phil Turner on a Destination Florida charity trip. He'd lost his leg unfortunately but I stayed in touch with him from when he was about 14. He's ended up working for me and was always speaking about this young lad coming through the ranks who was going to be great. He said he was a real prospect and that he was a pal of his. I got introduced to Crolla and he was everything on the tin, he was everything I'd heard about and more. He is one of the genuine guys. My two lads have learning difficulties and he's always gone out of his way to talk to them behind the scenes, even at busy times like at weigh-ins. He's just always had great time for them. He's become more a friend really, one of the lads you'd always want to have a beer with. He's a good soul from good stock.'

Eddie Hearn

'People talk about him being the nicest man in boxing and it is said a lot. There are a lot of incredible people in boxing, some really nice guys and some great stories – he's a combination of the two.

'I'm yet to meet anyone who could say a bad word about Anthony Crolla. He's incredibly tough and has earned every penny and every bit of adulation.

'By the flip of a coin, the Kieran Farrell fight or the Gavin Rees fight – he could've been in a nine-to-five now. The Manchester Arena is now his fortress and he's got what he's deserved. People will remember those nights forever. He has a résumé where you can say he's one of the greats of British boxing. You would never have thought that of Anthony Crolla.

'I want him to walk out of the game with his health intact, houses paid for and kids' education sorted. That's all that matters to me. It's so rare that nice guys do win. Anthony Crolla did win.'

Ricky Hatton

'Anthony should be an example to any youngsters coming through – you know, if you lose a couple of fights, you don't get disheartened. My son Campbell's lost a couple of fights and I always say to him, "It's not where you start, it's where you finish."

'When I promoted Anthony, he lost a six-rounder and he got stopped by Derry Mathews but went on to win a world title and fight the number one in the division. I think that just shows that if you've got the desire and the determination to learn from a defeat and not let it get you down, you can be a success story. Anthony's a real success story. You don't win a world title if you're not worthy of it.

'I learned in boxing that defeat is not the end of your career. Anthony's a perfect and shining example of that. Keep your pecker up, as they say!

'Anthony came on board with me but my job as a promoter was very hard. We had Joe Murray, Scott Quigg, Martin Murray, Denton Vassell – I had more champions than anyone, but I lost my dates with Sky and then it's very hard when you have lads knocking on the door of titles. They want to be on the TV and I couldn't provide that for them. I had no quarrels with letting them go and move on and it's nice to see them do well. If I complained, I'd be holding them back and that's not what I'm all about. It makes me feel very proud that I had that little small part to play years ago.

'People still come and ask me for advice. I've done a lot in boxing, I've been a world champion, I've trained a world champion, I've promoted a world champion. There's not much I haven't done, so it's nice that fighters who are challenging for titles hold me in high regard and ask me for advice.

'I'm very proud we've got lads like Crolla flying the flag for Manchester boxing.'